# Children's Rights
and the Law

# Children's Rights and the Law

Samuel M. Davis
University of Georgia

Mortimer D. Schwartz
University of California

**Lexington Books**
*D.C. Heath and Company/Lexington, Massachusetts/Toronto*

*Library of Congress Cataloging-in-Publication Data*
Main entry under title:

Davis, Samuel M.
  Children's rights and the law.

  Bibliography: p.
  Includes index.
  1. Children—Legal status, laws, etc.—United
States.  2. Parent and child (Law)—United States.
I. Schwartz, Mortimer D.  II. Title.
KF479.S38    1987    346.7301'35    78-14156
ISBN 0-669-02679-4 (alk. paper) 347.306135

Published simultaneously in Canada
Printed in the United States of America
Casebound International Standard Book Number: 0-669-02679-4
Library of Congress Catalog Card Number: 78-14156

The paper used in this publication meets the minimum requirements
of American National Standard for Information Sciences—
Permanence of Paper for Printed Library Materials, ANSI
Z39.48-1984. ∞ ™

87  88  89  90  91  8  7  6  5  4  3  2  1

# Dedication

The idea for this book was conceived by John C. Hogan, who died suddenly and unexpectedly just before work on the manuscript was to commence. At the time, John was a visiting professor in the Graduate School of Education at UCLA, after serving as an adjunct professor in the Education Department of the Claremont Graduate School, Claremont, California, while concurrently filling a full-time career as an administrator and then consultant specializing in publishing and copyright matters with the Rand Corporation, Santa Monica, California. With three degrees from UCLA, including a master's in political science and a doctorate in education and the law, John was a brilliant, energetic and imaginative scholar whose productive and creative talents are well reflected in the wide range of his studies embracing such diverse fields as space law, copyright law, education and the law, and legal history. John was a colleague who was also a friend, radiating with warmth, acceptance, and unselfishness, always available and always responsive. From his work in education and the law and in legal history, John developed a profound concern for the rights of children. Hence, it is not surprising that he should come up with the notion that a study which delved into historical and philosphical roots would produce a useful and interesting panorama for those seeking an informative understanding of children and the law. It was with the momentum of that notion and the encouragement given to us that we carried forward to produce this book, which we now dedicate to John C. Hogan.

# Contents

# Preface and Acknowledgments

"Children's rights" is a topic about which one hears much today. It is quite impossible, however, to examine children's rights in isolation, without examining the respective roles played by parents and the state. The study of "rights" is the study of power, control, and decision making. To the extent children have rights, they have the right to make choices for themselves and to exercise control over their lives. When children do not have certain rights, it is usually because someone else, either parents or the state, has power of control—and, therefore, decision-making power—over them. This book is an effort to identify and examine the various interests that favor decision making by parents, the state, or children themselves. As such, it is a study of the very delicate relationship between the family and the state in modern society.

The book originally was written for an intelligent lay audience. It should prove highly informative as well to judges, lawyers, educators, counselors, and other professionals who work with children or who have an interest in the welfare of children. Anyone, lay or professional, who desires a greater understanding of how the law relates to children will find the book very useful. Indeed, many may find the breadth of that relationship startling.

No major project of this nature is ever completed without the help of many persons. Professor Davis wishes to acknowledge the assistance of the following persons: Patricia Gail Singleton, who, as a third-year law student, conducted the research for and produced a draft of Chapter 6; Dean J. Ralph Beaird, who generously furnished the research support necessary for the project; Mary Crace, Emma Terrell, and Pixie Ryals, who typed (and retyped) the manuscript without complaint; and his wife and daughters, who sacrificed their time and lent personal support when it was greatest needed. Both authors acknowledge their intellectual debt to John C. Hogan, to whom this book is dedicated.

# 1
# Introduction: The Place of Children in the Law

> The law's concept of the family rests on a presumption that parents possess what a child lacks in maturity, experience, and capacity for judgment required for making life's difficult decisions. More important, historically it has recognized that natural bonds of affection lead parents to act in the best interests of their children. . . .
>
> Most children, even in adolescence, simply are not able to make sound judgments concerning many decisions. . . . Parents can and must make those judgments.
>
> —Chief Justice Warren E. Burger, *Parham v. J.R.*
> 442 U.S. 584, 602–03 (1979)

I f compelled to do so, we would say that in a nutshell this is a book about children's rights. The words *rights* is troublesome enough, and the book itself is testimony to the numerous problems associated with the term. The word *children* presents conceptual difficulties of its own. Children have been variously referred to in the law as *infants, minors, adolescents, youths, juveniles,* and the like. Sometimes particular terms are zealously touted; for example, a thousand-page casebook on juvenile justice has been criticized for not including *youth* or *adolescent* in its subject matter index.[1] We have adopted the terms *children* and *child* throughout this book for no better reason than that we are comfortable with these terms, which sound more humanistic and less clinical than the others.[2]

This is more than a book about children's rights, however. In a broader sense, as the title suggests, it is an examination of the relationships existing between children, their parents, and the state. Close observation of those relationships reveals that on a day-to-day, practical, functional basis they present a study of *authority*, a search for an answer to the question of *who* speaks for the child—parents, the state, or the child himself.

The complexity of the relationships does not lend itself to any single, simple answer. Depending on the circumstances and the context, children sometimes decide certain matters for themselves, especially if they are emancipated—that is, free from parental authority and control.[3] In other contexts the parents might make decisions for a child—for example, decisions regarding medical treatment[4] or commitment to a mental institution.[5]

In still other contexts the state might make decisions on the child's behalf, as on the question of adequate parenting[6] or even regarding medical treatment, especially in life-threatening situations.[7]

Unquestionably, young people frequently are subject to differential treatment whether they are labeled *children* or *adults*. In keeping with the current trend, we regard anyone under eighteen years of age as a child and anyone eighteen years of age or older as an adult.[8] Yet even some adults as so defined are denied certain rights or privileges; for example, in some states one must be twenty-one in order to make a will[9] or nineteen or older to purchase alcoholic beverages.[10] Such provisions are evidence of lingering uncertainty over the wisdom of lowering the age of majority from twenty-one to eighteen years of age. In contrast, the *Juvenile Justice Standards Relating to Rights of Minors* propose adoption of age eighteen as the age of majority for *all* purposes. Anything less, the proponents claim, is both inconsistent with the notion that an eighteen-year-old is capable of assuming adult responsibilities and demeaning to persons who for most purposes are regarded as adults.[11]

Certainly if one is regarded as a child differential treatment is common. For most purposes children are treated differently from adults, and some children are treated differently from other children. Thus, in private law, children are viewed as lacking capacity to enter into a binding contract[12] or to make a will[13] and as lacking freedom to work at certain occupations.[14] Emancipated children, however, are treated as adults for some purposes and therefore can make decisions for themselves and engage in certain activities that are denied to children generally.[15]

Where the Constitution has a role to play, children have the right to make some decisions for themselves. Thus, a state can not impose an absolute requirement of parental consent for a child to have an abortion.[16] Indeed, a mature minor[17] can decide for herself whether to have an abortion, and even if immature, she must be afforded an opportunity to persuade a court that the abortion would be in her best interests.[18]

Professor Frank Zimring has argued that no one, single age (such as eighteen) should be used in determining such matters as capacity or responsibility. Rather, he argues, the age should vary depending on the attribute of adulthood under consideration. He names three such attributes that often are associated with the age of majority: liberty, entitlement, and responsibility. Liberty entails the same exercise of free choice, as far as the state is concerned, enjoyed by adults generally—for example, the right to make decisions about medical care. Entitlements are "special opportunities the state might wish to provide only to those who have not yet reached adulthood," such as the Job Corps or the old Civilian Conservation Corps (CCC). Responsibility refers to one's accountability for misconduct under the criminal and civil law, as well as the burden of supporting oneself. He suggests that the age of majority for liberty be eighteen and for entitlement and responsibility twenty-one.[19]

Professor Zimring would not require that such determinations be wholly age-specific, however. He prefers to create a presumption that, depending on the purpose, one must have reached either age eighteen or age twenty-one before he is free to make a choice, entitled to some benefit or opportunity, or responsible for himself. The argument could be made in individual cases for a lower or higher age. The presumption should be a strong one, he argues, but deciding whether it has been overcome in individual cases would force us to articulate, examine, and constantly rethink the policy reasons underlying such age requirements.[20]

Age, in this sense, is being used as a proxy for the real, underlying issue—namely, the question of *who* decides for children. There the law is caught in a bind between competing interests: the desire to protect children from others, from harmful situations, and from their own improvidence and the desire to give children as much autonomy as they can bear, as soon as they can bear it.[21]

The nature of these competing interests constitutes one of the major themes of this book. In chapter 2 we examine traditional perceptions of children and the family as revealed in writings of the great historians, philosophers, and jurists. In chapter 3 we examine the conflicting views of children and their place in the law as developed in various areas of private law long before any aspect of family law came to be measured by a constitutional yardstick. In chapter 4 we present a broad constitutional perspective of the authoritative roles of children, parents, and the state as revealed in decisions of the United States Supreme Court. From there we examine specific aspects of children's rights, including the right to life (chapter 5), the right to liberty (chapter 6), the right to property (chapter 7), the right to an education (chapter 8), and the right to protection from inadequate parenting (chapter 9). Finally, in chapter 10 we will draw some conclusions from all of the above, particularly whether the prospect is likely that the law, and especially the United States Supreme Court, is capable of developing a coherent, consistent policy with respect to children's rights.

## Notes

1. F. Zimring, The Changing Legal World of Adolescence xii & n.6 (1982) [hereinafter cited as F. Zimring]. The book criticized was S. Fox, Cases and Materials on Modern Juvenile Justice (2d ed. 1981).

2. In his book Professor Zimring notes that lawyers have a language all their own that does not correspond to terminology found in social science literature. It was in this context that he criticized omission of *adolescent* or *youth* from the casebook mentioned in note 1. F. Zimring, *supra* note 1, at xi–xiii.

3. *See* the section on emancipation in chapter 3 *infra.*

4. *See* the material on medical decision making in chapter 5 *infra.*

5. *See* the discussion of Parham v. J.R., 442 U.S. 584 (1979), in chapter 4 *infra.*

6. *See* chapter 9 *infra.*

7. *See* the material on medical decision making in chapter 5 *infra*.

8. These definitions, particularly the use of age eighteen as a dividing line, are discussed generally in JUVENILE JUSTICE STANDARDS RELATING TO RIGHTS OF MINORS Standard 1.1 and Commentary at 17–20 (1980). Specific applications are discussed in the sections on testamentary transfer of property and emancipation in chapter 3 *infra*.

9. *See* the section on testamentary transfer of property in chapter 3 *infra*.

10. The experience in Michigan, as well as the problem generally of setting a legal drinking age, are recounted in F. ZIMRING, *supra* note 1, at 3–7. Of course, federal legislation now has been enacted and signed by President Reagan that seeks to coerce states into raising the legal drinking age to twenty-one by withholding up to 10 percent of federal highway construction funds from states that have not enacted such legislation by October 1, 1987. Some twenty-three states have already raised the legal drinking age to twenty-one. N.Y. Times, July 18, 1984, at A15, col. 1. Some whimsically have proposed raising the age to thirty-seven or thirty-eight or even forty. And one writer has proposed a *maximum* drinking age of fifty. Benson, *Hic*, N.Y. Times, at A15, col. 2.

11. JUVENILE JUSTICE STANDARDS RELATING TO RIGHTS OF MINORS Standard 1.1 and Commentary at 19 (1980).

12. *See* the section on contracts in chapter 3 *infra*.

13. *See* the section on testamentary transfer of property in chapter 3 *infra*.

14. *See* the section on regulation of child employment in chapter 3 *infra*.

15. *See* the section on emancipation in chapter 3. *infra*.

16. Planned Parenthood v. Danforth, 428 U.S. 52, 72–75 (1976).

17. *See* note 2 *supra*.

18. Bellotti v. Baird (II), 443 U.S. 622, 642–44 (1979). These rights were confirmed more recently in Planned Parenthood Ass'n v. Ashcroft, 462 U.S. 416 (1983), and City of Akron v. Akron Center for Reproductive Health, 462 U.S. 476 (1983). These cases and others are discussed in the material on medical decision making in chapter 5 *infra* and in connection with H.L. v. Matheson, 450 U.S. 398 (1981), in chapter 2 *infra*.

19. F. ZIMRING *supra* note 1, at 111.

20. *Id.* at 111–12. An excellent review of Professor Zimring's book is Hafen, *The Learning Years: A Review of* The Changing Legal World of Adolescence, 81 MICH. L. REV. 1045 (1983) [hereinafter cited as Hafen].

21. Some have argued in favor of virtual total autonomy for all children. *See, e.g.*, R. FARSON, BIRTHRIGHTS (1974); J. HOLT, ESCAPE FROM CHILDHOOD (1974). Others have argued in favor of increased parental control. *See, e.g.*, Goldstein, *Medical Care for the Child at Risk: On State Supervision of Parental Autonomy*, 86 YALE L.J. 645 (1977). Still others have argued for a moderate approach somewhere in between. *See, e.g.*, Hafen, *Children's Liberation and the New Egalitarianism: Some Reservations about Abandoning Youth to Their "Rights,"* 1976 B.Y.U. L. REV. 605.

In addition to the above works, a number of excellent books and articles have been written on the subject of children's rights generally and on particular aspects of children's rights. Among them are L. HOULGATE, THE CHILD AND THE STATE: A NORMATIVE THEORY OF JUVENILE RIGHTS (1980); R. MNOOKIN, CHILD, FAMILY AND STATE (1978): W. WADLINGTON, C. WHITEBREAD & S. DAVIS, CHILDREN IN THE LEGAL SYSTEM (1983); F. ZIMRING, *supra* note 1; Batey, *The Rights of Adolescents*, 23 WM. & MARY L. REV. 363 (1982); Foster & Freed, *A Bill of Rights for Children*, 6 FAM. L.Q.

343 (1972); Hafen, *The Constitutional Status of Marriage, Kinship, and Sexual Privacy—Balancing the Individual and Social Interests*, 81 MICH. L. REV. 463 (1983); Hafen, *supra* note 20; Kaufman, *Protecting the Rights of Minors: On Juvenile Autonomy and the Limits of Law*, 52 N.Y.U. L. REV. 1015 (1977); Wald, *Children's Rights: A Framework for Analysis*, 12 U.C.D. L. REV. 255 (1979).

# 2
# Natural Law and Children's Rights

> Adam had not, either by natural right of fatherhood or by positive donation from God, any such authority over his children . . . as is pretended.
>
> —John Locke
> *Two Treatises of Government*[1]

The rights of children, as well as the corresponding duties owed by children to their parents, have been examined in the writings of the classical historians, philosophers, and jurists. Comparison discloses a pattern, which has been given a name. Except for very ancient times, when among barbarian races and tribes male supremacy dominated and children's rights were nonexistent, civilized peoples have recognized a universal right of children to receive maintenance, protection, and education from their parents, which may be called the original obligation.

## The Original Obligation

Although an original obligation or duty to support and provide protection and education for one's offspring long has been recognized, it has not been universally imposed on the same parent or to the same-sex offspring, nor are the same reasons for its existence always given. A corresponding duty has been assigned to the offspring, which is to honor and care for the parent in old age or infirm health, again not always universally imposed on the same-sex offspring or always assigned for the same reasons.

Thus, the obligation can be stated or paraphrased in two parts:

1. The parent provides maintenance, protection, and education (any or all of these) for the child.
2. Reciprocally, the parent receives from the child honor and care in old age or infirmity.

The evolution of these concepts (one a right, the other a duty) is briefly traced below in the histories (Herodotus), the writings of the philosophers

(Aristotle, Hobbes, Locke, Hegel), and the works of the jurists (Pufendorf, Grotius, Blackstone) from the earliest times.

## The Historians

### Antiquity

Among uncivilized people children's rights and duties were nonexistent. The historians relate instances among numerous tribes where even the life of the child was viewed as of no consequence; thus, in *Orestes*, Electra asserts that Atreus slew the children of Thyestes and "feasted him on them."[2] The Thracians engaged in the custom of selling their children to traders.[3] Instances of child extinction were common: in *The Phoenician Maidens* Jocasta refers to "exposure" of her child by his father.[4] Members of the tribe of the Auseans neither married nor lived as families but "dwell[ed] together like the gregarious beasts," and when their children were grown they were brought before the assembly of men and assigned to those whom they most resembled.[5] Freud noted other instances of extreme cruelty in the relationship of father and son that have come down to us from the primeval ages of society in the form of mythology or folklore. These include Kronos, who devoured his children like a wild boar, and Zeus, who emasculated his father.[6] Under these conditions, children's rights and duties were nonexistent.

### The Egyptians

The historian Herodotus (circa 490–380 B.C.) recorded some unusual practices among the Egyptians:

> [T]he Egyptians themselves seem to have reversed the ordinary practices of mankind. For instance, women attend market and are employed in trade, while men stay home and do the weaving. . . . Sons are under no compulsion to support their parents if they do not wish to do so, but daughters must, whether they wish it or not.[7]

Thus, although the obligation was practiced in the reverse as we know it in the Western world, the principle was the same; the party responsible for earning the livelihood (that is, women) also had responsibility for the infirm parents' support or maintenance. Other instances of this reversal of roles as related to the obligation were noted in matriarchic societies, and in the absence of a contract, according to the philosopher Hobbes as noted below, it fell on the mother.[8]

## The Ancient Chinese

As one might expect to find, the obligation as practiced in the Oriental world involved "grave and unchangeable fundamental relations" as set forth in the Chinese Shu-King:

1.  those of the emperor and the people,
2.  those of fathers and children,
3.  those of an elder and a young brother,
4.  those of husband and wife,
5.  those of friend and friend.

The ancestral duties of the Chinese family were "absolutely binding and . . . established, and regulated by law."[9] It is significant that the relationship of fathers and their children is located immediately after the emperor and the people but before husband and wife in the Shu-King.

## The Greek and Roman Civilizations

A study of the history and culture of the Western world demonstrates a kind of continuity in thinking among the philosophers and jurists that placed the obligation of maintenance, protection, and education of offspring on the father and the duty to provide for the parents in old age and infirmity on the males in the family. Especially in later periods, with the rise of civilizations, these rights and duties of children and parents began to emerge more clearly.

By Aristotle's time, Greek philosophers were inquiring about the rights and duties of children with questions such as "whether one should in all things give the preference to one's father and obey him, or whether when one is ill one should trust a doctor?"[10] Obedience, thus, was questionable but not the child's obligation to provide for the parent, for example, in the matter of sustenance. Aristotle admonished that in the latter area there exists a duty to "help our parents before all others, since we owe our own nourishment to them."

Household management among the Greeks was viewed as consisting of three elements:

1.  the rule of a master over slaves,
2.  the rule of a father, and
3.  the rule of a husband.

According to Aristotle, the father's rule over children was a "royal rule," while that over his wife was a "constitutional rule." That is, the father ruled the children "by virtue both of love and of respect due age" and thus exercised a kind of royal power.[11]

**Protection.** Admitting that there might be exceptions to it, Aristotle nevertheless accepted male dominance in this area because "the male is by nature fitter for command than the female."[12] This superiority of fitness extended to physical matters, and the father was viewed as better able to provide for the protection of the child. Thus, because of his superiority, to the father fell the obligation to protect as well as maintain and educate the child.

**Maintenance.** Aristotle's theory of rearing (that is, maintaining) children was decidedly protectionist: control the food they eat, the motions they make with their bodies, their early-age adaptation to the cold—all this before age five—during which time no demand "should be made upon the child for study or labour."[13]

**Education.** Among the Greeks, education usually was regarded as a rigorous, highly developed science, yet according to Aristotle there was no agreement about what should be taught, particularly whether education should be concerned with practical, intellectual, or moral values: "The existing practice is perplexing; no one knows on what principle we should proceed—should the useful in life, or should virtue, or should the higher knowledge, be the aim of our training; all three opinions have been entertained." One thing, however, was clear to the philosopher: education should be regulated by law and should be a function of the state. But the character of public education and the manner in which children should be educated were questions that remained to be considered.[14]

In Roman times, elder daughters were entitled to education as were their male counterparts. Thus, Halicarnassus reports that Romulus "laid the citizens of Rome under an obligation to educate all their male children, and the eldest of their daughters"[15]—an early example of partial alleviation of discrimination based on sex.

Whereas the early philosophers argued whether what is natural is just, right, or correct, Justinian concluded that a "natural impulse, that is, affection, impels parents to bring up their children." Imposing the obligation on the man, he declared that "A father is obliged by nature herself to support a son or daughter."[16] This natural instinct is found in other living creatures who also provide nourishment of their offspring.[17]

*Transition*

In the *Summa Theologica,* Saint Thomas Aquinas recognized the parental obligation to provide education for the child with the observation that it was unlawful for persons having children to enter religion "so as to altogether set aside the care for their children, namely without providing for their education."[18] He cited Biblical scripture in support of this admonition.[19]

He further wrote that it "accidentally" belonged to the parent to be assisted by the child if the parent was in a condition of necessity. Consequently, when the parents were in such need that they could not be supported otherwise than by their children, the children might not lawfully enter religion "in despite of their duty to their parents." But if the parents' necessity were not great, then the children could enter religion despite the duty they owed the parents and even against the command of the parents.

The general obligation was formulated by Aquinas as follows: "He who is under a certain fixed obligation cannot legally set it aside as long as he is able to fulfil it."[20] Thus a person under an obligation of a fixed debt could not lawfully evade it by entering religion. Nor could a child avoid his obligations to his parents by entering religion for the same reasons.

## The Philosophers

The principal philosophers who commented on children's rights and parental obligations were Thomas Hobbes (1588-1679), John Locke (1632-1704), Jean Jacques Rousseau (1712-78), and George Wilhelm Hegel (1770-1831). To a lesser extent the subject also was addressed by Immanuel Kant (1724-1804), John Stuart Mill (1806-73), and a few others who are noted below. This group, which spanned some 300 years, discussed such matters as the origin of dominion that parents have over children and the education that necessarily must be provided a child. By this time in history, maintenance had become a state-regulated matter as had protection.

### Hobbes

Hobbes divided dominion into two kinds—paternal and despotical—and wrote that it is acquired in two ways—by generation and by conquest.[21] Arguing that no man can have two masters, he referred to the dominion of the male parent over the child as "paternal," deriving from the child's consent:

> The right of dominion by generation is that which the parent hath over his children, and is called paternal. And it is not so derived from the generation, as if therefore the parent had dominion over his child because he begat him, but from the child's consent, either express or by other sufficient arguments declared. . . . God hath ordained to man a helper, and there be always two that are equally parents: the dominion therefore over the child should belong equally to both, and he be equally subject to both, which is impossible; for no man can obey two masters.[22]

Noting that some societies attributed this dominion to the male only, Hobbes maintained that in commonwealths the controversy was decided by the civil law and that for the most part (but not always) the decision was in favor of the father. But Hobbes declared that in a state of nature, where there are no laws respecting matrimony or the education of children, where rather the laws of nature and of natural inclination govern, "either the parents themselves dispose of the dominion over the child by contract, or do not dispose thereof at all." As an example of this premise he cites the case of the Amazons, who contracted with their neighboring countries that male issue should be sent back but that females should remain with them "so that the dominion of the females was in the mother."[23]

Hobbes furnishes another example: if there be no contract, dominion is in the mother, for in the condition of mere nature, where there are no matrimonial laws, the identity of the father is unknown unless declared by the mother; "and therefore the right of dominion over the child dependeth on her will, and is consequently hers."[24] Hobbes also cites examples of dominion being acquired or lost (by women) by nourishment or by exposure of the child.

Hobbes further observed that because the first instruction of children depends on the care of their parents, obedience to parents is necessary while the children remain under their tuition, and also afterwards since gratitude requires they acknowledge the benefit of their education.[25]

### Locke

John Locke, on the other hand, argued that *paternal power*, was a misnomer and that it more properly should be called *parental power*, because power over children is shared by father and mother and she has equal title to it. He also cited the Scriptures in support of his argument—for example, "Honour thy father and thy mother" (*Exodus* 20:12).

Of the first part of the obligation Locke wrote that

> Adam and Eve, and after them all parents were, by the Law of Nature, under an obligation to preserve, nourish, and educate the children they had begotten, not as their own workmanship, but as the workmanship of their own, the Almighty.[26]

Thus, according to Locke, the power of parents over their children arises from this divine duty imposed on them. Concerning the second part of the obligation, Locke wrote that the support and gratitude due the parent flows from the benefits received by the child and is an "indispensable duty of the child and a proper privilege of the parent."[27]

Of the age of discretion, the point at which the child is deemed capable of knowing and choosing, Locke stated that in England it was by "law at the age of twenty-one, and in some cases sooner."[28]

Of the bonds of subjection to the rule and jurisdiction of their parents, Locke observed that age and reason in the child develop as they grow, loosening the bonds until at length they drop off. Persons laboring under any mental infirmity, however, are never set free from the government of their parents because they are deemed incapable of knowing the law and living within its rules.

## Rousseau

Rousseau, in *The Social Contract*, notes that "Man is born free; and everywhere he is in chains."[29] In the very next paragraph, however, he both affirms and contradicts this statement when speaking of the family and children and their attachment to their father: the oldest of all societies and the one that is most natural, he says, is the family, and the children remain attached to the father only as long as they need him for their preservation. As soon as this need ceases, the natural bond is dissolved: "The children, released from the natural obedience they owed to the father, and the father, released from the care he owed his children, return equally to independence."[30] If they remain united, they continue so no longer naturally but voluntarily, and the family itself is then maintained only by convention.

## Hegel

For Hegel, the family was a legal entity with the husband as its head controlling and administering the family's capital, which was the common property of the members of the family. Thus, "Children have the right to maintenance and education at the expense of the family's common capital."

The right of parents to the service of their children in his view was based on and restricted by the common task of looking after the family generally. Similarly, the right of parents over the wishes of their children was determined by the objectives in view—discipline and education. The punishment of children did not aim at justice as such: "The aim is more subjective and moral in character."[31]

Hegel offered the following rationale for the child's right to an education:

> Man has to acquire for himself the position he ought to attain; he is not already in possession of it by instinct. It is on this fact that the child's right to education is based.[32]

*Kant*

Immanuel Kant divided the topic parental right (parent and child) into two subtopics: (1) the relation of parent and child and (2) the rights of the parent. Of the first subtopic he observed that from the fact of procreation follows the parental duty of preservation and the corresponding congenital right (distinguished from a hereditary right) of children to be reared by the care of their parents until able to maintain themselves. The latter right of children he viewed as immediately theirs by law, without need of any particular judicial act.[33]

Of the second subtopic Kant wrote that from the foregoing duty of the parent "necessarily arises the right of the parents to the management and training" of the child, which continues as long as the child is incapable of proper use of the body and the mind.[34] "This involves its [the child's] nourishment and the care of its education."

Kant maintained that this training should continue until the child reached the "age of emancipation (*emancipatio*), as the age of practical self-support." The parents then would relinquish the right to command, and the children for their part would

> owe their parents nothing by way of legal debt for their education, just as the parents, on their side, are now released from their obligations to the children in the same way.[35]

## The Jurists

The jurists (Grotius, Pufendorf, and later, Blackstone) incorporated into their writings the earlier rationales for the obligation, which by now almost universally had become law with the responsibility fixed on the father.

*Grotius*

Grotius argued that a right could be acquired not only over things but also over persons and that such rights had their origins in (1) generation, (2) consent, and (3) crime. Parents acquired rights over children by generation, he maintained—"both parents, I mean, the father and the mother." However, if there was a variance in the exercise of these rights, then the right of the father was given preference "on account of the superiority of sex."[36]

In presenting his arguments, Grotius distinguished three periods:

1.  the period of "imperfect judgment" and lack of "discretion" (as in Aristotle's *Ethics* and in *Nicomachean Ethics*);

2. the period of "mature judgment" during which the son remains with the parents as a part of the family; and

3. the period commencing after the son has withdrawn from the family.

In the first period, Grotius said, "all the actions of the children are under the control of the parents," and the responsibility belongs first to the father, second to the mother.[37] In the second period, the child has matured with age, and no actions are subject to the rule of the parents except those that are important "for the position of the family in relation to the father and mother." In the third period, the child is for all purposes independent and his own master.

In the first and second periods, this control or right of the parent to govern the child "embraces also the right to chastise," and children must do their duty or else may be disciplined.[38]

Noting that it was a widely debated question in his time whether parents were under an obligation, legal or otherwise, to support their children and that some jurists, indeed, thought it in accord with "natural reason" that parents should have such a duty, Grotius concluded that "yet there is no legal duty."[39] Perhaps realizing that the word *duty* by itself was ambiguous, Grotius distinguished its several meanings, pointing out that

> The word sometimes is taken strictly for that obligation which is imposed by expletive justice; and sometimes, more freely, to indicate what cannot be neglected with honour, although in this case honour does not have its origin in expletive justice but in another source. We are concerned with duty in its larger sense, except when a human law intervenes.[40]

As examples of this reasoning, he quotes Valerius, who said that "parents by bringing us up have imposed upon us the duty of bringing up their grandchildren," and Plutarch's statement in *On the Love of Offspring* that "Children expect the inheritance as their due."

From Aristotle's reasoning that "Who gives the form gives what is necessary to the form," Grotius argued that

> Therefore the one who brings a human being into existence is under a duty to look out for it as much as he can, and as much as is necessary, in those things which are essential to human life, that is, for the natural social existence for which man was born.[41]

Grotius noted the existence of a "natural instinct" to provide nourishment and cited numerous examples from Euripides, Philostratus, and Oppian to illustrate that this affection is "inborn."

Whether unborn children can be deprived of a right, Grotius described as "an exceedingly difficult question," yet he concluded that a person not yet born has no rights, "just as a thing which does not exist has no attributes."[42] Therefore, abandonment of ownership and occupation does no injustice to those yet unborn because they have not yet acquired any right. This, he explained, is the law of nature, for the civil law (citing the *Digest*) had introduced other fictions such as that the law should defend the persons of those that do not yet exist and should hinder anything from being seized to their disadvantage.[43]

Grotius further stated that support likewise is due parents; this duty, he said, is fixed not only by laws but also by the common proverb that bids us "to cherish in return."[44] To Grotius, however, observance of the duty to parents was not as universal as the duty of parents to children.

Concerning ownership of property, Grotius said that in the first period (as described above) a son or daughter could own property according to "universal customary law," though exercise of the right would be hindered on account of their imperfection in judgment. He cited Plutarch's statement that children have the "right to possess" but not "to use" such property.[45]

Reaffirming that parental authority attached to the father and could not be taken away or transferred to another, Grotius nonetheless maintained that by natural right a father could "pledge" his son as security (if the civil law did not prevent it) and could even sell him if necessary and if there were no other means of supporting him.[46]

Distinguishing between the power of parents acquired by the law of nature and that conferred by municipal law, Grotius cited numerous examples from the Roman law of extensive powers of the father.

### Pufendorf

In the continuing discourse over the rights of children, the jurist Le Baron de Pufendorf stands at a crucial point in history. He contributed critical observations about the obligatory nature of the parental duty to support, protect, and provide education for the child, and these are found in his most famous work, which was translated into English under the formidable descriptive title:

> *Of the Law of Nature And Nations.* Eight Books. Written in Latin by the Baron Pufendorf, Counsellor of State to his late Swedish Majesty, and to the late King of Prussia. Done into English by Basil Kennett, D.D., late President of Corpus Christi College in Oxford. To which are added All the large Notes of Mr. Barbeyrac, translated from the best Edition; Together with Large Tables to the Whole. The Fourth Edition, carefully Corrected. To which is now prefixed Mr. Barbeyrac's Prefatory Discourse, Containing an Historical and Critical Account of the Science of Morality, and the Progress it has made in the World, from the earliest Times down to the

Publication of this Work. Done into English by Mr. Carew, of Lincoln's Inn. London: Printed for J. Walthoe, et al., 1729.[47]

Pufendorf posed a series of questions:

1. On what grounds is the "parental Right" over the child founded?
2. "[T]o which of the Parents this Right . . . doth most properly belong"?
3. "[H]ow far [doth] this Power of Parents over their Children [extend]; what are the proper Bounds and Measures of it"?
4. Whether the "perpetual Duty and Obligation" of children to their parents that remains after the father's power over them has expired, arise from:
   a. "the Act of Generation," or
   b. "the faithful Care and Labour of Breeding them up"?

   (Pufendorf noted that in his time this was a "Controversy that hath divided learned Men")
5. As a "common Question, Whether Children may dispose of themselves in Marriage against the Consent of their Parents"?[48]

"Children are the proper Fruit of Matrimony," wrote Pufendorf, who added that they are likewise the proper subjects of paternal dominion, the most ancient and most sacred kind of government by which children are engaged to acknowledge the superiority and to obey the commands of their parents.[49]

Pufendorf observed that Grotius (and other writers on this subject) referred to the act of generation as one in which parents in some manner resemble the Creator in making a person to exist who before had no being. Because both parents contributed equally, the other writers maintained that both acquired a right over their issue. But because they contended for power over the child and their contrary commands could not be obeyed, the father's authority carried precedence, not only on account of the advantage he had in sex but because the mother was placed under his direction and sway.[50]

In particular, Pufendorf examined the dominion by the father as expressed by Hobbes and concluded:

And, first of all, we think it may be settled as an undoubted Truth, that the Act of Generation doth yield an Occasion to the acquiring a Right over the Child which shall hold good. . . . We say an *Occasion*; because we are not persuaded that *Generation* alone is sufficient to give a full Dominion over human Issue.[51]

What, then, did Pufendorf view as the basis of parental dominion over children? This right, according to Pufendorf, is founded on two "Titles" or claims.

1.   First, it arises from the duty imposed on men by nature to take care of their offspring.

This duty (to care for offspring) cannot be exercised unless the parent has the power to direct and to govern the actions of the child.

2.   "Secondly, The Sovereignty of the Parents seems likewise to be built on the presumed Consent of the Children, and consequently on a tacit Pact."

The parent by the very act of rearing the infant declares himself ready to fulfill the obligation of nature and to provide education for his child, and the child by reason of this care and education acquires reciprocal duties toward its parents.[52]

Education was viewed by Pufendorf as the immediate foundation of paternal power and the duties of the father and child. "It is clear therefore," he said, "that the Power which Parents have over a Child, is then actually constituted, when they apply themselves to nourishing and educating him, and rendering him, so far as they are able, a useful Member of human Society."[53]

In response to the question to which of the parents does this duty most properly belong, Pufendorf concluded that in a commonwealth or otherwise where the parents are engaged to one another by a covenant, the power rightly lies with the father.[54]

How far does this power of the parents over their children extend? Pufendorf wrote,

> Now the Obligation, or Duty of a Father, as such, chiefly turns on this
> general Performance, that he duly educate his Children; that is, nourish,
> protect, inform, and govern them.[55]

Thus, for Pufendorf, education was the immediate foundation of parental power and of the rights and duties of father and child. He quotes a passage from Plutarch wherein he said that parents deserved censure if they committed their sons to the care of masters and instructors and then did not inquire into how the boy was doing but placed all hope and faith in the teachers.

Next, Pufendorf asked whether this "perpetual Duty and Obligation of Children" remaining after their father's power has expired arises from the act of generation or from the faithful care and labor in rearing them? Citing Plato and Socrates in support of his belief, Pufendorf answered:

> Yet we cannot but deliver it as our Persuasion that the Benefit of Educating is a much stronger Ground and Spring of filial Obligation, than the other of Begetting.[56]

To Pufendorf, the power of the father over the child by no means was of such a degree that "he may destroy the Child whilst in the Mother's Belly," unless the mother would otherwise perish, or after birth expose or give it away, "much less after the increase of Growth and Years."[57]

### Blackstone

Sir William Blackstone, in his classic work on the law of England, referred to the three elements of the obligation, and after citing (and sometimes quoting from) the works of Grotius, Pufendorf, and others, made the following observations about the obligation. In a chapter titled "Of Parent and Child," he wrote that the duties of parents to legitimate children consist of three particulars: their maintenance, their protection, and their education.

**Maintenance.** Blackstone assigned the duty of maintenance to natural law and cited Pufendorf to the effect that maintenance of children is a duty laid on parents not only by nature itself "but by their own proper act, in bringing them into the world." Thus, he concluded, children have a "perfect right" of receiving maintenance from their parents.[58]

"The municipal laws of all well-regulated states have taken care to enforce this duty: though providence has done it more effectually than any laws," Blackstone maintained, by implanting in every parent's breast an insuperable degree of affection for offspring.

In England, Blackstone noted, it was a "principle of law, that there is an obligation on every man to provide for those descended from his loins." He argued that the father, mother, grandfather, and grandmother of poor impotent persons were under a duty to maintain them by law and yet that no person was bound to provide maintenance of his issue unless the issue were impotent and unable to work. Thus,

> For the policy of our laws, which are ever watchful to promote industry, did not mean to compel a father to maintain his idle and lazy children in ease and indolences.[59]

**Protection.** Blackstone maintained that protection is likewise a natural duty, but one rather permitted than enjoined by municipal laws. (Thus, under English law, a parent could maintain and uphold his children in their lawsuits without fear of being charged with the crime of maintenance; so too a parent might justify assault and battery in defense of his children.)[60]

**Education.** Blackstone wrote that

> The last duty of parents to their children is that of giving them an education suitable to their station in life: a duty pointed out by reason, and by far the greatest importance of any.[61]

Citing Pufendorf, Blackstone observed that it is not easy to imagine a parent who would entirely neglect the culture and education of his child and permit him to grow up like a mere beast: "Yet the municipal laws of most countries seem to be defective in this point, by not constraining the parent to bestow a proper education upon his children." In contrast, English law provided for the apprenticing of poor children, Blackstone noted, yet

> The rich, indeed, are left at their own option, whether they will breed up their children to be ornaments or disgraces to their family.[62]

**Parental Authority over Children.** The power of parents over their children is derived from their duty, said Blackstone, this authority being given them to enable them to perform this duty more effectively and partly to compensate them for their care and trouble in performing the duty. Although Roman law gave the father the power of life and death over his children, the power of the father under English law was much more moderate but still designed to keep the child in order and obedience. Thus,

> He may lawfully correct his child being under age, in a reasonable manner; for this is for the benefit of his education.[63]

Further, he noted, the consent of the parent to marriage was absolutely required to protect the child from the "snare of artful and designing" persons and prevent the ill consequences of too early marriages.

Parental authority and control continued until the child was emancipated by age, Blackstone maintained:

> The legal power of a father (for a mother, as such, is entitled to no power, but only reverence and respect) power of a father, I say, over the persons of his children ceases at the age of twenty-one: for they are then enfranchised by arriving at years of discretion.[64]

The father also might delegate part of his power during his lifetime to a tutor or schoolmaster "who is then *in loco parentis,* and has such a portion of the power of the parent committed to his charge, *viz.* that of restraint and correction, as may be necessary to answer the purposes for which he is employed."[65]

**Duties of Children to Their Parents.** The duties owed by children to their parents, said Blackstone, arise from principles of natural justice and retribution: "For those, who gave us existence, we naturally owe subjection and obedience during our minority, and honour and reverence ever after."[66] Thus, the parents are entitled to protection in the infirmity of their old age and ought to be supported by their offspring if they are in need of assistance. On this principle proceed all the duties of children to their parents, including the duty to provide for them when they are fallen into poverty.

## Conclusion

The views of the ancient historians and the philosophers and jurists do not exist only in the abstract. The views of the philosophers were incorporated in those of the jurists, and many of these views achieved the status of law. Blackstone's *Commentaries,* for example, represented his views of the law of England.

Many modern legal rules respecting the rights, obligations, and incapacities of children have antecedents in these ancient customs and practices, except where the rules themselves have been overcome or changed by recent legislation or judicial decision. The modern views of children's rights and responsibilities are covered in the remainder of the book. In particular, the effect of the classical thinkers on the development of the parent/child/state relationship is seen most keenly in this book in the material on emancipation (chapter 3), the education cases decided by the United States Supreme Court (chapter 4), the material on medical decision making (chapter 5), the material on the right to an education (chapter 8), and the material on protection of children from inadequate parenting (chapter 9).

## Notes

1. J. Locke, Two Treatises of Civil Government 117 (1955) (1st ed. London 1690) [hereinafter cited as J. Locke].
2. "In silence will I pass the horrid banquet." Select Tragedies of Euripides (*Orestes*) 524 (Printed for N. Conant 1880).

3. HERODOTUS, THE HISTORIES 3 (A. Selincourt trans. 1955) [hereinafter cited as HERODOTUS].

4. SELECT TRAGEDIES OF EURIPIDES (*Phoenissae*) 2 (Printed for N. Conant 1880).

5. HERODOTUS, *supra* note 3, at 303.

6. S. FREUD, THE INTERPRETATION OF DREAMS (Fifth Lecture) 256 (1960) (1st ed. 1900).

7. HERODOTUS, *supra* note 3, at 115.

8. T. HOBBES, LEVIATHAN, OR THE MATTER, FORME, AND POWER OF A COMMONWEALTH, ECCLESIASTICALL AND CIVILL 131 (W. Marriott trans. 1955) [hereinafter cited as T. HOBBES].

9. G. HEGEL, LECTURES ON THE PHILOSOPHY OF WORLD HISTORY 200 (1975).

10. ARISTOTLE, NICOMACHEAN ETHICS, Bk. IX, 2. 1164b. (D. Ross trans. 1954).

11. ARISTOTLE, POLITICS, Bk. I, 12. 1259b. (D. Ross trans. 1954) [hereinafter cited as ARISTOTLE]. *Cf.* the saying of Amasis about his "foot-pan." HERODOTUS, *supra* note 3, at 170.

12. ARISTOTLE, *supra* note 11, Bk. I, 12. 1259b.

13. *Id.*, Bk. VII, 1. 1336a.

14. *Id.*, Bk. VII, 2. 1337a.

15. *Quoted in* B. DE MONTESQUIEU, 2 THE SPIRIT OF THE LAWS 509 (T. Nuget trans. 1900).

16. *Quoted in* H. GROTIUS, 2 DE JURE BELLI AC PACIS LIBRI TRES 270 (F. Kelsey trans. 1925) [hereinafter cited as H. GROTIUS]. *Compare* the comment by Chief Justice Burger in Parham v. J.R., 442 U.S. 584 (1979), at the beginning of chapter 1 *supra*.

17. H. GROTIUS, *supra* note 16, at 270.

18. ST. THOMAS AQUINAS, 47 SUMMA THEOLOGIAE 251 (1973) [hereinafter cited as ST. THOMAS ACQUINAS].

19. 1 *Timothy.* 5:8.

20. ST. THOMAS AQUINAS, *supra* note 18, at 253.

21. Dominion acquired by conquest or victory in war is also called *despotical* from the Greek *despotis*.

22. T. HOBBES, *supra* note 8, at 130–31.

23. *Id.* at 131. Montesquieu referred to the "natural obligation of the father to provide for his children," which he maintained established marriage, "which makes known the person who ought to fulfill this obligation." B. DE MONTESQUIEU, 1 THE SPIRIT OF THE LAWS 112–13 (T. Nuget trans. 1900).

24. T. HOBBES, *supra* note 8, at 131. Montesquieu refers to the "natural obligation of the father to provide for his children," which, he maintains, established marriage "which makes known the person who ought to fulfill this obligation." 2 THE SPIRIT OF THE LAWS 485.

25. T. HOBBES, *supra* note 8, at 131.

26. J. LOCKE, *supra* note 1, at 28–29.

27. *Id.* at 35.

28. *Id.* at 30. *See* the section on emancipation in chapter 3 *infra*.

29. J. ROUSSEAU, THE SOCIAL CONTRACT AND DISCOURSES 3 (G. Cole trans. 1950).

30. *Id.* at 4.

31. G. HEGEL, HEGEL'S PHILOSOPHY OF RIGHT 117 (1942).

32. *Id.* at 265.

33. I. KANT, SCIENCE OF RIGHT, II, 28 (W. Hastie trans. 1887).

34. *Id.* at 29.

35. *Id.* at 30. *See* the section on emancipation in chapter 3 *infra.*

36. H. GROTIUS, *supra* note 16, at 231.

37. *Id.* at 231 & n.1, citing SENECA, CONTROVERSIES, III, xix: "The first place belongs to the father, the second to the mother."

38. *Id.* at 232.

39. *Id.* at 269.

40. *Id.*

41. *Id.* at 270.

42. *Id.* at 226.

43. *Id.* at 227.

44. *Id.* at 271.

45. *Id.* at 232.

46. *Id.* at 232–33.

47. Chapter II, Book VI, of Pufendorf concerns "Paternal Power," at 598, which deals with such subjects as the origin of paternal power, Hobbes on the original power of the mother over the children, the reasons on which paternal authority is grounded, the extent to which the father has more rights than the mother, and so forth [hereinafter cited as PUFENDORF].

48. *Id.* at 600–602, 610, 612.

49. *Id.*

50. *Id.*

51. *Id.* at 600.

52. *Id.* at 601.

53. *Id.*

54. *Id.* at 601–02. *Compare* H. GROTIUS, *supra* note 16 and accompanying text, and ARISTOTLE, *supra* note 11 and accompanying text.

55. PUFENDORF, *supra* note 47, at 603.

56. *Id.* at 610.

57. *Id.* at 603.

58. 1 BLACKSTONE, COMMENTARIES ON THE LAWS OF ENGLAND *447.

59. *Id.* at *449.

60. *Id.* at *450.

61. *Id.*

62. *Id.* at *451.

63. *Id.* at *452.

64. *Id.* at *453.

65. *Id.*

66. *Id.*

# 3
# Private Law and Children's Rights

> A stranger must think it strange that a minor in certain cases may be liable for his torts and responsible for his crimes and yet is not bound by his contracts. Of course there are exceptions and qualifications to this general proposition. However, the common-law conception that a minor does not possess the discretion and experience of adults and therefore must be protected from his contractual follies generally holds sway today.
> —Chief Justice Frank R. Kenison
> *Porter v. Wilson*
> 106 N.H. 270, 271, 209 A.2d 730, 731 (1965)

## Introduction

In the private law context, law has assumed sometimes confusing and often conflicting attitudes toward children. In the areas of contract and property law, for example, the law traditionally has viewed children as being incapable of entering into binding contracts or disposing of their property and in need of protection from more experienced adults. The law, therefore, has assumed a protective posture in dealing with children in these areas. On the other hand, in the area of tort law, children traditionally have been regarded as liable for their torts where they have caused injury to others or property damage. In contrast to the protective role assumed by the law in other areas, the law here has accorded children a certain degree of autonomy.

These contrasting attitudes of the law toward children, from one area of private law to the next, probably are the result of independent development of each area of law without any thought given to the status of children generally under the law. Regardless of the reasons that conflicting attitudes developed, the fact undeniably remains that such conflicting attitudes exist. These attitudes are presented and discussed in the sections that follow. The chapter culminates with a discussion of the doctrine of emancipation that attempts to resolve some of the inconsistencies in the law's attitudes toward children; emancipation allows some children, at least, to decide some matters for themselves as though they were adults.

## Torts

In 1863 in the case of *Huchting v. Engel*[1] the Wisconsin Supreme Court held that a six-year-old child was liable in trespass for damages for "breaking and entering the plaintiff's premises, and breaking down and destroying his strawberries and flowers therein standing and growing"—despite the claim that the child was "'of such tender years that a suit at law could not be maintained against him.'" One might suppose that because of the date of the decision it represents an antiquated view no longer followed today. In truth, however, the proposition stated by the Wisconsin court—that children can be held liable for their torts—is as valid today as it was in 1863.[2]

A word of caution is in order. The rule is simply that children—like adults—*can* be held liable for their torts. Put another way, children *as a class* are not immune from liability solely because of their age.

As with virtually every rule some qualification is in order. Thus, although children do not enjoy absolute immunity as such, a particular child may escape liability because he lacks the mental state required for liability. For example, because of his age, inexperience, and limited intelligence he may be incapable of forming the intent required for commission of an intentional tort such as battery, and he may be incapable of negligence as well in that he can not comprehend risks of which an adult would—or should—be aware.[3]

On the latter score especially—that is, where a child is alleged to have caused injury or property loss negligently—a child's immaturity and lack of experience are often taken into account. In judging whether an adult has acted negligently the law typically employs what is referred to as the *reasonable man* standard—that is, the inquiry is into whether the subject exercised the sort of care exercised by the reasonable, ordinary person, or put another way, whether the reasonable, ordinary person would have been aware of the risk of which the subject was unaware.[4] Children, however, are not expected to measure up to the adult standard. Consequently, the standard for children is more subjective—that is, a child's conduct is measured against what reasonably would be expected of a child of like age, intelligence, and experience.[5]

Most of the case law on the subject has arisen in the context of cases in which children were plaintiffs and their contributory negligence was raised as a defense. Rather than allow children's claims to be defeated simply because their conduct fell short of the norm when measured by adult standards, courts have preferred application of the more subjective children's standard for evaluating the reasonableness of their conduct. This view might be attributable to a protective concern—that is, that children with valid claims for personal injury or loss be able to seek redress for the injury or loss.[6]

Recent commentary has suggested that no good reason appears why a child's conduct should not be judged on the basis of the "children's" standard regardless of whether the child is plaintiff or defendant. Hence, the trend is toward adoption of the subjective standard both where the child is defendant in a lawsuit and where the child is plaintiff and is alleged to have been contributorily negligent.[7] The one limitation on this view is that if the child is engaged in an adult activity, such as driving a car or piloting an airplane, he is held to the adult standard.[8]

Occasionally parents are held responsible for torts committed by their children, usually as a result of statutes providing for parental responsibility. These statutes typically provide for a fairly low ceiling for damage awards against parents.[9] Louisiana's statute is by far the broadest in scope. It provides for parental liability for torts committed by children with no limitation on damages[10] and without regard to the child's ability or lack thereof to discern right from wrong.[11] Although Louisiana's parental responsibility statute is one of long standing, most of the others are recent enactments designed to encourage increased parental supervision of children as a curb against vandalism.

To be distinguished from these statutory approaches, which flatly hold parents vicariously liable for the negligent and intentional acts of their children, is a separate theory of parental liability under which parents are held accountable for acts of their children on the ground that the parent was independently negligent in failing to supervise the child properly. For example, in *Moore v. Crumpton*,[12] in which a rape victim sued the parents of the unemancipated seventeen-year-old assailant, the court acknowledged that parental liability can be established where the parent (1) had the ability and opportunity to control the child and (2) knew or should have known of reasons requiring exercise of such control.[13] In such cases the parent is independently negligent for failing to exercise proper control, whereas under the parental liability statutes previously mentioned, the child's negligence (or intent) is imputed to the parent.

Another facet of tort liability affecting children is the doctrine of parent/child, or intrafamily, immunity. A novel idea when it was first announced in an 1891 decision,[14] the doctrine quickly became the established rule in this country. The immunity doctrine states that neither parent nor child is liable to the other for tortious acts committed by one against the other.[15] The chief reason offered in its favor is that it promotes family harmony, although one might question whether having an uncompensated tort in the family promotes harmony between its members, particularly in the case of an intentional, even brutal, tort.[16]

Perhaps in response to such concerns, over half the states have abrogated the parent/child immunity doctrine either by court decision or legislation. Today in these states either parent or child may bring an action against the other for the other's tortious act.[17] One exception, however, is that courts have declined to recognize the right of a child to bring an action against a parent for inadequate parenting.[18] On the latter point, an interesting obsrvation is that children generally have become more litigious in recent years, seeking to vindicate their rights not only against parents for inadequate parenting[19] and wrongful life[20] but against school authorities for infliction of excessive corporal punishment[21] and for what has been labeled *educational malpractice*.[22] For the most part their efforts have met with little or no success.

## Contracts

In contrast to the law's view that children may be held accountable for their tortious acts, the law takes a protective view of children when they enter into contractual agreements with others. The vehicle for this protective attitude is the doctrine of *disaffirmance,* which refers to the power of a child to avoid or disavow a contract into which he has entered.[23]

Suppose, for example, a child and an adult enter into a contract by which the adult agrees to sell and the child agrees to purchase an automobile. The child makes a downpayment and the car is delivered to the minor on his promise to pay a stated sum per month until the purchase price is paid in full, at which time the seller agrees to deliver title to the car. The minor enjoys use of the car for a couple of months and makes his monthly payments. Everyone is happy, and the deal is proceeding as planned. Then, however, for whatever reason—defects real or imagined or pure whim—the child decides to back out of the agreement, and he returns the car and insists on return of all money paid. The law is of the view that the minor has the absolute power to disaffirm his contract; therefore, he is entitled to return of his money and release from any further obligation.[24]

Dissaffirmance is wholly the child's option. Thus, if the child stops making payments, and the seller brings suit to collect on the contract, the child may raise minority as a defense and thereby avoid the contract.[25] Moreover, if the seller decides for whatever reason that he has made a bad bargain, he is nevertheless bound by the agreement; he may not seek to have the contract set aside for the reason of the child's minority.[26]

Presumably, the basis for the doctrine is that children, because of their age and inexperience, are in need of protection from their own improvidence and from more experienced adults who might take unfair advantage of them.[27] At the same time, however, this policy is in conflict with another equally compelling policy in contract law—the policy that favors protection of the other party's expectations, which has particular application here if the adult has dealt fairly and in good faith with the child.[28]

Perhaps because of the hardship that might be imposed on an adult who has dealt fairly with the minor, there are a number of limitations either on the doctrine itself or on the consequences of its application. The most obvious limitation is that for the purpose of determining who is a child with power to disaffirm, most states have lowered the arbitrary age limit from twenty-one to eighteen in keeping with lowering of the age of majority to eighteen in general.[29]

Although the latter reform has the effect of removing the power of disaffirmance from persons eighteen or older who enter into contracts, it does not automatically mean that on reaching the age of eighteen a child immediately loses the power to disaffirm a contract into which he previously entered. To the contrary, a child retains the power of disaffirmance for a reasonable period after reaching the age of majority, and there are instances in which even a delay of several years did not affect the power of disaffirmance where the other party had not relied on the transaction.[30]

On the other hand, a child on reaching majority may, by word *or conduct*, ratify a contract into which he had entered previously. An example of the doctrine of ratification is found in *Jones v. Dressel*.[31] In that case a seventeen-year-old boy entered into a contract for use of the defendant's skydiving facilities. The contract contained an exculpatory clause and a provision whereby the user of services agreed not to sue the defendant. Ten months after becoming eighteen the plaintiff, now an adult, was injured in the crash of an airplane furnished by the defendant. Subsequently the plaintiff filed suit against the defendant, alleging that he had disaffirmed the contract within a reasonable time after reaching adulthood. The court, however, held that the trial court properly determined that by accepting the benefits of the contract after he reached adulthood, the plaintiff ratified the contract and was bound by its terms, including the covenant not to sue.

Another limitation on the power of disaffirmance is sometimes created by statute for children who are professional athletes or entertainers or who have contracted for "necessaries" (food, shelter, clothing, and the like). Such contracts cannot be disaffirmed, although typically court approval of the contract is required.[32] Some proposals, such as the *Juvenile Justice Standards Relating to Rights of Minors,* would go even further by removing the child's power to disaffirm a contract to which the child's parent or guardian has consented in writing, a contract entered into by a child who has misrepresented his age where a reasonable person would have believed the representation, and a contract in which the child was a purchaser and is unable to return the goods to the seller in substantially original condition because they have been lost or destroyed, consumed, or given away.[33]

A contemporary example of the latter kind of statutory limitation is found in the attempt by Brooke Shields to prevent publication of nude photographs taken when she was ten years old and working as a model. Section 51 of New York's Civil Rights Law creates a civil cause of action for use of a living person's name, portrait, or picture for advertising purposes without written consent of the person, or if the person is a child, his or her parent or guardian. Shields brought suit against the photographer who took the pictures, seeking to disaffirm the consent executed by her mother on her behalf.

The New York Court of Appeals, while conceding that under principles of common law a child has the power to disaffirm a contract, concluded that the legislature has the authority to abrogate a child's right to disaffirm and intended to do so in this instance by providing for consent on a minor's behalf by a parent or guardian.[34] Therefore, Shields was bound by the consent executed by her mother on her behalf and could not disaffirm it.

In situations in which a child unquestionably has the power to disaffirm, questions nevertheless arise with respect to the consequences resulting from the disaffirmance, especially whether and to what extent the child has to make restitution to the other party. The traditional rule is that the child need return only what remains in his possession. To return to the example used earlier, if a child contracts for the purchase of an automobile and he later disaffirms the contract, he is entitled to return of all money paid, and for his part he need return only the automobile as is. If it is wrecked, he must return the wreckage; if it is lost or totally destroyed he has nothing to return and is under no further obligation.[35] At least one court has made a departure from the traditional rule, holding the child accountable for the value of the benefit actually received, not to exceed the price he agreed to pay for the goods.[36] The latter view is particularly compelling where the child is engaged in business for himself.[37]

Several exceptions to the traditional rule operate to mollify the hardship that otherwise would result to a party entering into a contract with a minor. One exception is that a child is liable for the reasonable value of necessaries where the parent has failed to meet the child's needs. What constitutes a "necessary" is a mixed question of fact and law; certainly it is something necessary for survival, such as food, shelter, or clothing, but could include medical care and transportation as well.[38] If the child has obtained the goods on his parent's credit and not on his own credit, then the parent, not the child, is liable.[39]

Another exception sometimes is allowed where the child as plaintiff seeks to recover money already paid, as opposed to where the child as defendant claims his minority as a defense. Thus, if the child receives the property and makes partial payment, then disaffirms and seeks a return of his money, he is entitled to avoid the contract but must restore the property to the seller and make restitution to the seller for the value of benefits received. The value of benefits received normally is equal to the depreciation of the property during the time the child held it, which is probably equal to the amount of payments actually made to the seller.[40]

The latter exception is based on the notion that a child's minority should be used as a shield but not as a sword.[41] As a practical result, one who furnishes goods or services to a minor for cash is entitled to restitution in full if the child disaffirms and then seeks a return of his money, whereas one who furnishes goods or services on credit is not. From the child's perspective, if he improvidently pays cash in full or a cash downpayment for goods or services, he must account in full or to the extent of the downpayment, but if he obtains the goods on credit he is not held accountable.[42]

Another exception is allowed where the child has misrepresented his age. A number of courts have held that if the child misrepresents his age and the seller reasonably relies on the representation, the child is obligated to make restitution for the depreciation of the property, typically a vehicle of some kind.[43] The underlying rationale for this view is that children are liable for their torts (see the preceding section on torts) and the child's fraudulent misrepresentation of age is a tort if the other party relied on it. Because reliance occasioned the furnishing of goods or services, and the other party suffered loss because of the child's disaffirmance, the loss is viewed as caused by the misrepresentation; restitution in full, therefore, is dictated.[44] Some courts go further, taking the position that because of his misrepresentation a child is estopped (that is, prevented under the law because of his misconduct) from asserting minority as a defense and is liable not just for restitution but on the contract itself.[45]

The fact of the limited number and scope of these exceptions bears witness to the reluctance of most courts to depart from the traditional rules allowing disaffirmance but not requiring restitution. As one court has put it, to do otherwise would "force the minor to bear the cost of the very improvidence from which the infancy doctrine is supposed to protect him."[46]

## Regulation of Child Employment

From a very early time the law has assumed a protective attitude toward children in the area of employment.[47] In response to humanitarian concerns for children working in hazardous occupations, for young children working at any occupation, for children working excessively long hours, and for conditions in the work place generally, laws regulating various aspects of child employment were enacted to protect children from physical danger and exploitation.[48]

Concerns for the welfare of children are real. Perhaps no other contemporary example illustrates them so dramatically as the incident that occurred on July 23, 1982, when during the filming of a movie at 2:30 in the morning a helicopter fell out of control, crashing into and killing veteran actor Vic Morrow and two child actors, six and seven years old. Questions surfaced immediately regarding why children of that age were engaged in such an activity at that time of day.[49]

Both federal and state laws regulate child labor practices. Included in the federal Fair Labor Standards Act,[50] for example, are numerous provisions relating to child employment. The act prohibits an employer involved in interstate commerce or in production of goods for interstate commerce from engaging in "oppressive child labor" practices.[51] Violations are punishable with civil and criminal penalties.[52] *Oppressive child labor* is defined under the act as employment of children under the minimum legal age for a particular type of employment.[53]

Generally, the minimum age for employment is eighteen for nonagricultural occupations that have been declared by the Secretary of Labor as posing a significant health or safety hazard to children.[54] Occupations that currently have been designated as hazardous or detrimental to the health or well-being of children include mining; logging and sawmilling; slaughtering, meat packing, or processing and rendering; manufacture of brick, tile, and explosives (including storage of explosives); wrecking, demolition, and shipbreaking; roofing; excavation; and any type of occupation involving operation of certain types of machinery or exposure to radioactive materials.[55]

Employment in other occupations, even those designated as hazardous agricultural occupations,[56] generally is permissible for children who are age sixteen or older.[57] Children age fourteen or older may be employed in some occupations, but not manufacturing or mining, where specific precautions have been taken to assure their safety.[58]

Finally, special allowance is made for children engaged in agricultural occupations. Generally, children age fourteen or older may work after school hours in agricultural occupations other than those deemed hazardous (see above).[59] Also, children under age twelve may be employed in nonhazardous agricultural occupations on the family farm, and children ages twelve and thirteen may be employed in nonhazardous agricultural occupations with parental consent or where the parent is employed on the same farm.[60]

An exemption from the age and occupation requirements of the act is allowed for children employed as actors or performers in motion pictures, radio, theater, or television.[61] Perhaps this exemption exists for reasons similar to those supporting special treatment of contracts entered into by children who are professional athletes or entertainers,[62] although the entertainment industry poses hazards of its own for children (as indicated by the helicopter incident mentioned above).

Individual states also have laws regulating child employment.[63] State laws apply in addition to federal laws; in fact, if state law imposes stricter requirements than those imposed under federal law, federal law adopts the state's stricter requirements.[64] Moreover, state law might apply exclusively in a situation to which federal law is inapplicable—for example, employment that does not touch on interstate commerce in any way or employment exempted from federal law but not from state law.[65]

Aside from civil penalties and criminal fines, what are the consequences, to an employer, of violation of laws regulating employment of children? The case of *Vincent v. Riggi & Sons*[66] furnishes an example. In that case, a builder hired a thirteen-year-old boy to mow the lawn of a newly constructed house, and the boy accidentally cut off three of his toes while mowing the lawn with his father's power mower. State law prohibited employment of children under age fourteen in "any trade, business or service." The boy brought suit against the builder for his injuries, but the jury returned a verdict for the defendant, largely because the jury was not told of the employment prohibition but was told that they could consider the boy's contributory negligence.

On appeal, the New York Court of Appeals reversed, holding that the jury should have been told of the prohibition against employing children under age fourteen and should not have been told that they could consider the boy's contributory negligence. The policy behind child employment regulations, the court said, is to protect children from exploitation and from their own negligence. If a child's negligence could be considered against him, he would lose the very protection the statute was designed to afford.[67] Therefore, an employer of child labor, in violation of law, is liable regardless of the child's contributory negligence.

Federal and state laws also impose wage requirements for employment of children and adults, typically in the form of a minimum wage. Under current federal law, for example, the minimum wage generally is $3.35 per hour.[68] The Fair Labor Standards Act, however, provides numerous exemptions, some of which specifically apply to children and others of which by implication include children. For example, the act allows an exemption for learners, apprentices, and messengers[69] and provides that full-time students, under special circumstances, may be paid at a rate not less than 85 percent of the minimum wage for employment in retail and service establishments.[70] Moreover, newspaper carriers and persons engaged at home in making natural evergreen wreaths are exempted,[71] as are some children engaged in certain agricultural occupations.[72]

In 1981 a subminimum wage for persons in the sixteen to nineteen age group was proposed. It immediately drew opposition from organized labor. One union leader dubbed the proposal the "McDonald's windfall gift amendment" because of the savings that would result for the fast-food chain, an employer of large numbers of teenage workers.[73] The proposal was not adopted. In 1984 the proposal resurfaced in a form that would authorize a subminimum wage of $2.50 per hour for persons between ages sixteen and twenty-one employed during the summer months. The National Conference of Black Mayors endorsed the proposal because of their concern over "the persistence of the tragedy of youth unemployment, particularly the problem of minority youth unemployment."[74] Substantiating their concern, Labor Department figures for April 1984 showed an unemployment rate of 19.4 percent among sixteen-to-nineteen-year-old youth generally and for blacks in the same age group a rate of 42.9 percent.[75]

Organized labor has been critical of such proposals because of the fear a lower minimum wage for youth inevitably would mean displacement of adult workers.[76] Moreover, contrary to earlier indications, fast-food chains are skeptical of a subminimum wage for youth because of speculation it would prompt a higher minimum wage for adults.[77] The proposal also has been criticized because it is not comprehensive enough and fails to take into account the correlation between educational deficiencies and unemployment; what is needed, it is claimed, is a program that creates opportunities and incentives "to acquire basic educational skills crucial to success in the job market."[78]

## Testamentary Transfer of Property

At common law a male who had reached fourteen years of age or a female of twelve years of age was deemed capable of disposing of his or her personal property by will, but a disposition of real property by will was valid only if the person had reached the age of majority—that is, twenty-one years of age.[79] In England after the Wills Act[80] in 1837, however, the age requirement was the same—that is, twenty-one for disposition of both realty and personalty.[81]

In the United States in 1929, eleven states employed different ages for disposition of personal as opposed to real property.[82] In all but one of these states today, however, the age requirement is the same for testamentary disposition of both realty and personalty.[83]

Adoption of a common age in these states is but a part of a larger development that has taken place in recent years. With three exceptions,[84] all states and the District of Columbia have adopted eighteen as the age at which one can make a valid will, regardless of the nature of the property.[85] This development probably reflects widespread acceptance of eighteen as the age of majority as well as recognition that at age eighteen young people possess sufficient intelligence and understanding to dispose of real property as well as personal property.[86]

One might reasonably ask why capacity to make a will is age specific at all in the case of children. One might compare, for example, the attitude of the law toward older persons who make wills. In such a case, the law disregards age and asks only whether the person had testamentary capacity —that is, whether he had sufficient mental capacity to understand the nature of his act in making the will, to understand and recall the nature and location of his property, and to understand and recall his relations, who are the natural objects of his bounty and whose interests would be affected by the will.[87] In fact, a presumption exists that one has testamentary capacity, and the burden to show otherwise is placed on the party challenging the will.[88] As a practical matter, the presumption is difficult to overcome.[89]

Why, then, should minors, wholly for the reason of age, be regarded as incompetent to dispose of their property by will, especially since they are held liable for their torts[90] and in some instances are bound by their contracts?[91] Why should not a child who, as an entertainer or professional athlete may be bound by his contracts with other persons, also be capable of disposing of his property by testamentary gift?

In California, for example, one must be age eighteen or older to make a will.[92] California law provides elsewhere, however, that an emancipated minor[93] is regarded as an adult for certain purposes, such as determining capacity to enter into a contract and, more recently, to make a will.[94] The comments following this statute indicate that because entering into a contract requires greater capacity than that required to make a will, it made little sense to allow emancipated minors to enter into binding contracts, which they could do under existing law, while denying them the right to dispose of their property by will.[95] Perhaps for similar reasons other states allow persons under age eighteen to make wills where they have been emancipated by marriage,[96] service in the armed forces or merchant marine,[97] or by judicial decree of emancipation.[98]

Children generally can inherit property from others if provision is made for them.[99] Little protection exists, however, against outright disinheritance. Thus, if a parent wishes to disinherit a child he need only mention the child by name in the will and disinherit him.[100] Despite disinheritance, however, children may be entitled to certain protections such as a "family allowance" during the time the estate is being administered,[101] temporary possession of the family residence,[102] and even continued use and enjoyment (that is, ownership) of the family residence.[103]

The most troublesome cases have been those in which the child was born after the will was made or, though born, simply was not mentioned in the will. Pretermitted children (that is, children not mentioned in the will) and afterborn children usually are entitled to a share of the parent's estate. In California, for example, with some exceptions a pretermitted child *born or adopted* after execution of the will is entitled to a share of his parent's estate equal to the share he would have received if the parent had died intestate (that is, without a will).[104] The exceptions cover situations in which it appears the omission was intentional.[105] In the case of any other pretermitted child, such child is protected only if the omission occurred either because the decedent erroneously thought the child was dead or because he was unaware of the child's birth.[106]

Another limited protection recognized by some states is a restriction on the amounts designated for charities where there are surviving children.[107] This type of limitation is fast declining,[108] perhaps because of the ease with which it is circumvented.[109]

Special provision generally is made for inheritance rights of adopted children. Traditionally, they could inherit both from their natural parents and adoptive parents. Under many modern statutes, however, adopted children are recognized fully as part of their adoptive families and therefore can inherit only from their adoptive parents.[110] Allowance is sometimes made in two instances: (1) where the child's natural parent remarries and the stepparent adopts the child, the child may inherit from the natural parent;[111] and (2) where one of the child's natural parents dies, the surviving natural parent remarries, and the stepparent adopts the child, the child may inherit from the deceased natural parent.[112]

In some states (for example, California), an adopted child can inherit not only from the adoptive parents[113] but in some instances from the natural parents as well,[114] although the natural parents may not always inherit from the child.[115]

As further protection, unless a contrary intent appears, an adopted child usually is included in any bequest or devise to a class described generally as *children, issue,* or *heirs.*[116]

## Statutes of Limitation

All states impose time limitations, known as statutes of limitation, within which one having a cause of action must bring it or else be foreclosed from bringing it in the future. Different time limits apply to different causes of action. For example, California provides that the statute of limitations for any action on a written contract is four years;[117] on an oral contract the statute of limitations is two years.[118] For some actions the statute of limitations is longer; for example, for a cause of action against a developer, contractor, or architect based on a claim of faulty design it is ten years.[119]

As another example of the law's protective attitude toward children, statutes of limitation do not run during a child's minority for any cause of action arising during minority. Thus, in California, for any of the causes of action mentioned above, the statute of limitations does not begin to run against a minor until the age of majority is reached.[120] The same is true of any other cause of action accruing during minority—that is, the statute is "tolled" during minority.[121]

If the purpose of statutes of limitation is to encourage—indeed, require —persons with knowledge of legitimate claims to seek timely relief, such purpose is thwarted under provisions tolling statutes of limitation during minority. One readily can see that from the potential defendant's perspective the possibility of legal action may be outstanding for a number of years—perhaps twenty or more—if the statute of limitations does not begin to run until a child reaches the age of majority. What social value—other than the law's patronage of children—offsets the considerable disadvantage imposed on potential defendants? The case law has been somewhat revealing as discussed below.

In recent years some states have created exceptions to the tolling of statutes of limitation during minority, in at least two kinds of cases: (1) medical malpractice actions and (2) paternity actions. In California, for example, the statute of limitations for medical malpractice actions generally is three years from the date of injury or one year from the date the injured party discovers or through reasonable diligence should have discovered the injury, whichever occurs first.[122] For a child also the statute of limitations is three years, except in the case of a child under the full age of six years, the action must be commenced within three years or before the child's eighth birthday, whichever is the longer period.[123]

A similar statute in Texas recently was declared unconstitutional by the Texas Supreme Court in *Sax v. Votteler*.[124] The state has a legitimate interest, the court conceded, in increasing the availability and quality of health care in the state, which can be furthered by limiting lawsuits against providers of health-care services in order to hold malpractice insurance rates to a reasonable level and to increase availability of such insurance. The state's interest is not as great, however, as to justify foreclosure of a child's claim where the parent has failed to act timely on the child's behalf. A child must depend on parents to bring an action on his behalf. If they fail to do so within the prescribed time, the child is foreclosed from bringing suit on his own behalf because he cannot bring suit during his minority and cannot sue the parent for negligence (in failing to meet the two-year statute of limitations) because of the parent/child immunity.[125]

The Texas statute, therefore, was held to violate a provision of the state constitution guaranteeing access to courts for vindication of lawful and just claims, which the court characterized as a due process provision. The current Texas statute provides that a child under age twelve has until his fourteenth birthday to bring an action or to have one brought on his behalf; otherwise, the statute of limitations is two years, the same as for adults.[126]

An Ohio statute similar to the current Texas statute recently was held unconstitutional by the Ohio Supreme Court in *Schwan v. Riverside Methodist Hospital*.[127] The Ohio statute provides that a child under ten years of age has until his fourteenth birthday to file a claim for medical malpractice, whereas the statute of limitations for a child ten years of age or older is the same as for adults, four years.[128] Any other statute of limitations is tolled during a child's minority.[129]

In the Ohio case, also, the court acknowledged the state's interest in ensuring continuation of health care to its citizens. The court held the statute to be a denial of equal protection of the laws, however, because it did not rationally further the state's worthy goal of ensuring quality health care for its citizens. It only created a distinction, without reasonable grounds for doing so, between medical malpractice litigants who are under age ten and those who are age ten or older but still minors. The court added the observation that only the age of majority establishes a rational distinction.

Statutes shortening the time for bringing paternity actions have fared no better. Paternity actions typically are brought as a means of establishing an illegitimate child's right to support from his father. In *Gomez v. Perez*[130] the United States Supreme Court held unconstitutional a Texas statutory scheme that allowed legitimate children a right of support from their fathers while denying any such right to illegitimate children. The Court recognized the validity of the state's desire to avoid the difficult problems of proof often associated with paternity cases but observed that such concern did not justify erection of an "impenetrable barrier" in the path of an illegitimate child's right to support.[131]

In *Mills v. Habluetzel*[132] the Court held unconstitutional a Texas statute requiring that a paternity action be filed within one year of the child's birth.[133] Writing for the Court, Justice Rehnquist observed that "in response to the constitutional requirements of *Gomez,* Texas has created a one-year window in its previously 'impenetrable barrier' through which an illegitimate child may establish paternity and obtain parental support."[134] He further observed that "It would hardly satisfy the demands of equal protection and the holding of *Gomez* to remove an 'impenetrable barrier' to support only to replace it with an opportunity so truncated that few could utilize it effectively."[135] Thus, the one-year period was characterized as "unrealistically short."[136]

The state had argued that the shortened period was necessary because of the problems of proof in paternity actions generally, problems made worse by passage of time. A concurring opinion by Justice O'Connor noted that problems of proof are presented in other civil cases as well, yet a paternity case is one of the few causes of action singled out for special treatment.[137]

*Mills v. Habluetzel* could be viewed as simply condemning an "unreasonably short" one-year statute of limitations, but for the Court's subsequent decision in *Pickett v. Brown*[138] holding Tennessee's two-year statute of limitations[139] unconstitutional as well. Specifically, the Court held that the two-year period was not long enough to afford an adequate opportunity to bring a paternity suit. Even in a two-year period, the mother might not be inclined to bring such a suit because of continuing affection for the child's father, a desire to avoid disapproval of family and community, emotional strain and confusion, or other reasons.

Moreover, the statute did not bear a substantial relationship to the state's interest in avoiding problems of proof. For example, the two-year limitation was not imposed on the state's right to bring a paternity suit in a case in which the child was or was likely to become a public charge, even though evidence would be just as stale in these cases as in others. This exception belied the state's asserted interest in avoiding evidentiary difficulties. And, as in *Mills v. Habluetzel,* the fact remained that in most other civil actions statutes of limitation were tolled during a child's minority. All of these considerations suggested illegitimate children were being discriminated against without valid purpose.[140]

In the last two Supreme Court decisions one of the concerns expressed by the Court was that paternity actions were singled out for different treatment from most other causes of action involving children. Perhaps this concern is limited to paternity actions because of the Court's "heightened scrutiny" of any statutes that discriminate against illegitimate children.[141] Especially when taken with the actions of the Texas and Ohio courts in the medical malpractice cases, however, the Court's concern may be a signal that *any* statute of limitations that is shortened for children for one cause of action, to the exclusion of other causes of action, is going to be viewed with suspicion.

## Emancipation

The doctrine of emancipation has existed since common law times.[142] In its simplest terms the doctrine means that a child is free from parental authority and regarded as an adult for some purposes if the child (1) is married, (2) has joined the military, (3) is living separate and apart from the parents, or (4) is otherwise economically self-supporting.[143] If a child is considered emancipated, the new status has a bearing on such matters as (1) application of intrafamily tort immunity, (2) the child's right to wages and damages, (3) the child's right to sue and be sued, (4) the child's right to parental support, (5) the child's choice of domicile, (6) the child's power to disaffirm contracts, (7) the child's ability to enlist in the military, and (8) the child's attainment of majority itself.[144]

Whether a child is deemed emancipated traditionally has been a determination made by the courts in highly particularized circumstances. For example, in *Accent Service Co. v. Ebsen*[145] the question before the court was whether an eighteen-year-old boy or his mother was liable for payment of medical care furnished the boy by the plaintiff hospital. The court held that the evidence was sufficient to establish that the boy was emancipated at the time the medical care was furnished, by virtue of the facts that he had moved out of his mother's home and become self-supporting prior to the injury for which he was treated. Thus the boy, not the mother, was liable for payment of the hospital bill.

Of course, lowering of the age of majority from twenty-one to eighteen years of age has diminished the overall significance of the emancipation doctrine because many of the litigated cases involved "children" in the eighteen-to-twenty-one age group.[146] In recent years, however, the common law doctrine of emancipation has been augmented by legislation allowing persons under eighteen years of age to petition the courts for a declaration of emancipation. Some first-generation statutes have been around for many years but characteristically lack details and objective standards by which emancipation determinations are to be made and more often than not require the petition to be brought by someone other than the child.[147] More recently, a second generation of statutes has opted for a more comprehensive approach.[148]

California is typical of the latter group. The California Civil Code allows a child age fourteen or older to petition the court for emancipation on a showing that the child lives separate and apart from the parents with the parents' consent and is self-supporting.[149] The child's parent, guardian, or custodian is entitled to notice of the hearing on the petition.[150] The petition is granted if the court finds the information contained in it to be true and that emancipation would not be adverse to the child's best interests.[151] If the petition is sustained and a declaration of emancipation is issued,[152] the child thereafter is considered an adult for a number of purposes:

(a) For the purpose of consenting to medical, dental, or psychiatric care, without parental consent, knowledge, or liability.

(b) For the purpose of the minor's capacity to do any of the following:

(1) Enter into a binding contract.

(2) Buy, sell, lease, encumber, exchange, or transfer any interest in real or personal property, including, but not limited to, shares of stock in a domestic or foreign corporation or a membership in a nonprofit corporation.

(3) Sue or be sued in his or her own name.

(4) Compromise, settle, arbitrate, or otherwise adjust a claim, action, or proceeding by or against the minor.

(5) Make or revoke a will.

(6) Make a gift, outright or in trust.

(7) Convey or release contingent or expectant interests in property, including marital property rights and any right of survivorship incident to joint tenancy, and consent to a transfer, encumbrance, or gift of marital property.

(8) Exercise or release his or her powers as donee of a power of appointment unless the creating instrument otherwise provides.

(9) Create for his or her own benefit or for the benefit of others a revocable or irrevocable trust.

(10) Revoke a revocable trust.

(11) Elect to take under or against a will.

(12) Renounce or disclaim any interest acquired by testate or intestate succession or by inter vivos transfer, including exercising the right to surrender the right to revoke a revocable trust.

(13) Make an election or an election and agreement referred to in Section 649.1 of the Probate Code.

(c) For the purpose of the minor's right to support by his or her parents.

(d) For purposes of the rights of the minor's parents or guardian to the minor's earnings, and to control the minor.

(e) For the purpose of establishing his or her own residence.

(f) For purposes of the application of Sections 300 and 601 of the Welfare and Institutions Code [dealing with dependent children and habitually disobedient or truant minors].

(g) For purposes of applying for a work permit pursuant to Section 49110 of the Education Code without the request of his or her parents or guardian.

(h) For the purpose of ending all vicarious liability of the minor's parents or guardian for the minor's torts; provided, that nothing in this section shall affect any liability of a parent, guardian, spouse, or employer imposed by the Vehicle code, or any vicarious liability which arises from an agency relationship.

(i) For the purpose of enrolling in any school or college.[153]

Before amendment in 1980 a Connecticut statute allowed a minor age sixteen or older to petition for emancipation on the ground, among others, "that the parent-child relationship has irretrievably broken down,"[154] raising the specter that courts would grant children something akin to a divorce from their parents on a showing of family disharmony. The statute currently provides for judicial emancipation if the child is married, on active duty in the military service, is living separately from the parents with or without their consent, and is self-supporting, *or* "for good cause shown, it is in the best interests of either or both parties" that the court declare the child emancipated.[155] If the child is declared emancipated, the declaration is effective for purposes similar to those contained in the California statutes.[156]

Some have argued that such an approach does not go far enough, that what is needed are specific legislative provisions dealing with emancipation in each substantive area of law. Thus, the *Juvenile Justice Standards* recommend that the statutes dealing with contract law, the making of wills and so forth should include provisions addressing the issue of when and under what circumstances children may, for example, enter into binding contracts and make wills.[157] The *Standards* specifically provide that a child is entitled to his own wages and that child and parent can sue one another for tortious behavior.[158] They also contain specific provisions on child support,[159] consent for medical care,[160] youth employment,[161] and contracts.[162]

Areas of substantive law containing no provision on the effect of minority or emancipation would be governed by a general statute that treats as emancipated any child who is living separately from his parents, with or without their consent, and is self-supporting.[163] Unlike the California and Connecticut provisions mentioned above, however, the *Standards* would not authorize judicial decrees of emancipation because of the unresolved problems of children who might be unaware of the emancipation procedures or who, for whatever reason, have not obtained a decree of emancipation but yet might be functioning independently of parental support and control.[164]

Whether one favors the approach of the *Standards* or that found in the new emancipation statutes, most commentators are in agreement that reform is needed.[165] Indeed, the purpose of this chapter is to demonstrate the law's need of a consistent, coherent position regarding the circumstances under which children ought to be regarded as adults and the purposes for which they should be so regarded. Fulfilling this need does not necessarily require that for *all* purposes children should be regarded as adults *at the same age,* but it does require that such decisions in each area of private law be made in reference to and not independently of all other areas of private law, as has been the case traditionally.

Thus, the law should not take one attitude toward a child's capacity to enter into a binding contract and a different attitude toward a child's responsibility for his tortious behavior, without in either instance considering the law's attitude toward children in other areas of private law. The law needs to develop a general view of a child's capacity to make decisions and to be responsible for his actions and his property, and if there are specific areas in which the rule should be otherwise, for example, the age at which one is able to purchase alcoholic beverages, those should be set out and rationally explained.[166]

## Notes

1. 17 Wis. 237 (1863).
2. W. Page Keeton, Prosser & Keeton on Torts 1071 and cases cited in n.2. (5th ed. 1984) [hereinafter cited as W. Page Keeton].
3. *Id.*
4. *Id.* at 169–70, 173–74.
5. *Id.* at 179 and cases cited in n.47; Restatement (Second) of Torts § 283(A) (1977). For a recent example of judicial adoption of the Restatement's special standard for children, *see* Standard v. Shine, 278 S.C. 337, 295 S.E.2d 786 (1982).
6. W. Page Keeton, *supra* note 2, at 181; Restatement (Second) of Torts § 283(A), comment a (1977).
7. *Id.* Again, a recent case in which the court adopts the children's standard in both kinds of cases is Standard v. Shine, 278 S.C. 337, 295 S.E.2d 786 (1982).
8. W. Page Keeton, *supra* note 2, at 181; Restatement (Second) of Torts § 283(A), comment c (1977).

9. *See, e.g.,* GA. CODE § 52-2-3 ($5,000.00); MASS. GEN. LAWS ANN. ch. 231, § 85G ($1,000.00); S.C. CODE § 20-7-340 ($1,000.00).

10. LA. CIV. CODE ANN. art. 2318.

11. Turner v. Bucher, 308 So. 2d 270 (La. 1975).

12. 306 N.C. 618, 295 S.E.2d 436 (1982).

13. In the *Moore* case, however, the court affirmed a summary judgment in favor of the defendant parents because the evidence established that at the time the rape occurred the parents lacked the opportunity to control the child and also had no reason to believe such control was necessary.

14. Hewlett v. George, 68 Miss. 703, 9 So. 885 (1891).

15. For a general discussion of the doctrine of parent/child immunity, *see* W. PAGE KEETON, *supra* note 2, at 904–07.

16. This and other arguments are presented and discussed in *id.* at 905. In *Hewlett v. George,* for example, the tort complained of was false imprisonment in that the parent allegedly had caused the child to be committed to an insane asylum.

17. *See generally* W. PAGE KEETON, *supra* note 2, at 907 and cases and statutes cited therein at nn. 62 & 63. The first court decision to abandon parent/child immunity was Goller v. White, 20 Wis. 2d 402, 122 N.W.2d 193 (1963), but one of the leading and most influential cases is Gibson v. Gibson, 3 Cal. 3d 914, 479 P.2d 648, 92 Cal. Rptr. 288 (1971).

18. Burnette v. Wahl, 284 Or. 705, 588 P.2d 1105 (1978).

19. *Id.*

20. *See, e.g.,* Zepeda v. Zepeda, 41 Ill. App. 2d 240, 190 N.E.2d 849 (1963), *cert. denied,* 379 U.S. 945 (1964).

21. *See, e.g.,* Ingraham v. Wright, 430 U.S. 651 (1977).

22. *See, e.g.,* Donohue v. Copiague Union Free School Dist., 47 N.Y.2d 440, 391 N.E.2d 1352, 418 N.Y.S.2d 375 (1979); Peter W. v. San Francisco Unified School Dist., 60 Cal. App. 3d 814, 131 Cal. Rptr. 854 (1976).

23. For an excellent discussion of the disaffirmance doctrine, more broad-ranging than is possible here, see A. FARNSWORTH, CONTRACTS 216–20 (1982) [hereinafter cited as A. FARNSWORTH]. Scholarly comment, for most part critical of the doctrine of disaffirmance and proposing various reforms, includes Edge, *Voidability of Minors' Contracts: a Feudal Doctrine in a Modern Economy,* 1 GA. L. REV. 205 (1967); Navin, *The Contracts of Minors Viewed from the Perspective of Fair Exchange,* 50 N.C.L. REV. 517 (1972); Note, *Restitution in Minors' Contracts in California,* 19 HASTINGS L. REV. 1199 (1968); 52 MARQ. L. REV. 437 (1969).

24. *See, e.g.,* Halbman v. Lemke, 99 Wis. 2d 241, 298 N.W.2d 562 (1980).

25. A. FARNSWORTH, *supra* note 23, at 217.

26. *Id.* at 216–17.

27. Kiefer v. Fred Howe Motors, 39 Wis. 2d 20, 24, 158 N.W.2d 288, 290 (1968).

28. A. FARNSWORTH, *supra* note 23, at 214–15.

29. *Id.* at 216.

30. *Id.* at 219 & n.15, *citing* Cassella v. Tiberio, 150 Ohio St. 27, 80 N.E.2d 426 (1948) (eleven years).

31. 623 P.2d 370 (Colo. 1981).

32. *See, e.g.,* CAL. CIV. CODE § 36 (contracts for necessaries cannot be disaffirmed; contracts for artistic or creative services and professional sports contracts cannot be disaffirmed if they have been approved by the appropriate court); N.Y.

Arts & Cult. Aff. Law § 35-03 (contracts entered into by child athletes and per-forming artists, if approved by the court, cannot be disaffirmed).

33. Juvenile Justice Standards Relating to Rights of Minors, Standard 6.1(A). Nevertheless, the standard provides that a contract of a minor under the age of twelve is void. *Id.,* Standard 6.1(B).

34. Shields v. Gross, 58 N.Y.2d 338, 448 N.E.2d 108, 461 N.Y.S.2d 254 (1983).

35. *See, e.g.,* Halbman v. Lemke, 99 Wis. 2d 241, 298 N. W.2d 562 (1980).

36. Hall v. Butterfield, 59 N.H. 354 (1879). The court more recently has adhered to its rule. Porter v. Wilson, 106 N.H. 270, 209 A.2d 730 (1965).

37. The New Hampshire court, for example, held in one case that a child engaged in the milk delivery business was bound by his contract with his supplier to pay for the benefits he actually received—that is, the reasonable value of the goods furnished him pursuant to his contract. Bartlett v. Bailey, 59 N.H. 408 (1879). Indeed, some states by statute declare children engaged in business bound by their contracts entered into in the course of that business. *See, e.g.,* Ga. Code § 13-3-21; Kan. Stat. Ann. § 38-103; Va. Code § 8.01-278(A).

38. *See generally* A. Farnsworth, *supra* note 23, at 221–22 and cases cited therein. A car, for example, might be considered a necessity where the child uses it in the conduct of his business, school, and social activities. Rose v. Sheehan Buick, 204 So. 2d 903 (Fla. Dist. Ct. App. 1967).

39. A. Farnsworth, *supra* note 23, at 223.

40. *See, e.g.,* Rice v. Butler, 160 N.Y. 578, 55 N.E. 275 (1899).

41. *Id.* at 582–83, 55 N.E. at 276, quoting 2 J. Kent, Commentaries on Ameri-can Law *240.

42. A. Farnsworth, *supra* note 23, at 223.

43. *See, e.g.,* Cain v. Coleman, 396 S.W.2d 251 (Tex. Civ. App. 1965). If there is no misrepresentation, however, the traditional rule applies—that is, the seller is entitled to return of the property "as is." *See, e.g.,* Rutherford v. Hughes, 228 S.W.2d 909 (Tex. Civ. App. 1950).

44. A. Farnsworth, *supra* note 23, at 223–24 and cases cited in nn. 21 & 22. Some courts, however, take the view that if the child has not actively misrepresented his age but rather merely has signed a standard form containing an affirmation that the purchaser is an adult, no misrepresentation has occurred and the traditional rule of restitution applies. *Id.* at 224 and cases cited in n.23. Moreover, some courts reject the misrepresentation rationale altogether, reasoning that treatment of mis-representation of age as a tort indirectly involves enforcement of the contract, which is contrary to the doctrine of disaffirmance. *Id.* at 224 and cases cited in n.24.

45. *Id.* at 224 and cases cited in n.25. Some courts also have employed the estoppel theory where the misrepresentation consisted not of words but silence or conduct. *Id.*

46. Halbman v. Lemke, 99 Wis. 2d 241, 251, 298 N.W.2d 562, 567 (1980).

47. The state's interests in the welfare of children generally, and in particular the welfare of children in the work place were discussed in the Supreme Court's decision in Prince v. Massachusetts, 321 U.S. 158, 165, 168–70 (1944). Prince v. Massachusetts is presented in chapter 4 *infra.*

48. For historical background of the child labor laws, *see* 1 G. Abbott, The Child and the State (1938). A good overview of the various kinds of legislative restrictions, plus an analysis of contemporary issues, is McGovern, *Children's*

*Rights and Child Labor: Advocacy on Behalf of the Child Worker,* 28 S.D.L. REV. 293 (1983). Other commentary includes Note, *Child Labor Laws—Time to Grow Up,* 59 MINN. L. REV. 574 (1975); JUVENILE JUSTICE STANDARDS RELATING TO RIGHTS OF MINORS, Standards 5.1–5.4, commentary at 87–100 (1980).

49. L.A. Times, July 24, 1982, pt. 1, at 1, col. 2. Under the Fair Labor Standards Act, 29 U.S.C.A. §§ 201 et seq., an exemption from the act's regulation of child labor is created for children employed as actors or performers in motion pictures, radio, theater, or television. 29 U.S.C.A. § 213(c) (3). Under applicable state law, however, such an exemption might not exist. *See, e.g.,* CAL. LABOR CODE § 1308.5.

50. 29 U.S.C.A. §§ 201 et seq. (1938).

51. *Id.* § 212(c).

52. *Id.* §§ 215(a) (4), 216(a), (e).

53. *Id.* § 203(l).

54. *Id.*

55. 29 C.F.R. §§ 570.51–570.68.

56. Fair Labor Standards Act, 29 U.S.C.A.§ 213(c) (2). For a list of agricultural occupations deemed hazardous, *see* 29 C.F.R. § 570.71. For the most part they deal with operation of or exposure to certain types of machinery, exposure to certain animals, or exposure to toxic chemicals.

57. Fair Labor Standards Act, 29 U.S.C.A. § 203(l); 29 C.F.R. § 570.2(a) (1).

58. Fair Labor Standards Act, 29 U.S.C.A. § 203 (l); 29 C.F.R. §§ 570.2(a) (1), 570.31–570.38.

59. Fair Labor Standards Act, 29 U.S.C.A. § 213(c) (1) (C), (c) (2).

60. *Id.* § 213 (c) (1) (A)–(B), (c) (2).

61. *Id.* § 213(c) (3).

62. *See* discussion in the preceding section on contracts.

63. Because of the breadth and diversity of such laws, the reader is referred to the sources cited in note 48 *supra* for an overview of some of the state laws.

64. Fair Labor Standards Act, 29 U.S.C.A. § 218; 29 C.F.R. §§ 570.50(a), 570.129.

65. As an example of the latter, under federal law an exemption is allowed for children employed as actors or performers in motion pictures, radio, theater, and television. Fair Labor Standards Act, 29 U.S.C.A. § 213(c) (3). Under California law, however, no exemption is allowed, and a special permit must be granted for child performers. CAL. LABOR CODE § 1308.5. California law also provides that generally children under age sixteen cannot work before 5:00 A.M. or after 10 P.M. CAL. LABOR CODE § 1391. To return to the incident in which Vic Morrow and the two child-actors were killed, *supra* note 49 and accompanying text, apparently no violation of federal law occurred, but unless a special work permit had been issued, there did appear to be a violation of state law. In fact, an official at the time stated that normally children under age eight cannot work past 7:00 P.M. unless a special waiver is granted, and no such waiver had been sought. L.A. Times, July 24, 1982, pt. 1, at 1, col. 2.

66. 30 N.Y.2d 406, 285 N.E.2d 689, 334 N.Y.S.2d 380 (1972).

67. *Compare* the Wisconsin Supreme Court's similar sentiments in the contracts context in Halbman v. Lemke, 99 Wis. 2d 241, 298 N.W.2d 562 (1980).

68. Fair Labor Standards Act, 29 U.S.C.A. § 206.

69. *Id.* § 214(a).

70. *Id.* § 214(b).

71. *Id.* § 213(d).

72. *Id.* § 213(a) (6) (B)–(D).

73. N.Y. Times, Mar. 26, 1981, at B15, col. 5.

74. *Id.*, April 21, 1984, § 1, at 20, col. 6.

75. *Id.*, May 6, 1984, § 1, at 25, col. 1.

76. *Id.*

77. *Id.*, May 17, 1984, at B14, col. 4.

78. Hawkins, *Promoting Jobs for Youth,* N.Y. Times, June 26, 1984, at A25, col. 1. Augustus F. Hawkins, a Democrat from California, is chairman of the House Education and Labor Committee's subcommittee on employment opportunities.

79. T. ATKINSON, HANDBOOK OF THE LAW OF WILLS 229–30 (2d ed. 1953); *see* Banks v. Sherrod, 52 Ala. 267 (1875). Sometimes the common law age requirement for disposition of personalty was said to be fourteen without qualification as to sex. *See* Deane v. Littlefield, 18 Mass. (1 Pick.) 239 (1822).

80. 1 Vict. ch. 26, § 7 (1837).

81. T. ATKINSON, HANDBOOK OF THE LAW OF WILLS 230 (2d ed. 1953).

82. Bordwell, *The Statute Law of Wills,* 14 IOWA L. REV. 172, 179 (1929).

83. ALA. CODE § 43-8-130; ARK. STAT. ANN. § 60-401; COLO. REV. STAT. § 15-11-501; MD. EST. & TRUSTS CODE ANN. § 4-101; MO. ANN. STAT. § 474.310; N.Y. EST. POWERS & TRUSTS LAW § 3-1.1; S.C. CODE ANN. § 21-7-10; TENN. CODE ANN. § 32-1-102; VA. CODE §§ 64.1-46, -47; W. VA. CODE §§ 41-1-1, -2. The lone holdout is Rhode Island, which follows the common law rule—that is, in order to make a will one must be twenty-one years of age, although a person age eighteen or older may dispose of personalty by will. R.I. GEN. LAWS §§ 33-5-2, -3.

84. The exceptions are Rhode Island, where one must be age twenty-one in order to make a valid will, *supra* note 83; Wyoming, where one must be age nineteen in order to make a valid will, WYO. STAT. § 2-6-101 (one must be "of legal age," defined in § 2-1-301 (xvii) as the age of majority, or nineteen); and Louisiana, where a minor age sixteen or older can make a will, LA. CIV. CODE ANN. art. 1477 (even though age of majority is eighteen, art. 37).

85. In addition to the statutes set forth in note 83, *supra, see* CAL. PROB. CODE §§ 6100, 6220; FLA. STAT. ANN. § 732.501; ILL. ANN. STAT. ch. 110½, § 4-1; MASS. GEN. LAWS ANN. ch. 191, § 1; MICH. COMP. LAWS ANN. § 700.121; N.J. STAT. ANN. § 3B:3-1; OHIO REV. CODE ANN. § 2107.02; 20 PA. CONS. STAT. ANN. § 2501; TEX. PROB. CODE ANN. § 57.

86. For example, in Arkansas, which formerly allowed testamentary disposition of personalty at age eighteen but did not allow disposition of realty until age twenty-one, the law was changed to allow disposition of all types of property at age eighteen. The Committee Comment following § 60-401 of Arkansas Statutes Annotated explains:

> The committee feels that no distinction should be made between the right to dispose of personalty and the right to dispose of realty, and that the general intelligence and business judgment of minors has been raised substantially since the adoption of the [statutes] now in force.

87. *See, e.g., In re* Estate of Lockwood, 254 Cal. App. 2d 309, 62 Cal. Rptr. 230 (1967).

88. *Id.; In re* Estate of Goetz, 253 Cal. App. 2d 107, 61 Cal. Rptr. 181 (1967); *In re* Estate of Wynne, 239 Cal. App. 2d 369, 48 Cal. Rptr. 656 (1966).

89. For cases in which the decedent was found to have testamentary capacity despite evidence of mental infirmity and eccentric behavior, *see In re* Estate of Goetz, 253 Cal. App. 2d 107, 61 Cal. Rptr. 181 (1967); *In re* Estate of Wynne, 239 Cal. App. 2d 369, 48 Cal. Rptr. 656 (1966); *In re* Estate of Sanderson, 171 Cal. App. 2d 651, 341 P.2d 358 (1959). For a case in which the decedent was found to lack testamentary capacity, *see In re* Estate of Lockwood, 254 Cal. App. 2d 309, 62 Cal. Rptr. 230 (1967).

90. *See* the section on torts *supra*.

91. *See* the section on contracts *supra*.

92. Cal. Prob. Code §§ 6100, 6220.

93. Cal. Civ. Code § 62 defines *emancipated minor* as

Any person under the age of 18 years...
(a) Who has entered into a valid marriage, whether or not such a marriage was terminated by dissolution; or,
(b) Who is on active duty with any of the armed forces of the United States of America; or
(c) Who has received a declaration of emancipation pursuant to Section 64 [of the Emancipation of Minors Act].

Emancipation is discussed further in a subsequent section.

94. Cal. Civ. Code § 63(b) (1), (b) (5).

95. *Id.*, Law Revision Commission Comment.

96. Idaho Code §§ 15-1-201(14), 15-2-50; Iowa Code Ann. §§ 599.1, 633.264; Kan. Stat. Ann. §§ 38-101, 59-601 (age sixteen or older and married); Neb. Rev. Stat. §§ 30-2209(26), 30-2326; N.H. Rev. Stat. Ann. § 551:1; Or. Rev. Stat. § 212.225; Tex. Prob. Code Ann. § 57.

97. Ind. Code Ann. § 29-1-5-1; Tex. Prob. Code Ann. § 57.

98. Kan. Stat. Ann. §§ 38-108 to -110, 59-601.

99. Much of the discussion of inheritance rights of children that follows is taken from W. Wadlington, C. Whitebread & S. Davis, Children in the Legal System 29–31 (1983).

100. An exception exists under Louisiana civil law, which contains a limitation on a decedent's power to exclude children. Depending on the number of children he leaves, they are entitled to a stated share of his estate, and they cannot be excluded without just cause set forth in the will itself. La. Civ. Code Ann. arts. 1493, 1495.

101. *See, e.g.*, Cal. Prob. Code § 6540.

102. *Id.* § 6500. The surviving spouse and children also may be given use of any other property of the decedent that is exempt from a money judgment. *Id.* § 6510.

103. *Id.* §§ 6520–6521.

104. *Id.* § 6570. This provision is based on Unif. Prob. Code § 2-302(a) (1969).

105. Thus, such a child is disinherited if (1) it appears from the will itself that the omission was intentional; (2) when the will was executed the decedent had children and left substantially all of the estate to the other parent of the omitted child; or (3) the decedent provided for the child outside the will and it appears that he intended such provision to be in lieu of a testamentary share of the estate. Cal. Prob. Code § 6571. These exceptions are taken from Unif. Prob. Code § 2-302(a) (1969).

106. In either event the child is entitled to a share of his parent's estate equal to the share he would have received if his parent had died intestate. CAL. PROB. CODE § 6572. The provision that entitles the child to a share of the estate if his parent erroneously thought he was dead is taken from UNIF. PROB. CODE § 2-302(b) (1969).

107. *See, e.g.,* GA. CODE § 53-2-10 (one-third of the first $200,000); MISS. CODE ANN. § 91-5-31 (one-third).

108. In 1950, five states had statutes limiting the portion of a decedent's estate that could be left to charitable organizations. Note, *Standing to Contest Wills Violating Charitable Bequest Statutes,* 50 COLUM. L. REV. 94 & nn. 1 & 3 (1950). Three of these states have since repealed their statutes. CAL. PROB. CODE § 41, repealed, 1971 Cal. Stats., ch. 1395, p. 2747, § 1; IOWA CODE ANN. § 633.266, repealed, 1980 Iowa Acts (68 G.A.), ch. 1064, § 2; N.Y. EST. POWERS & TRUSTS LAW § 5-3.3, repealed, 1981 N.Y. Laws, ch. 461, § 1. Of course, some states have added such provisions since 1950. *See, e.g.,* FLA. STAT. ANN. § 732.803; OHIO REV. CODE ANN. § 2107.06.

109. For example, in New York the statute was repealed in part because it had been a source of frequent litigation and much confusion and in part because a testator could avoid the limitation, for example, by making charitable gifts of his property during his lifetime. N.Y. EST. POWERS & TRUSTS LAW § 5-3.3, Supplementary Practice Commentaries. As an example of litigation resulting from a challenge by surviving children of their father's charitable bequest, *see* Estate of Rothko, 98 Misc. 2d 718, 414 N.Y.S.2d 444 (Sur. Ct. 1979).

110. *See, e.g.,* ALASKA STAT. § 25.23.130 (unless the adoption decree expressly provides for continued inheritance rights from the natural parents); MASS. GEN. LAWS. ANN. ch. 210, § 7; N.Y. DOM. REL. LAW § 117; OHIO REV. CODE ANN. § 3107.15; WIS. STAT. ANN. § 851.51(1).

111. *See* the Alaska, New York, Ohio, and Wisconsin statutes cited in note 110 *supra.*

112. *See* the Alaska, Massachusetts, Ohio, and Wisconsin statutes cited in note 110 *supra.*

113. CAL. PROB. CODE § 6408(a) (2). The adoptive parents can also inherit from the adopted child. *Id.*

114. *Id.* §§ 6408(a) (3), 6408.5(a).

115. *Id.* § 6408.5.

116. *Id.* §§ 6151, 6152(a); N.Y. EST. POWERS & TRUSTS LAW § 2-1.3; WIS. STAT. ANN. § 851.51(3).

117. CAL. CIV. PROC. CODE § 337.

118. *Id.* § 339.

119. *Id.* § 337.15(a).

120. *Id.* § 352(a).

121. *See, e.g., id.* § 328 (statute is tolled during minority for any action to recover real property); OHIO REV. CODE ANN. § 2305.16; VA. CODE § 8.01-229(A).

122. CAL. CIV. PROC. CODE § 340.5.

123. *Id.*

124. 648 S.W.2d 661 (1983).

125. *See* the section on torts *supra* for a discussion of parent/child immunity.

126. TEX. REV. CIV. STAT. ANN. art. 4590i, § 10.01.

127. 6 Ohio St. 3d 300, 452 N.E.2d 1337 (1983).

128. OHIO REV. CODE ANN. § 2305.11(B).

129. *Id.* § 2305.16.

130. 409 U.S. 535 (1973).

131. *Id.* at 538.

132. 456 U.S. 91 (1982).

133. In 1981 the statute was amended to allow a four-year period in which suit could be brought. In 1983 it was amended again to allow bringing of a paternity action any time prior to two years after the child reaches the age of majority. TEX. FAM. CODE ANN. § 13.01.

134. 456 U.S. at 95.

135. *Id.* at 97.

136. *Id.* at 101.

137. *Id.* at 104.

138. 462 U.S. 1 (1983).

139. In 1984 the Tennessee statute was amended to allow a paternity action to be filed any time prior to one year after the child reaches the age of majority. TENN. CODE ANN. § 36-2-103(b).

140. 462 U.S. at 12-16.

141. *See id.* at 7-8.

142. For a history of the emancipation doctrine and its variations and development at common law, *see* H. CLARK, THE LAW OF DOMESTIC RELATIONS IN THE UNITED STATES 240-44 (1968); JUVENILE JUSTICE STANDARDS RELATING TO RIGHTS OF MINORS, Standard 2.1, commentary at 21-23 (1980); Cady, *Emancipation of Minors,* 12 CONN. L. REV. 62 (1979) [hereinafter cited as Cady]; Katz, Schroeder & Sidman, *Emancipating Our Children—Coming of Legal Age in America,* 7 FAM. L.Q. 211 (1973) [hereinafter cited as Katz, Schroeder & Sidman].

143. *See* JUVENILE JUSTICE STANDARDS RELATING TO RIGHTS OF MINORS, Standard 2.1, commentary at 27-30 (1980).

144. *See* Cady, *supra* note 142, at 65-67; Katz, Schroeder & Sidman, *supra* note 142, at 219-32; JUVENILE JUSTICE STANDARDS RELATING TO RIGHTS OF MINORS, Standard 2.1, commentary at 24-27 (1980). The effect of emancipation on a child's capacity to enter into binding contracts and to dispose of property was discussed in the sections on contracts and testamentary transfer of property *supra.*

145. 209 Neb. 94, 306 N.W.2d 575 (1981).

146. *See, e.g.,* Lev v. College of Marin, 22 Cal. App. 3d 488, 99 Cal. Rptr. 476 (1971); Vaupel v. Bellach, 261 Iowa 376, 154 N.W.2d 149 (1967); In re Fiihr, 289 Minn. 322, 184 N.W.2d 22 (1971); Accent Service Co. v. Ebsen, *supra* note 145.

147. Comment, *The Uncertain Status of the Emancipated Minor: Why We Need a Uniform Statutory Emancipation of Minors Act (USEMA),* 15 U.S.F.L. Rev. 473, 477-79 (1981) [hereinafter cited as Comment].

148. *See, e.g.,* ALASKA STAT. § 09.55.590; CAL. CIV. CODE §§ 60 et seq.; CONN. GEN. STAT. ANN. §§ 46b-150 et seq.; TEX. FAM. CODE ANN. §§ 31.01 et seq. Others are listed in Comment, *supra* note 147, at 479 & n.34.

149. CAL. CIV. CODE § 64(a).

150. *Id.* § 64(b).

151. *Id.* § 64(c).

152. *Id.* § 64(d).

153. *Id.* § 63. The California emancipation statutes are discussed in Note,

*California's Emancipation of Minors Act: The Costs and Benefits of Freedom from Parental Control*, 18 CAL. W.L. REV. 482 (1982).

154. 1979 Conn. Acts, P.A. No. 79-397, § 3 (Reg. Sess.), amended by 1980 Conn. Acts, P.A. No. 80-283, § 1 (Reg. Sess.). Before its amendment, the Connecticut provision was discussed and criticized in Cady, *supra* note 142, at 81-85. *See also* Hafen, *Children's Liberation and the New Egalitarianism: Some Reservations About Abandoning Youth to Their "Rights,"* 1976 B.Y.U. L. REV. 605, 608-09.

155. CONN. GEN. STATS. ANN § 46b-150b. The petitioner must be at least sixteen years of age. *Id.* § 46b-150.

156. *Id.* § 46b-150d.

157. JUVENILE JUSTICE STANDARDS RELATING TO RIGHTS OF MINORS, Standard 2.1(A) and commentary at 30-31 (1980); *see* the earlier sections in this chapter on contracts and testamentary transfer of property.

158. *Id.*, Standard 2.1(B) and commentary at 31-32.

159. *Id.*, Standards 3.1-3.4.

160. *Id.*, Standards 4.1-4.9.

161. *Id.*, Standards 5.1-5.8.

162. *Id.*, Standard 6.1.

163. *Id.*, Standard 2.1(C) and commentary at 32-33.

164. *Id.* and commentary at 33.

165. *Id.*, Standard 2.1, commentary at 21-24, 30-33; Comment, *supra* note 147.

166. Refer generally back to the subject matter of chapter 1 and specifically to F. ZIMRING, THE CHANGING LEGAL WORLD OF ADOLESCENCE 111-15 (1982).

# 4

# "Life, Liberty and Property": The Supreme Court and Children's Rights

> The child is not the mere creature of the state; those who nurture him and direct his destiny have the right, coupled with the high duty, to recognize and prepare him for additional obligations.
>
> —Justice James C. McReynolds
> *Pierce v. Society of Sisters*
> 268 U.S. 510, 535 (1925)

> [N]either rights of religion nor rights of parenthood are beyond limitation. Acting to guard the general interest in youth's well being, the state as *parens patriae* may restrict the parent's control by requiring school attendance, regulating or prohibiting the child's labor, and in many other ways.
>
> —Justice Wiley B. Rutledge
> *Prince v. Massachusetts*
> 321 U.S. 158, 166 (1944)

## Introduction

Over a period of years the United States Supreme Court has decided numerous cases touching on children's rights. We have chosen 1923, when the Supreme Court decided the case of *Meyer v. Nebraska*,[1] as the beginning point of this philosophical odyssey, which culminates in the Court's decision in *New York v. Ferber*[2] in 1982. The membership—and therefore the philosophy and jurisprudence—of the Court has changed considerably since 1923. Some have argued that over the years the Court has failed to develop a consistent theory of children's rights, and we will draw certain conclusions of our own at the end of this chapter.

We should point out two matters that probably are self-evident in any event. First, the cases are discussed in chronological order. Any attempt to arrange them by subject area—such as the education cases, the abortion cases, and so forth—would be, in our view, futile, frustrating, and difficult for the reader to follow. Rather, we set them out in the chronology in which they were decided to give the reader an accurate if sometimes puzzling sense of the Supreme Court's historical framework for deciding such cases. Second, we have not included any of the juvenile justice cases[3] because of our strong feeling that those cases deal with different kinds of children's rights—namely, those analogous to rights of adult defendants in the criminal process, and such are beyond the scope of this book.[4]

What is presented in this chapter is the Supreme Court's analytical framework for deciding children's rights issues, with emphasis on the competing interests favoring, on the one hand, increased autonomy for children at an earlier age than traditionally has been the case and, on the other hand, increased parental supervision over children or increased state intervention into the lives of children to protect them from perceived harms or risks. The reader will observe, no doubt, that from one context to the next, and from one historical time period to the next, the balance between children's autonomy, parental control, and state authority ebbs and flows, which has generated some uncertainty over the Supreme Court's ability, as an institution reflecting and influencing societal values over the long term, to develop a consistent, cohesive policy toward children and their position in the law. Judge for yourself.

## Meyer v. Nebraska

*Meyer v. Nebraska*[5] was an appeal by a Nebraska teacher from a conviction in state court for violation of a state statute that prohibited the teaching of any foreign language in public or private schools. The question presented was whether the statute unreasonably infringed on his liberty interest guaranteed under the fourteenth amendment's due process clause, which provides that "No state . . . shall deprive any person of life, liberty, or property without due process of law."

As such, the case really was not a children's rights case at all, although the Court, perhaps inevitably, addressed the total relationship between child, parent, teacher, and state in determining whether the state had overreached its authority: "That the state may do much, go very far, indeed, in order to improve the quality of its citizens, physically, mentally, and morally, is clear; but the individual has certain fundamental rights which must be respected."[6] And elsewhere: "His [the teacher's] right thus to teach and the right of parents to engage him so to instruct their children, we think, are within the liberty of the Amendment."[7]

What was the "liberty" guaranteed under the fourteenth amendment? What must be remembered about this case is that until the Supreme Court's decisions much later in *Griswold v. Connecticut*[8] and *Loving v. Virginia*,[9] the Court's decision in *Meyer v. Nebraska* was the only pronouncement on the meaning of due process of law in the family context. The Court went through a litany of due process rights, some of which touched on the family:

> [I]t [due process] denotes not merely freedom from bodily restraint, but also the right of the individual to contract, to engage in any of the common occupations of life, to acquire useful knowledge, to marry, establish a home and bring up children, to worship God according to the dictates of his own conscience, and, generally, to enjoy those privileges long recognized at common law as essential to the orderly pursuit of happiness by free men.[10]

Having found that the teacher's right to teach foreign language was within the liberty so described, the Court further judged that the state's ban on teaching of foreign languages unduly "interfere[d] with the calling of modern language teachers, with the opportunities of pupils to acquire knowledge, and with the power of parents to control the education of their own."[11] The Court thus came down squarely in favor of parents and the family against what it perceived as unreasonable and unwarranted interference and stifling regulation by the state.

## Pierce v. Society of Sisters

In *Meyer v. Nebraska* the Court said that "The power of the state to compel attendance at some school and to make reasonable regulations for all schools . . . is not questioned."[12] School attendance, of course, was not at issue in *Meyer v. Nebraska*. It was *the* issue in *Pierce v. Society of Sisters*.[13] The Oregon statute in question required every school-age child, with certain exemptions, to attend *public* school. The Court reiterated its view taken in *Meyer v. Nebraska:* "No question is raised concerning the power of the state . . . to require that all children of proper age attend some school."[14]

The appellees, both private schools, objected that the statute interfered with "the right of parents to choose schools where their children will receive appropriate mental and religious training, the right of the child to influence the parents' choice of a school, [and] the right of schools and teachers therein to engage in a useful business or profession."[15] As in *Meyer v. Nebraska*, the Court viewed this as more of a parents' rights case and, relying on *Meyer*, was of the opinion that the statute "unreasonably interfere[d] with the liberty of parents and guardians to direct the upbringing and education of children under their control."[16]

Once again the Court came down strongly on the side of parents in a conflict between parental authority and state authority in educational matters. Moreover, the Court implied that parental authority extended to "upbringing" as well as to educational matters. A policy favoring parental control over state interference in family matters seemed to be emerging, underscored by the poignant statement quoted at the beginning of this chapter.[17]

## Prince v. Massachusetts

By the time *Prince v. Massachusetts*[18] was decided in 1944, a parent would have expected, based on *Meyer* and *Pierce*, to prevail against the state on the issue of control over a child's upbringing. This expectation, quite reasonable in itself, would have been enhanced by the added presence of a first amendment religious freedom claim. Yet the result in *Prince v. Massachusetts* went counter to such an expectation.

*Prince* involved the constitutionality of Massachusetts statutory provisions prohibiting children from engaging in sales of magazines, newspapers, and the like in a public place and punishing as a criminal offense the furnishing of such goods to a child for sale in a public place. The appellant, who was the aunt and custodian of the children involved, was convicted of a violation of the statutes for furnishing to the children for subsequent sale copies of a religious pamphlet. She appealed her conviction on two bases: that the statutes violated her due process rights under the Constitution in that they represented undue interference by the state with her parental right to control the activities of her children and that they violated her first amendment rights by unduly inhibiting her free exercise of religion.

Unlike in *Meyer* and *Prince,* however, in this case the Court found a substantial state interest to be weighed against the individual interests asserted: "Against these sacred private interests, basic in a democracy, stand the interest of society to protect the welfare of children, and the state's assertion of authority to that end."[19] The Court went on to observe that neither freedom of religion nor parental authority is absolute: "Acting to guard the general interest in youth's well being, the state as *parens patriae* may restrict the parent's control by requiring school attendance, regulating or prohibiting the child's labor, and in many other ways."[20]

In a move that both strengthened the state's assertion of authority in this case and that also had implications for future cases,[21] the Court concluded that a state may regulate the activities of children to a greater extent than it can those of adults, particularly in the case of public activities and in matters of employment. The state may do so, the Court asserted, because of its interest in protecting the welfare of children:

A democratic society rests, for its continuance, upon the healthy, well-rounded growth of young people into full maturity as citizens, with all that implies. It may secure this against impending restraints and dangers, within a broad range of selection. Among evils most appropriate for such action are the crippling effects of child employment, more especially in public places, and the possible harms arising from other activities subject to all the diverse influences of the street.[22]

The Court foresaw "possible" harms to children resulting from the public exposure inherent in street preaching—namely, "emotional excitement and psychological or physical injury."[23] To prevent such potential harm, the Court concluded, the state could regulate, even prohibit, such activities by children.

The perceived harms were not imminent enough for Justice Murphy, who dissented based on the religious freedom issue. He concluded that

> The reasonableness that justifies the prohibition of the ordinary distribution of literature in the public streets by children is not necessarily the reasonableness that justifies such a drastic restriction when the distribution is part of their religious faith. If the right of a child to practice its religion in that manner is to be forbidden by constitutional means, there must be convincing proof that such a practice constitutes a grave and immediate danger to the state or to the health, morals or welfare of the child.[24]

Perhaps *Prince* can be distinguished from its predecessors on the basis that for the first time the Court was presented with a substantial state interest to weigh against the considerable parental interests at stake. In any event, the practical consequence of the *Prince* decision was to signal that parental authority was not without limits. Future cases would be decided by balancing the individual rights involved against the state's authority to impose reasonable and necessary restrictions in order to achieve some legitimate purpose.

## Ginsberg v. New York

Almost twenty-five years passed before the balancing test of *Prince* was applied next in *Ginsberg v. New York*.[25] At issue in *Ginsberg* was the validity of a New York statute that prohibited the sale to minors under age seventeen of material defined to be obscene for minors, without regard to whether it would be obscene for adults.

Ever since the Supreme Court's decision in *Roth v. United States*[26] the Court consistently has held that obscenity is not within the area of protected speech or press. The task that has plagued the Court has been that of defining obscenity. As though the task were not perilous enough, the *Ginsberg* case compounded it by raising the issue of whether there could be a variable standard for defining obscenity, depending on one's status as an adult or a child.

Appellant, owner and operator of a store at which "girlie" magazines were sold to minors, appealed his conviction under the statutes relying on *Meyer* and *Pierce* for the proposition that his first amendment rights had been infringed on by an overreaching state just as the state had infringed on parental rights in the two earlier cases. In upholding the conviction, however, the Court found *Prince* to be more applicable to this case in two respects: (1) the state has greater authority to regulate the conduct of children than it has in the case of adults, even where important rights are infringed on; and (2) the state has a significant interest, in its own right and as a proxy for parents, in the well-being of its children. Whereas in *Meyer* the Court had found no harm inherent in a child's learning a foreign language, in this case the Court found considerable risk posed by exposure of minors to sexual material of the kind covered by the New York statutes.[27]

The Court in both *Prince* and *Ginsberg* seemed to be moving away from protection of individual rights—for example, the parental right to rear children in an appropriate manner, freedom of religion, and freedom of expression—and more toward protection of societal interests as defined and asserted by the state. Moreover, in protecting the latter interests, the Court was assuming a more protective attitude toward children generally, perceiving the state's role as being one of acting in the child's best interests, sometimes, as in *Prince,* even against the wishes of the parents.

## Tinker v. Des Moines Independent Community School District

The conflict between individual rights and societal interests was renewed only a year after *Ginsberg* in *Tinker v. Des Moines Independent Community School District.*[28] *Tinker* was the first "pure" children's rights case decided by the United States Supreme Court. Although *Meyer* and *Pierce* had elements of children's rights to choose their school subjects and the school they would attend, the central focal point of those cases was on the parental right to make those decisions for their children and the rights of school authorities to engage in the business of education and to choose what subjects would be taught in schools. *Tinker,* on the other hand, was concerned with *children's* first amendment freedom of expression in the school environment.

The *Tinker* case arose out of the act of a number of students in wearing black armbands to school to protest American military involvement in Vietnam, in defiance of a school policy banning the wearing of armbands. The students wore the armbands to school and were suspended and sent home when they refused to remove them. They filed a complaint in federal court through their fathers, claiming their civil rights had been denied. The federal district court dismissed their complaint on the basis that the action of school authorities was reasonably calculated to prevent disturbances at school. This decision was upheld on appeal to the Eighth Circuit Court of Appeals.

The Supreme Court posed the conflict between competing values clearly:

> First Amendment rights, applied in light of the special characteristics of the school environment, are available to teachers and students. It can hardly be argued that either students or teachers shed their constitutional rights to freedom of speech or expression at the schoolhouse gate. . . .
> . . . On the other hand, the Court has repeatedly emphasized the need for affirming the comprehensive authority of the States and of school officials, consistent with fundamental constitutional safeguards, to prescribe and control conduct in the schools. Our problem lies in the area where students in the exercise of First Amendment rights collide with the rules of the school authorities.[29]

Just as it had in *Meyer* and *Pierce* the Court in this case found no state concern of such significance to warrant infringement of individual liberties. The evidence showed that in fact no disturbances had occurred at school to warrant the ban imposed by school officials.[30] The Court referred to two lower court decisions in which the same court on the same day reached opposite results in two separate cases involving school board action in banning the wearing of freedom buttons; the distinguishing feature was that in one case, in which the court enjoined the school board from enforcing its ban, no disturbances had occurred, whereas in the other case, in which the court declined to enjoin enforcement of the ban, students wearing the buttons harassed other students and created disturbances.[31]

The Court in *Tinker* concluded that

> In order for the State in the person of school officials to justify prohibition of a particular expression of opinion, it must be able to show that its action was caused by something more than a mere desire to avoid the discomfort and unpleasantness that always accompany an unpopular viewpoint. Certainly where there is no finding and no showing that engaging in the forbidden conduct would "materially and substantially interfere with the requirements of appropriate discipline in the operation of the school," the prohibition cannot be sustained.[32]

For the moment, then, the Court returned to the position taken earlier in *Meyer* and *Pierce* of championing individual rights against state infringement. It simply asserted the view that the state's authority, though powerful, is not absolute, especially, as in *Prince*, in the absence of any significant state concern:

> Students in school as well as out of school are "persons" under our Constitution. They are possessed of fundamental rights which the State must

respect, just as they themselves must respect their obligations to the State.
. . . In the absence of a specific showing of constitutionally valid reasons
to regulate their speech, students are entitled to freedom of expression of
their views.[33]

Two points should be kept in mind about the *Tinker* case. First of all,
it was a first amendment case, and the Court has a long tradition of zealous
protection of first amendment rights.[34] Although courts have tended to
protect students' first amendment rights in other respects,[35] one might ask
whether other constitutional rights would be protected to the same extent.[36]

Second, although *Tinker* was characterized earlier as the first real
children's rights case, it could also be viewed as a parents' rights or family
rights case because the views of the children in *Tinker*, in fact, mirrored the
views of their parents. Viewed in this way, one might ask whether the Court
would be as protective of children's rights if their views were contrary to
parental wishes.[37]

## Wisconsin v. Yoder

All states and the District of Columbia have compulsory school attendance
laws—laws that require parents to send their children to school until a
certain age, typically sixteen.[38] Wisconsin's law became the focus of attention in 1972 in the case of *Wisconsin v. Yoder*,[39] in which the Supreme
Court was confronted with the issue of whether Amish parents could refuse
to send their children to school beyond the eighth grade (when they were
age fourteen or fifteen) based on their claim of free exercise of religion under
the first amendment.

The Amish parents were convicted in criminal court for failure to send
their children to school in accordance with state law. The Wisconsin
Supreme Court reversed their convictions on the ground that their first
amendment right to free exercise of religion, guaranteed to them against
state infringement under the fourteenth amendment, had been violated.
The state applied for and was granted review by the Supreme Court.

Not since *Prince v. Massachusetts* had a religious freedom claim been
before the Supreme Court. Moreover, not since *Prince* had the balance of
interests been so finely tuned: on the one hand the parents' claim of authority plus their religious freedom claim, and on the other hand the state's
interest, not insubstantial, in having an educated citizenry. Perhaps hint-
ing at how it would decide the case, the Court began its analysis with a
reference to *Pierce v. Society of Sisters*, observing that

> a State's interest in universal education, however highly we rank it, is not
> totally free from a balancing process when it infringes on fundamental
> rights and interests, such as those specifically protected by the Free Exercise

Clause of the First Amendment, and the traditional interest of parents with respect to the religious upbringing of their children so long as they, in the words of *Pierce,* "prepare [them] for additional obligations."[40]

The Court's inquiry was threefold: (1) whether the Amish religious beliefs were sincere; (2) whether the state's compulsory attendance requirement placed an undue burden on the free exercise of Amish religious beliefs; and (3) whether in any event the state had an interest so compelling as to outweigh the interest claimed under the free exercise clause.

As to the first inquiry, the state conceded that the Amish religious beliefs were sincerely held. Their belief was that if their children attended school past the eighth grade the children would be exposed to values and influences that were in such conflict with their simple lifestyle that the continued existence of the Amish community would be threatened.

In response to the second inquiry, the Court concluded that enforcement of the state's requirement of compulsory school attendance would have a serious impact on the Amish lifestyle. Because their lifestyle and religious faith were "inseparable and interdependent," enforcement of state law "would gravely endanger if not destroy the free exercise of respondents' religious beliefs."[41]

The Court spent the greatest part of its discussion on the third point of inquiry, examining the weight of the state's interest. The state has a significant interest, the Court conceded, in promoting an educated citizenry in a participatory democracy such as ours, and in preparing its citizens to be self-reliant, self-sufficient members of society. The Court concluded, however, that because the Amish give their children vocational skills that are useful in Amish society and marketable in the outside world should they choose to leave the Amish community, and because the Amish have a 300-year history of self-reliance and independence as a society, and because the children were not threatened with any sort of harm or evil of the kind present in *Prince,* the state's interests were insufficient to outweigh the Amish claim of religious freedom. Indeed, the state's interests were being furthered by Amish practice of their religious beliefs.

Two observations can be made at this point regarding the *Yoder* decision. First, as with *Tinker* before it, *Yoder* could be characterized as a case that vindicated the rights of parents rather than those of children. In fact, Justice Douglas dissented in part because no delineation had been drawn between the parents' religious beliefs and those of their children.[42] The lower courts and the majority of the Supreme Court, he argued, had assumed an identity of interests. If parents are allowed a religious exemption, the effect is to impose the parents' views on the children, whose rights are being infringed if they, in fact, hold views different from those of their parents. If an Amish child wishes to attend high school, he continued, perhaps the state should be able to override the parents' religious objections.

Second, the *Yoder* decision is a very narrow decision in terms of its potential value as precedent. It probably has no application to any group other than the Amish, as recognized by the Court itself:

> [C]ourts must move with great circumspection in performing the sensitive and delicate task of weighing a State's legitimate concern when faced with religious claims for exemption from generally applicable educational requirements. It cannot be overemphasized that we are not dealing with a way of life and mode of education by a group claiming to have recently discovered some "progressive" or more enlightened process for rearing children for modern life.
>
> . . . In light of [the convincing showing made by the Amish in this case], one that probably few other religious groups or sects could make, and weighing the minimal difference between what the State would require and what the Amish already accept, it was incumbent on the State to show with more particularity how its admittedly strong interest in compulsory education would be adversely affected by granting an exemption to the Amish.[43]

## Stanley v. Illinois

In the chronology of cases pursued thus far the focal point shifts for the moment from cases involving children in schools to those concerned with another aspect of the child/parent/state relationship that has been the subject of judicial scrutiny for the last fifteen to twenty years—illegitimacy. *Stanley v. Illinois*,[44] which dealt with custodial rights of fathers of illegitimate children, was decided in 1972, but movement in this area began earlier.

In 1968 the Supreme Court decided two companion cases, *Levy v. Louisiana*[45] and *Glona v. American Guarantee & Liability Insurance Co.*,[46] both of which involved different Louisiana wrongful death statutes. In *Levy* the court held it unconstitutional for a state to deny illegitimate children the right to bring an action for the wrongful death of a parent while providing such a cause of action for legitimate children. Similarly, in *Glona* the Court held unconstitutional a Louisiana statute that denied a mother of illegitimate children the right to bring an action for the wrongful death of a child while creating a cause of action for the parent of a legitimate child.[47]

Commencing with *Labine v. Vincent*[48] in 1971 and culminating in *Lalli v. Lalli*[49] in 1978, the Court decided a series of cases that to some extent, at least, protects the inheritance rights of illegitimate children. Some qualification is necessary here because although the Court has held unconstitutional a statutory scheme that totally precluded illegitimate children from inheriting from their father,[50] it has upheld, in *Lalli*, certain procedural requirements that must be met by illegitimate children before they can inherit from their fathers.[51]

In *Weber v. Aetna Casualty & Surety Co.*[52] the Court held unconstitutional a Louisiana statute barring illegitimate children from bringing a worker's compensation claim on behalf of their deceased father. In *Gomez v. Perez*[53] the Court held that a state can not constitutionally deny illegitimate children the right to parental support while granting a right to support to legitimate children.

One concludes from a reading of these cases that the Court will not condone any statutory scheme that, as the Court put it, poses an "impenetrable barrier"[54] to illegitimate children seeking some entitlement or opportunity to which legitimate children are given access. As a concession to the state's concern for problems of proof of paternity, the Court has been tolerant of procedural barriers that make it difficult but not impossible for illegitimate children to inherit, sue, file claims, and the like. Against this analytical framework *Stanley v. Illinois* was decided.

Joan and Peter Stanley lived together off and on for eighteen years. During this time they had three children. When she died, under Illinois law the children became wards of the state, despite the fact that they had a surviving father with whom they lived. Their father claimed the statutory scheme was unconstitutional because he had been deprived of the custody of his children without a hearing and a showing of unfitness on his part, both of which would have been required in the case of a married father or an unwed mother. The state's response was that the statutory scheme was validly based on the presumptive unfitness of unwed fathers.

Once again the Court engaged in a balancing approach. The individual interest, the Court said, is the interest that a parent—any parent—has in the children he has fathered and, in this case, reared. The state's interest, it continued, is the familiar one of preserving and promoting the well-being of its children. The Court captured the essence of the case when it observed that "we are here not asked to evaluate the legitimacy of the state ends, rather, to determine whether the means used to achieve these ends are constitutionally defensible."[55]

Very early in the opinion the Court announced its decision that Stanley's due process rights had been violated in that he had been denied a hearing on the question of his fitness as a father, and he had been denied equal protection of the laws in that he had been treated differently from a married father without any significant reasons for the differential treatment.

Stanley presented a very sympathetic case. The Court observed that it may well be true, as Illinois asserted, that most unwed fathers are uncaring, never know their children, and never assume parental responsibilities. This was certainly not true in Stanley's case, however. Because of the likelihood that there were other fathers like Stanley who have assumed parental responsibilities, the Court felt the presumption of unfitness employed by

Illinois was inappropriate. Thus, the state, if it would remove custody from an unwed father, must hold a hearing at which it would have the burden of proving the father's unfitness as a parent.

Another factor that made Stanley's case so appealing was the fact that his assumption of parental responsibility actually furthered the state's interest in the welfare of children. The state actually was placed in the role of the heavy, the party who, contrary to the state's own asserted interest, was stepping in to break up a viable, ongoing family unit.

In subsequent decisions the Court has signaled that these cases are going to be decided on a case-by-case basis, depending on the nature and extent of the father's relationship, if any, with his children. In *Quilloin v. Walcott*[56] the Court unanimously upheld a lower court decision terminating the rights of an unwed father to his children and ordering their adoption by a step-parent where the natural father had never established a meaningful relationship with his children or sought to assume parental responsibility in any way. In this case, the natural father was in the role of the interloper, and the state was in the role of protector, seeking to preserve an ongoing family unit.

In *Caban v. Mohammed*,[57] on the other hand, a closely divided Court ruled in favor of the natural father because he had established a continuing, meaningful relationship with his children and desired to continue his role as parent. Again, as in *Stanley,* the father was in the role of promoting continuity and stability, and the state was in the role of the intervenor.

Finally, in *Lehr v. Robertson*[58] the Court upheld a New York statutory scheme under which an unwed father's rights to his child, whom he had rarely seen since her birth and never supported, were terminated without notice. The statutes listed several bases on which an unwed father would be entitled to notice and a hearing, most of which centered on whether the father had ever maintained any sort of relationship with his child. None of them applied in Lehr's case, and the Court made it clear that an unwed father does not have an absolute right to notice.

### Goss v. Lopez

All of the prior school cases decided by the Supreme Court were concerned with *substantive* due process, which means that before the state can deprive a person of a substantive right such as life, liberty, or property, the state must have a legitimate objective (for example, in *Prince* the protection of children from potential harms on the streets) and the means employed must be reasonably calculated to achieve that objective. In *Goss v. Lopez,*[59] however, the issue was *procedural* due process, which means that before a person may be deprived of his rights the state must afford him notice and a hearing (as in *Stanley,* a nonschool case).

In *Goss* students who had been suspended from school for misconduct for periods up to ten days without notice or a hearing brought suit against school officials seeking to have Ohio's laws authorizing such suspensions declared unconstitutional. The federal district court held the Ohio statute and its implementing regulations unconstitutional. The state appealed.

The Court first dismissed the state's claim that because there is no constitutional right to education[60] the due process clause does not protect students against expulsions or suspensions. The Court observed that the due process clause protects persons against unlawful deprivation of life, liberty, or property and that property interests normally are not created by the Constitution but rather by state law or regulations. In this case Ohio law created an entitlement to a free public education on behalf of all citizens between five and twenty-one years of age. Having created such a property interest, Ohio could not withdraw it without due process of law—that is, without "fundamentally fair procedures to determine whether the misconduct has occurred."[61]

The Court also found a liberty interest to be at stake here because the disciplinary action called into question the students' reputations, honor, and integrity:

> School authorities here suspended appellees from school for periods of up to 10 days based on charges of misconduct. If suspended and recorded, those charges could seriously damage the students' standing with their fellow pupils and their teachers as well as interfere with later opportunities for higher education and employment.[62]

Moreover, in response to the state's claim that the ten-day loss was neither severe nor grievous, the Court expressed the view that

> as long as a property deprivation is not *de minimis,* its gravity is irrelevant to the question whether account must be taken of the Due Process Clause. A 10-day suspension from school is not *de minimis* in our view and may not be imposed in complete disregard of the Due Process Clause.[63]

Having determined that due process applies, the Court proceeded to determine what process is due. Consistent with its earlier procedural due process decisions, the Court held that "At the very minimum . . . students facing suspension and the consequent interference with a protected property interest must be given *some* kind of notice and afforded *some* kind of hearing."[64]

As to the *kind* of notice and hearing to be afforded, the Court's requirements were minimal:

> [D]ue process requires, in connection with a suspension of 10 days or less, that the student be given oral or written notice of the charges against him

and, if he denies them, an explanation of the evidence the authorities have and an opportunity to present his side of the story.[65]

Such minimal requirements, the Court said, are necessary to safeguard against both "unfair or mistaken findings of misconduct and arbitrary exclusion from school."[66]

On the matter of timing, the Court stated that "Since the hearing may occur almost immediately following the misconduct, it follows that as a general rule notice and hearing should precede removal of the student from school."[67] However, "Students whose presence poses a continuing danger to persons or property or an ongoing threat of disrupting the academic process may be immediately removed from school. In such cases, the necessary notice and rudimentary hearing should follow as soon as practicable."[68]

The hearing to be held in the case of a short suspension is rudimentary indeed. It may be held without the presence of counsel and without the opportunity to confront and cross-examine adverse witnesses or the opportunity to call friendly witnesses. The Court cautioned, however, that once alerted to a dispute about facts, a disciplinarian might wish to "summon the accuser, permit cross-examination, and allow the student to present his own witnesses," and in difficult cases, "permit counsel."[69]

The Court added a final caution: "Longer suspensions or expulsions for the remainder of the school term, or permanently, may require more formal procedures." The Court also raised the possibility that even in cases of short suspensions, "unusual situations" might require more formal procedures.[70]

*Goss* was decided by the narrowest of margins, a five-to-four vote. The dissenters, led by Justice Powell, expressed the fear that the Court's decision "unnecessarily opens avenues for judicial intervention in the operation of our public schools that may affect adversely the quality of education."[71] As will be seen in the next case, their view was soon vindicated.


## Ingraham v. Wright

*Ingraham v. Wright,*[72] decided two years after *Goss,* involved the constitutionality of use of corporal punishment as a disciplinary measure in public schools. Two constitutional claims were raised: (1) whether paddling constituted cruel and unusual punishment within the meaning of the eighth amendment and (2) whether if constitutionally permissible, paddling nevertheless required prior notice and a hearing under due process considerations.

The case had an interesting journey through the courts. The federal district court found no constitutional basis for relief. A panel of the court of appeals voted to reverse on both the eighth amendment and fourteenth amendment (due process) grounds, but on rehearing *en banc* (before the entire court) the court of appeals affirmed the district court. The Supreme Court granted the students' petition for writ of certiorari (application for review).

The four dissenters from *Goss* were joined by Justice Stewart to form a new majority that upheld the use of corporal punishment in schools. Justice Powell wrote the opinion of the Court. The remaining members of the old majority, led by Justice White, who wrote the majority opinion in *Goss*, and joined by Justice Stevens, who had replaced Justice Douglas, dissented in *Ingraham*. Justice White wrote the dissenting opinion.

The Court began its analysis by observing that corporal punishment as a means of discipline has been around for a long time—in this country since the colonial period. Since its inception use of corporal punishment by school personnel has been limited by the same principle governing its use by parents: reasonable but not excessive force may be used to discipline a child. If the force used is excessive (that is, unreasonable), school personnel are subject to the common law remedies of civil and criminal liability. Whether punishment is reasonable depends on

> the seriousness of the offense, the attitude and past behavior of the child, the nature and severity of the punishment, the age and strength of the child, and the availability of less severe but equally effective means of discipline.[73]

The Court then turned to the eighth amendment claim. Drawing a distinction between the school environment and the criminal and correctional process, the Court concluded that the prohibition against cruel and unusual punishment was intended to apply only to the latter:

> The prisoner's conviction entitles the State to classify him as a "criminal," and his incarceration deprives him of the freedom "to be with his family and friends and to form the other enduring attachments of normal life.". . .
>
> The school child has little need for the protection of the Eighth Amendment. Though attendance may not always be voluntary, the public school remains an open institution. . . . [A]t the end of the school day, the child brings with him the support of family and friends and is rarely apart from teachers and other pupils who may witness and protest any instances of mistreatment.
>
> The openness of the public school and its supervision by the community afford significant safeguards against the kinds of abuses from which the Eighth Amendment protects the prisoner.[74]

In light of this contrast, the Court was inclined to view the common law remedies for use of excessive force as an effective deterrent to abuse.

Turning to the fourteenth amendment due process claim, the Court employed the same twofold inquiry utilized in *Goss:* (1) is a constitutionally protected interest (that is, life, liberty, or property) implicated, and if so, (2) what process is due? As it had in *Goss* the Court easily concluded that a constitutionally protected liberty interest was at stake in this case. A person has a fundamental right to be free from bodily restraint and punishment except in accordance with due process of law.

The Court's departure from *Goss* (and therefore its chief point of disagreement with the dissenters) was over the question of what process is due. The Court might have been inclined to require the same procedural safeguards imposed by *Goss* but for two factors: the common law privilege permitting teachers to use reasonable corporal punishment as a disciplinary measure and the availability of civil and criminal remedies for abuse.

The Court employed a three-point inquiry that would be used in subsequent cases[75] to determine the adequacy of existing safeguards: (1) what is the private interest that will be affected, (2) what is the risk of an erroneous deprivation of such interest and the likely value of any other or additional safeguards, and (3) what is the state interest affected in terms of the fiscal and administrative cost of other or additional safeguards that might be imposed? The three-prong approach can be seen as nothing more than a cost/benefit analysis.

The Court already had recognized the importance of the liberty interest as the private interest to be affected. The real inquiry was into the practicality or necessity of requiring other or additional safeguards. The Court found that additional safeguards were unnecessary and too costly. The existing safeguards of potential civil and criminal liability act as a deterrent to abuse, therefore minimizing the risk of erroneous decision making by school personnel. Moreover, even if added safeguards furnished an incremental benefit, the cost of requiring notice and a hearing in potentially every case would be a cost too high for school personnel to bear because it would reduce the administrative effectiveness and efficiency of the operation of schools.

The Court summarized its rationale:

> In view of the low incidence of abuse, the openness of our schools, and the common-law safeguards that already exist, the risk of error that may result in violation of a schoolchild's substantive rights can only be regarded as minimal. Imposing additional administrative safeguards as a constitutional requirement might reduce that risk marginally, but would also entail a significant intrusion into an area of primary educational responsibility.[76]

With this last statement, the majority in this case, the same group, plus one, who had dissented in *Goss*, was able to vindicate its concern over unnecessary judicial intervention into the educational process.

In a footnote the Court distinguished this case from *Goss:*

> Unlike *Goss v. Lopez* . . . , this case does not involve the state-created property interest in public education. The purpose of corporal punishment is to correct a child's behavior without interrupting his education.[77]

The implication is that additional safeguards were necessary in *Goss* because the consequences to the child were more serious than in this case—in *Goss* the child was suspended and his education was disrupted, whereas here the child was only paddled and sent back to the classroom.

What makes this observation interesting is the experience related by a student who was enrolled in the Dade County, Florida, school system—the school system at issue in *Ingraham*—at the time the case was decided.[78] According to this student, if a student misbehaved he was called to the front of the room, where he was given a choice—several licks with a paddle or a trip to the principal's office. The students knew that a trip to see the principal, who was sensitive to due process concerns as a result of *Goss v. Lopez*, meant an automatic ten-day suspension, complete with notice and hearing.

The school's policy was that absences of nine days or more during the term precluded a student from receiving credit for that term, necessitating enrollment in summer school to make up the deficiency. Faced with a choice of taking their licks or going to the principal's office, where they would be accorded full due process of law—and also would face going to summer school—most students chose the paddle. This experience makes the Court's comparison of *Goss* and *Ingraham* appear totally unrealistic, a view urged, in fact, by the dissenters in *Ingraham*.[79]

The dissenters disagreed with the majority's conclusion that the eighth amendment applies only to the criminal and correctional processes:

> If there are some punishments that are so barbaric that they may not be imposed for the commission of crimes, designated by our social system as the most thoroughly reprehensible acts an individual can commit, then, *a fortiori*, similar punishments may not be imposed on persons for less culpable acts, such as breaches of school discipline.[80]

"The relevant inquiry," the Court said, "is not whether the offense for which a punishment is inflicted has been labeled as criminal, but whether the purpose of the deprivation is among those ordinarily associated with punishment, such as retribution, rehabilitation, or deterrence."[81]

Moreover, the Court concluded, "if a punishment is so barbaric and inhumane that it goes beyond the tolerance of a civilized society, its openness to public scrutiny should have nothing to do with its constitutional validity."[82] The dissenters fell short, however, of concluding that *all* corporal punishment in the schools is prohibited by the eighth amendment; rather, they disagreed with the majority's conclusion that corporal punishment in the schools is *never* limited by the eighth amendment.

They also disagreed with the majority's conclusion as to the adequacy of existing safeguards. Under Florida law, they argued, a student erroneously punished cannot recover from a teacher acting in good faith on information furnished by others. The civil remedy, therefore, is virtually nonexistent. Even if a student could sue successfully for a good-faith error in imposition of a punishment, the remedy would still be inadequate: "The infliction of physical pain is final and irreparable; it cannot be undone in a subsequent proceeding."[83] The safeguards of notice and hearing, as required by *Goss*, would produce the kind of exchange between student and disciplinarian that would avoid much erroneous—and needless—infliction of pain.

## *Parham v. J.R.*

*Parham v. J.R.*,[84] also a procedural due process case, was a class action challenging the constitutionality of Georgia's statutory scheme allowing the voluntary commitment of a child by the child's parent or guardian to a mental institution. Under that scheme, on the parent's application the superintendent of the hospital is authorized to admit the child temporarily for observation and diagnosis. If the superintendent finds evidence of mental illness he is authorized to admit the child for a longer period of time for treatment. Any child who has been hospitalized for more than five days may be discharged at the parent's request and, in any event, must be discharged by the superintendent if the child has recovered or has improved to the point where hospitalization is no longer necessary.

The federal district court held Georgia's statutory scheme unconstitutional because a liberty interest was implicated (in terms of freedom from restraint and freedom from emotional and psychic harm caused by the hospitalization) and the process designed to protect that interest was inadequate. At a minimum, the district court held, notice and a hearing before an impartial panel were required. The state appealed.

In analyzing the case, the Supreme Court applied the familiar three-pronged approach employed in *Ingraham*. In analyzing the individual interests affected the Court conceded that a child, like an adult, has a substantial, protectible interest in freedom from unnecessary bodily restraint as well as freedom from being erroneously labeled mentally ill. Parents have the same interest in a child's freedom and well-being, but on the whole parents reasonably are expected to act in a child's best interests because they "possess what a child lacks in maturity, experience, and capacity for judgment required for making life's difficult decisions."[85]

Discussion of the state's interests was very brief. For the most part the Court only listed them: the state's interests (1) "in confining the use of its costly mental health facilities to cases of genuine need," (2) "in not imposing unnecessary procedural obstacles that may discourage the mentally ill or their families from seeking needed psychiatric assistance," and (3) "in allocating priority to the diagnosis and treatment of patients as soon as they are admitted to a hospital rather than to time-consuming procedural minuets before the admission."[86]

The Court devoted the greatest part of its analysis to examining the risk of error and what process adequately safeguards against it without unnecessarily burdening the state. The Court concluded that although there is some risk of erroneous judgment, the procedures outlined in the statutory scheme are fairly calculated to offset or minimize it. Neither an outside panel nor a formal hearing is required to make what is essentially a medical judgment. The Court summarized:

> In general, we are satisfied that an independent medical decisionmaking process, which includes the thorough psychiatric investigation described earlier followed by additional periodic review of a child's condition, will protect children who should not be admitted; we do not believe the risks of error in that process would be significantly reduced by a more formal, judicial-type hearing.[87]

In light of the Court's minimalization of the risk of error and its conclusion regarding the adequacy of existing safeguards, one might recall, with some irony, the case of *Hewlett v. George*[88] mentioned in chapter 3. *Hewlett v. George* was the first case in which a court adopted the doctrine of parent/child tort immunity, which holds that neither parent nor child is liable to the other for tortious acts committed by one against the other. In that case, the tort alleged was false imprisonment in that the defendant mother had caused her child to be committed without cause to an insane asylum. Under the doctrine of parent/child immunity, of course, the child's suit was precluded, ostensibly on the theory that allowing such a suit would disrupt family harmony.

The Court in *Parham v. J.R.* observed that Georgia's statutory scheme is typical of a model generally followed in more than thirty states. This statement concedes that in some states the Georgia model is not followed and *Parham v. J.R.* does not prevail. In *In re Roger S.*,[89] for example, the California Supreme Court held that children fourteen years of age or older who object to hospitalization for mental disorders constitutionally are entitled to notice and a hearing on the propriety of commitment.[90]

## H.L. v. Matheson

*H.L. v. Matheson*[91] was a substantive due process case concerning a challenge to Utah's statutory requirement that a physician notify, if possible, the parents or guardian of a minor before performing an abortion on the minor. The notice requirement was alleged by the minor to violate her constitutional right to privacy as recognized in earlier decisions.

In one of those earlier decisions, *Bellotti v. Baird*,[92] the Court held unconstitutional a statute imposing a requirement of parental *consent* for a minor to obtain an abortion, although the Court intimated in that case that parents might have *some* role to play. The fatal flaw in the statute was that it failed to allow "mature minors" (that is, those capable of mature, informed decision making) to decide for themselves whether to undergo an abortion. Thus, a four-member plurality was of the view that a minor should be afforded an alternative—either to obtain consent of her parents or to obtain consent of an impartial judicial or administrative panel on a showing that she is a mature minor capable of making her own decisions or, even if immature, that the abortion would be in her best interest.[93]

In *Matheson* the Court found no constitutional infirmity with a statute that merely required parental notification and did not give parents a veto power over the minor's decision. Requiring parental notification, the Court found, furthers the legitimate state objectives of encouraging parent/child communication with regard to a very important medical decision and affording parents an opportunity to furnish medical and other information to the physician.

The dissenters objected on the ground that notification of parents would mean intrusion by the parents into the minor's right of private choice, which would have the effect in most cases of denying her the right of private choice altogether. The majority, however, came down very strongly in favor of parental authority in the home, perhaps giving some indication of what the Court meant in *Bellotti v. Baird* that parents might have *some* role to play.

Citing and quoting from an array of its earlier decisions (such as *Ginsberg, Quilloin v. Walcott, Yoder, Stanley, Meyer, Prince, Parham v. J.R.,* and *Pierce*), the Court concluded that " 'constitutional interpretation has consistently recognized that the parents' claim to authority in their own household to direct the rearing of their children is basic in the structure of our society.' "[94] The Court thus read its earlier recitations of parental authority as supporting parental participation in, and even influencing of, a minor's decision whether to bear a child. Such a parental role is consistent with, as the Court put it, "the important considerations of family integrity and protecting adolescents."[95]

*H.L. v. Matheson* represents a fairly narrow holding, applicable only to cases of immature, dependent minors. The Court itself narrowed the scope of the case before it:

> The only issue before us, then, is the facial constitutionality of a statute requiring a physician to give notice to parents "if possible," prior to performing an abortion on their minor daughter, (a) when the girl is living with and dependent upon her parents, (b) when she is not emancipated by marriage or otherwise, and (c) when she has made no claim or showing as to her maturity or as to her relations with her parents.[96]

The Court thus left open the question of the constitutionality of a parental notification requirement as applied to mature or emancipated minors.

### New York v. Ferber

In *Prince* the Supreme Court first intimated that the state can regulate the activities of children to a greater extent than it can those of adults,[97] and in *Ginsberg* the Court relied heavily on *Prince* in upholding a New York statute prohibiting the sale to minors of material defined to be obscene for minors without regard to whether it would be obscene for adults.[98] The state has a strong interest, it was said in both cases, in protecting the well-being of its children.

In *New York v. Ferber*[99] the Court upheld a New York statute prohibiting the knowing promotion of sexual performances by children under age sixteen by distributing material depicting such performances. Although recognizing the hazards of attempts by states to regulate any sort of expression, the Court relied on *Prince* and *Ginsberg* in concluding that states have greater freedom to regulate pornographic depictions of children. Its reasons were several but the very first mentioned was the state's significant interest in the well-being of children.

The Court also upheld the statute against the claim that it was overbroad in that it prohibited distribution of protected nonobscene material—that is, material with serious literary, scientific, or educational value.[100] In so holding the Court reasoned that any such material—such as illustrations in medical textbooks and pictorials in *National Geographic*—would make up such a small percentage of materials within the reach of the statute as to be insubstantial.

*Ferber*, like *Prince* and *Ginsberg* before it, is another example of the Court upholding a statute designed to protect children from their own improvidence and from harmful influences, perhaps in some instances (such as *Prince*) against the wishes of the child or his parents.

## Conclusion

It is readily apparent from the foregoing synopses of Supreme Court decisions that the Court has granted children some rights and has not granted them certain others. Less obvious is the conclusion that the Supreme Court has failed to develop a consistent theory as to *why* it has decided these cases in such a disparate manner.

One clear sign of the Court's failure is the fact that so many of its decisions were very narrow in scope and application, evidencing the absence of any cohesive underlying policy base. In addition to the limiting language just quoted from *H.L. v. Matheson,*[101] the following limitation is found in *Prince:*

> Our ruling does not extend beyond the facts the case presents. We neither lay the foundation "for any [that is, every] state intervention in the indoctrination and participation of children in religion" which may be done "in the name of their health and welfare" nor give warrant for "every limitation on their religious training and activities."[102]

In a particularly revealing comment in *Ginsberg* the Court also drew a narrow perspective:

> We have no occasion in this case to consider the impact of the guarantees of freedom of expression upon the totality of the relationship of the minor and the State. . . . It is enough for the purposes of this case that we inquire whether it was constitutionally impermissible for New York . . . to accord minors under 17 a more restricted right than that assured to adults to judge and determine for themselves what sex material they may read or see.[103]

In *Tinker,* also, the Court narrowed its focus:

> The problem posed by the present case does not relate to regulation of the length of skirts or the type of clothing, to hair style, or deportment. It does not concern aggressive, disruptive action or even group demonstrations. Our problem involves direct, primary First Amendment rights akin to "pure speech."[104]

The Court's reluctance, in constitutional cases, to make pronouncements any broader than necessary to decide a case is understandable. At the same time it is equally clear that what the Court was reluctant to do in *Ginsberg*—that is, examine "the totality of the relationship of the minor and the State—is precisely what is required if it is to develop a consistent analytical approach in children's cases.

Instead, what is seen in this chapter, dealing with public law (that is, constitutional) issues, resembles the picture *seen* in the previous chapter dealing with private law issues. The law—as exemplified by the actions of legislatures and the courts—in both private and public law contexts, has failed to reexamine the traditional roles of children, parents, and the state and in particular has failed to reexamine the bases for traditional rules limiting the rights and opportunities of children.

Professor Michael Wald has categorized children's rights into four groups: (1) rights against the world (freedom from discrimination and poverty), (2) the right to adequate care (freedom from neglect, abuse, and exploitation), (3) the right to adult legal status (entitlement to constitutional and other rights that adults enjoy), and (4) rights versus parents (freedom from parental control or guidance).[105]

The first two groups he refers to as *protections,* in that children are in need of protection from endangering surroundings and influences and occasionally from themselves.[106] Few would argue that children are not in need of some protection.[107] If a child is employed in the making of pornographic films, the child's reaction—indeed, the reaction of his family—might be: "Hey, I'm having fun and making lots of money. Leave me alone."[108] Yet most people would agree that despite the wishes of the child or his parents, the child is in need of protection from exploitation and the risk of permanent emotional injury.[109]

The second two groups are viewed by Wald as embracing *rights* in the traditional sense, as evidenced by the subject matter of this chapter and to a large degree the preceding chapter. Most limitations on children's rights, Wald points out, are based on the judgments that children lack capacity to make decisions for themselves and that parents must make decisions for them,[110] and that parental control and authority are necessary to preserve the stability of the family unit, which is crucial to our societal structure.[111]

Wald urges that legislatures and courts—the Supreme Court included—reexamine these assumptions of incapacity in light of changes in our social structure and in the rate of development of children and, to the extent limitations are based on invalid assumptions, that they be eliminated. In some cases an age restriction may not be necessary at all; in others if restriction is needed, it need not be wholly age-specific but rather based on other criteria and rationally related to capacity to engage in a particular activity.[112] He further urges rethinking of the roles of parents and the state in decision making for children because in many instances less interference by parents or state may be more conducive to a child's well-being.[113]

The need to reassess traditional roles and assumptions of incapacity applies equally whether in the case of a child's capacity to enter into a contract, make a will, or engage in a particular occupation[114] or a child's capacity to decide what he will or will not read or view, whether she will obtain an abortion or whether he will wear an armband in school or pass out leaflets on the streets. Reassessment does not mean abandonment. Many age restrictions or other constraints on children's rights might be retained, but if they are their retention presumably would be based on current knowledge about child development and parental and other roles.

Against this backdrop, admittedly painted with very broad brush strokes, the remaining chapters of this book are devoted to a study of decision making by and for children in a number of important areas implicating the constitutional rights to life (medical decision making for children), liberty (freedom of children), and property (protected entitlements of children), as well as the right to an education and the right to protection from inadequate parenting.

## Notes

1. 262 U.S. 390 (1923).
2. 458 U.S. 747 (1982).
3. For example, New Jersey v. T.L.O., 469 U.S. 325 (1985); Schall v. Martin, 467 U.S. 253 (1984) (preventive detention of juveniles before hearing); Breed v. Jones, 421 U.S. 519 (1975) (application of prohibition against double jeopardy to juvenile cases); McKeiver v. Pennsylvania, 403 U.S. 528 (1971) (right to jury trial in juvenile cases); *In re* Winship, 397 U.S. 358 (1970) (requirement of proof beyond a reasonable doubt in deliquency cases); *In re* Gault, 387 U.S. 1 (1967) (right to counsel, privilege against self-incrimination, and rights to confrontation and cross-examination at an adjudicatory hearing); Kent v. United States, 383 U.S. 541 (1966) (right to a waiver hearing).
4. Indeed, we have given some thought to a separate book on children in the juvenile justice system that would be a companion volume to this book.
5. 262 U.S. 390 (1923).
6. *Id.* at 401.
7. *Id.* at 400.
8. 381 U.S. 479 (1965) (statute prohibiting use of contraceptives unconstitutional as undue infringement on the right to privacy).
9. 388 U.S. 1 (1967) (statutory ban on interracial marriage unconstitutional).
10. 262 U.S. at 399.
11. *Id.* at 401.
12. *Id.* at 402.
13. 268 U.S. 510 (1925).
14. *Id.* at 534.
15. *Id.* at 532.
16. *Id.* at 534–35.
17. *See* page 51 *supra.*
18. 321 U.S. 158 (1944).
19. *Id.* at 165.
20. *Id.* at 166.
21. *See, e.g.,* Ginsberg v. New York, 390 U.S. 629 (1968).
22. 321 U.S. at 168.
23. *Id.* at 170.
24. *Id.* at 173–74.
25. 390 U.S. 629 (1968).
26. 354 U.S. 476 (1957).
27. More recently, the Court upheld a New York statute prohibiting the knowing promotion of a sexual performance by a child under age sixteen by distributing material depicting such a performance, without regard to whether the material is obscene. New York v. Ferber, 458 U.S. 747 (1982). Sexual exploitation of minors as a form of child abuse is covered in chapter 9.
28. 393 U.S. 503 (1969).
29. *Id.* at 506–07.
30. Justice Black in a dissenting opinion disagreed with the majority's conclusion that no disruption had occurred:

While the record does not show that any or these armband students shouted, used profane language, or were violent in any manner, detailed testimony by some of them shows their armbands caused comments, warnings by other students, the poking of fun at them, and a warning by an older football player that other, nonprotesting students had better let them alone. There is also evidence that a teacher of mathematics had his lesson period practically "wrecked" chiefly by disputes with Mary Beth Tinker, who wore her armband for her "demonstration." Even a casual reading of the record shows that this armband did divert students' minds from their regular lessons, and that talk, comments, etc., made John Tinker "self-conscious" in attending school with his armband. While the absence of obscene remarks or boisterous and loud disorder perhaps justifies the Court's statement that the few armband students did not actually "disrupt" the classwork, I think the record overwhelmingly shows that the armbands did exactly what the elected school officials and principals foresaw they would, that is, took the students' minds off their classwork and diverted them to thoughts about the highly emotional subject of the Vietnam war.

*Id.* at 517–18.

31. The cases, noted in footnote 1 of the Supreme Court's opinion in *Tinker,* are Burnside v. Byars, 363 F.2d 744 (5th Cir. 1966) (enforcement of rule enjoined), and Blackwell v. Issaqueena County Bd. of Educ., 363 F.2d 749 (5th Cir. 1966) (enforcement of rule not enjoined).

32. 393 U.S. at 509.

33. *Id.* at 511.

34. *See, e.g.,* Cox v. Louisiana, 379 U.S. 559 (1965) (freedom of speech and assembly); New York Times v. Sullivan, 376 U.S. 254 (1964) (freedom of press); Sherbert v. Verner, 374 U.S. 398 (1963) (freedom of religion); Herndon v. Lowry, 301 U.S. 242 (1937) (freedom of speech). One might suppose, obviously, that the first amendment rights—freedom of speech, press, religion, and assembly—were placed in the first amendment because they were deemed most important of all the protections of the Bill of Rights. One should not be surprised, therefore, that the Supreme Court has been most zealous in its safeguarding of these rights. The preferential status of first amendment rights has been argued on numerous occasions. *See, e.g.,* New York Times v. Sullivan 376 U.S. 254, 267–83 (1964) (Brennan, J., majority opinion); West Virginia State Bd. of Educ. v. Barnette, 319 U.S. 624, 638–40 (1943) (Jackson, J., majority opinion); United States v. Carolene Products, 304 U.S. 144, 152 n.4 (1938) (Stone, J., majority opinion); Whitney v. California, 274 U.S. 357, 375–79 (1927) (Brandeis, J., concurring); Abrams v. United States, 250 U.S. 616, 624–31 (1919) (Holmes, J., dissenting); *see also* Kovacs v. Cooper, 336 U.S. 77, 90–97 (1949) (Frankfurter, J., concurring) (summary—and criticism—of "preferred position" argument).

35. For example, courts have frowned on attempts at prior restraint of material intended for publication in school newspapers. *See, e.g.,* Gambino v. Fairfax County School Bd., 429 F. Supp. 731 (E.D. Va.), *aff'd,* 564 F.2d 157 (4th Cir. 1977); Bright v. Los Angeles Unified School Dist., 18 Cal. 3d 450, 556 P.2d 1090, 134 Cal. Rptr. 639 (1976).

36. One might compare with *Tinker,* for example, the Supreme Court's recent decision in New Jersey v. T.L.O., 469 U.S. 325 (1985), in which the Court accorded less than full fourth amendment protection to students in public schools.

37. More recently, for example, the Court upheld a school district's action in disciplining a student for making a nomination speech before an assembly in which he referred to his candidate in terms of "an elaborate, graphic, and explicit sexual metaphor." Bethel School Dist. v. Fraser, 106 S. Ct. 3159 (1986). For further discussion of this point, *see* Garvey, *Child, Parent, State, and the Due Process*

*Clause: An Essay on the Supreme Court's Recent Work*, 51 So. CAL. L. REV. 769, 785 (1978); Hafen, *Children's Liberation and the New Egalitarianism: Some Reservations about Abandoning Youth to Their "Rights"*, 1976 B.Y.U. L. REV 605, 646.

38. Mississippi repealed its compulsory attendance law in 1956 but enacted a new law in 1977, thus making the requirement universal in the United States. For general works on the history of education in America and on the development of compulsory attendance laws in particular, *see* F. BUTTS & L. CREMIN, A HISTORY OF EDUCATION IN AMERICAN CULTURE (1953), and N. EDWARDS & H. RICHEY, THE SCHOOL IN THE AMERICAN SOCIAL ORDER (2d ed. 1963). A current summary of caselaw, particularly with respect to exemptions from compulsory school attendance laws, is found in W. WADLINGTON, C. WHITEBREAD & S. DAVIS, CHILDREN IN THE LEGAL SYSTEM 108–13 (1983).

39. 406 U.S. 205 (1972).

40. *Id.* at 214.

41. *Id.* at 215, 219.

42. *Id.* at 241–46 (Douglas, J., dissenting in part).

43. *Id.* at 235–36. As an example of a case illustrating the narrowness of the *Yoder* decision, *see In re* McMillan, 30 N.C. App. 235, 226 S.E.2d 693 (1976) (affirming determination that American Indian children were neglected because of parents' refusal to send them to school, over parents' objection that their refusal was based on deeply held cultural convictions, which, like religious beliefs, were entitled to constitutional protection). *See also* Duro v. District Attorney, 712 F.2d 96 (4th Cir. 1983), *cert. denied*, 465 U.S. 1006 (1984); State v. Shaver, 294 N.W.2d 883 (N.D. 1980).

44. 405 U.S. 645 (1972).

45. 391 U.S. 68 (1968)

46. 391 U.S. 73 (1968).

47. More recently, in Parham v. Hughes, 441 U.S. 347 (1979), the Court upheld a Georgia statutory scheme allowing the mother of an illegitimate child to bring an action for the wrongful death of the child but precluding the father from doing so unless he had legitimated the child. The Court's rationale was that paternity of illegitimate children, unlike maternity, is fraught with problems of proof, and to alleviate these problems of proof, Georgia could reasonably require the father to assume parental responsibility and legitimate the child; moreover, the reality was that in Georgia only a father could legitimate a child by unilateral court action.

48. 401 U.S. 532 (1971).

49. 439 U.S. 259 (1978).

50. In Trimble v. Gordon, 430 U.S. 762 (1977), the Court held unconstitutional an Illinois statutory scheme that barred illegitimate children from sharing in the distribution of intestate property. Without specifically stating so, the Court effectively overruled Labine v. Vincent, 401 U.S. 532 (1971), in which it had upheld a similar Louisiana statutory scheme.

51. Specifically, the New York statute at issue in Lalli v. Lalli required that a paternity order issue during the father's lifetime before a child, still illegitimate, would be allowed to inherit from the father's estate. The Court found this requirement, which did not constitute a total ban, to be reasonably related to the state's legitimate concern over problems of proof.

52. 406 U.S. 164 (1972).

53. 409 U.S. 535 (1973).

54. *Id.* at 538.

55. 405 U.S. at 652.

56. 434 U.S. 246 (1978).

57. 441 U.S. 380 (1979).

58. 463 U.S. 248 (1983).

59. 419 U.S. 565 (1975).

60. *See* chapter 8 in this book on the right to an education.

61. 419 U.S. at 574

62. *Id.* at 574–75.

63. *Id.* at 576.

64. *Id.* at 579.

65. *Id.* at 581.

66. *Id.*

67. *Id.* at 582.

68. *Id.* at 582–83.

69. *Id.* at 584.

70. *Id.*

71. *Id.* at 585 (Powell, J., dissenting).

72. 430 U.S. 651 (1977).

73. *Id.* at 662.

74. *Id.* at 669–70.

75. *See* Parham v. J.R., 442 U.S. 584 (1979), discussed later in this chapter.

76. 430 U.S. at 682.

77. 430 U.S. at 674 n. 43.

78. The student related this experience as a member of the class in the Children in the Legal System course taught at the University of Georgia School of Law in spring 1985.

79. 430 U.S. at 692–700 (White, J., dissenting).

80. *Id.* at 684.

81. *Id.* at 686–87.

82. *Id.* at 690.

83. *Id.* at 695.

84. 442 U.S. 584 (1979).

85. *Id.* at 602. One might ask in light of the Court's view on this point, why we have a system of laws designed to handle cases of neglect and abuse of children by parents. *See* chapter 9 in this book.

86. *Id.* at 604–05.

87. *Id.* at 613.

88. 68 Miss. 703, 9 So. 885 (1891).

89. 19 Cal. 3d 921, 569 P.2d 1286, 141 Cal. Rptr. 298 (1977).

90. As a followup on the case and its impact on mental health commitment procedures, *see* Dillon, Roisman, Sanders & Adler, *In re* Roger S.: *The Impact of a Child's Due Process Victory on the California Mental Health System*, 70 CALIF. L. REV. 373 (1982).

91. 450 U.S. 398 (1981).

92. 443 U.S. 622 (1979).

93. In two subsequent cases the Court reached different results over whether

challenged statutes met the alternative procedure approved in Bellotti v. Baird. *Compare* City of Akron v. Akron Center for Reproductive Health, 462 U.S. 416 (1983) (city ordinance unconstitutional), with Planned Parenthood Ass'n v. Ashcroft, 462 U.S. 476 (1983) (statute constitutional).

94. 450 U.S. at 10.

95. *Id.* at 411.

96. *Id.* at 407.

97. *See* notes 21–23 and accompanying text, *supra*.

98. *See* notes 25–27 and accompanying text, *supra*.

99. 458 U.S. 747 (1982).

100. In Miller v. California, 413 U.S. 15 (1973), the Court defined *obscene material* as material lacking serious literary, scientific, or educational value calculated to appeal primarily to prurient interests.

101. *See* note 96 and accompanying text, *supra*.

102. 321 U.S. at 171.

103. 390 U.S. at 636–37.

104. 393 U.S. at 507–08.

105. Wald, *Children's Rights: A Framework for Analysis*, 12 U.C.D. L. Rev. 255, 260 (1979) [hereinafter cited as Wald].

106. Wald's second category, the right to adequate care, is the subject of chapter 9 of this book *infra*.

107. Some have urged, however, that children be granted full autonomy in all matters. *See, e.g.*, R. Farson, Birthrights (1974); J. Holt, Escape from Childhood (1974).

108. The example is from Wald, *supra* note 105, at 263.

109. The Supreme Court's decisions in New York v. Ferber, 458 U.S. 747 (1982), and Prince v. Massachusetts, 321 U.S. 158 (1944), support this view. *See generally* chapter 9 in this book on protection of children from inadequate parenting, especially the discussion of sexual exploitation as a form of abuse.

110. Wald, *supra* note 105, at 259. For an expression of the incapacity theory, *see* the quote from Parham v. J.R., 442 U.S. 584 (1979), at the beginning of chapter 1.

111. Wald, *supra* note 105, at 259. Professor Bruce C. Hafen has also supported the idea of parental authority as the necessary element to secure the well-being of children and to strengthen the family as the basic unit in our societal structure. Hafen, *Children's Liberation and the New Egalitarianism: Some Reservations about Abandoning Youth to Their "Rights,"* 1976 B.Y.U. L. Rev. 605. The Supreme Court's decisions in Wisconsin v. Yoder, 406 U.S. 205 (1972), and H.L. v. Matheson, 450 U.S. 398 (1981), contain strong statements supporting parental authority.

112. Wald, *supra* note 105, at 266–69.

113. *Id.* at 270–81.

114. Recall that the matter of rethinking assumptions of a child's incapacity to engage in these and other activities was raised in chapter 3 of this book.

# 5
# Life: Medical Decision Making for Children

Parental autonomy is not . . . absolute. The state is the guardian of society's basic values. Under the doctrine of *parens patriae*, the state has a right, indeed, a duty, to protect children. State officials may interfere in family matters to safeguard the child's health, educational development and emotional well-being.

One of the most basic values protected by the state is the sanctity of human life. Where parents fail to provide their children with adequate medical care, the state is justified to intervene. However, since the state should usually defer to the wishes of the parents, it has a serious burden of justification before abridging parental autonomy by substituting its judgment for that of the parents.

—Justice Thomas W. Caldecott
*In re Phillip B.*
92 Cal. App. 3d 796,
156 Cal. Rptr. 48 (1979)

## Introduction

In his *Two Treatises on Government* John Locke spoke of man's right to "life, liberty and property."[1] The Virginia Bill of Rights, adopted on June 12, 1776, declared that

all men are by nature free and independent, and have certain inherent rights, . . . namely, the enjoyment of life and liberty, with the means of acquiring and possessing property, and pursuing and obtaining happiness and safety.[2]

The Declaration of Independence, adopted shortly thereafter, states:

We hold these truths to be self-evident: that all men are created equal; that they are endowed by their Creator, with certain unalienable rights; that among these are life, liberty, and the pursuit of happiness.[3]

And the fifth amendment to our Constitution states, in language later echoed in the due process clause of the fourteenth amendment:

> No person shall be . . . deprived of life, liberty, or property, without due process of law.[4]

If one of the "blessings of liberty"[5] is the right to life, what is it? In an influential piece written in 1890, two eminent jurists and scholars wrote of the "older" views of life, liberty, and property and how they had changed in "recent" times:

> That the individual shall have full protection in person and in property is a principle as old as the common law; but it has been necessary from time to time to define anew the exact nature and extent of such protection. . . . Thus, in very early times, the law gave a remedy only for physical interference with life and property, for trespasses *vi et armis*. Then the "right to life" served only to protect the subject from battery in its various forms; liberty meant freedom from actual restraint; and the right to property secured to the individual his lands and his cattle. Later, there came a recognition of man's spiritual nature, of his feelings and his intellect. Gradually the scope of these legal rights broadened; and now the right to life has come to mean the right to enjoy life,—the right to be let alone; the right to liberty secures the exercise of extensive civil privileges; and the term "property" has grown to comprise every form of possession—intangible, as well as tangible.[6]

The "right to life" could be presented in many different ways. The means chosen here is to examine the conflict between the state and parents and even the child in some instances, in the matter of medical decision making for children. Perhaps in no other area is the conflict between the competing goals of autonomy and protection so keenly felt.

Medical decision making for children is also an emotion-laden area, cutting across the whole range of human behavior affected. Once again, as mentioned in the introduction to this book, the central issue is authority. Who shall speak for the child? Who should decide whether a child may have an abortion? The child? The parents? The courts? Who should decide whether a defective newborn should be allowed to die or whether extraordinary means should be employed to save it? If the parents decline, does the state have the authority to act for the child because the child cannot speak for itself?

In light of these profound questions, it is interesting that in their article quoted above, Warren and Brandeis viewed changes in the concepts of life, liberty, and property as wrought by "recognition of man's spiritual nature, of his feelings and his intellect." Certainly these same qualities guide current thinking about medical decision making for children, although the decisions themselves do not come any easier, nor is the law's task in formulating policy and rules made any less difficult.

## The "Life-Threatening" Criterion

Consent is a basic requirement for medical treatment. Medical treatment without consent constitutes a trespass, an actionable tort. To be valid, consent must be informed—that is, the person giving it must have been apprised of and understand the risks entailed in the medical procedure. Moreover, the person must possess legal capacity to consent to medical treatment. Hence, children, unless they are emancipated or an emergency exists and the parent is unavailable, cannot consent for themselves; rather, a parent's consent is required.[7]

Suppose, however, that a child faces a medical emergency and the parent is present but refuses to consent to medical treatment. A well-settled exception to the parental consent requirement is the life-threatening scenario in which the child requires immediate medical attention in order to preserve his life. In such cases courts have felt compelled to intervene on the child's behalf, even over parental objection.

A leading case is *People ex rel. Wallace v. Labrenz,*[8] in which the parents, Jehovah's Witnesses, refused to consent to a blood transfusion for their child based on Biblical teachings that blood is the *life* of the flesh and that it should not be consumed in any way,[9] which they read as an admonition against any injection of blood into the body. The court upheld the trial court's finding that the child was a dependent child and its order placing the child in the custody of a guardian for the purpose of the guardian giving consent to the transfusion.

The court found the child to be dependent or neglected within the meaning of the applicable statute, despite the fact that the parents had not failed her in any other respect:

> Neglect . . . is the failure to exercise the care that the circumstances justly demand. It embraces wilful as well as unintentional disregard of duty. It is not a term of fixed and measured meaning. It takes its content always from specific circumstances, and its meaning varies as the context of surrounding circumstances changes. . . . We entertain no doubt that this child, whose parents were deliberately depriving it of life or subjecting it to permanent mental impairment was a neglected child within the meaning of the statute.[10]

More important, in formulating the life-threatening exception, the court engaged in a balancing of risks:

> The short answer is that the facts here disclose no . . . perilous undertaking, but, on the contrary, an urgently needed transfusion—virtually certain of

success if given in time—with only such attendant risk as is inescapable in all of the affairs of life.[11]

In other words, the medical procedure itself posed very little or no risk, whereas forgoing it because of the parents' refusal posed a certainty of either loss of life or permanent brain damage. Under these circumstances the court felt intervention by the state, pursuant to its strong interest in preserving the well-being of its children, was proper even against the important individual interests of religious freedom and parental authority. Other courts followed this lead.[12]

## Baby Doe Cases

In recent years a particular class of life-threatening cases has posed a more complicated medico/legal/ethical dilemma than that presented in the *Labrenz* case. These are the Baby Doe cases, which in one sense are the same as the usual life-threatening cases but in another sense are different. They are identical in that, absent surgery or some other medical procedure, the attendant risk is loss of life. They are different in that the life itself may be regarded by the parents and perhaps their doctors as "hopeless" because the child is born with a severe birth defect and accompanying medical complications.

A transitional case between the typical life-threatening cases such as *Labrenz* and the more recent Baby Doe cases is *In re Cicero*.[13] In that case the court over parental objection appointed a guardian to consent to surgery on a newborn infant to correct a spina bifida condition. The prognosis was fairly good. With the operation the child would have only minimal handicaps. She would be able to walk with short braces, and her intellectual development would be normal.

The court did not view this as an extreme or hopeless case: "This is not a case where the court is asked to preserve an existence which cannot be a life."[14] Further: "There is a hint in this proceeding of a philosophy that newborn, 'hopeless' lives should be permitted to expire without an effort to save those lives. Fortunately, the medical evidence here is such that we do not confront a 'hopeless' life."[15]

The court's decision in *Cicero* was made easier, then, by the fact that it was not presented with a hopelessly defective newborn. Nor was it faced with a classic confrontation between parents who, in the best interests of the child and the family, might wish to allow the baby to die, and the state, which might seek to intervene because of its paramount interest in preservation of life. What position might courts be expected to take if faced with such a confrontation, in cases where the prognosis on the infant is far less favorable than that of the infant in *Cicero?*

Two Baby Doe cases have gained national attention in recent years, and both have prompted considerable legislative, judicial, and administrative response at the federal and state levels. The first concerned Infant Doe, a Down's syndrome child born in an Indiana hospital in April 1982. The infant had a serious respiratory condition with the attendant risk of heart complications, requiring major corrective surgery. The parents declined to consent to surgery, apparently based on the medical prognosis that while the chances of successfully remedying the respiratory ailment were even, the Down's syndrome condition was not treatable. The trial court's refusal to interfere with the parents' decision was allowed to stand when the Indiana Supreme Court declined review. Infant Doe died while state authorities were seeking intervention by the United States Supreme Court.[16]

Response to the Infant Doe case was immediate. The Secretary of Health and Human Services sent letters to some 6,800 hospitals receiving federal funding warning them that withholding medical treatment from handicapped infants could violate section 504 of the Rehabilitation Act of 1973.[17] Violators, he warned, could lose their federal funding.[18]

Further, the Secretary published a set of regulations on March 7, 1983, requiring hospitals receiving federal funds to post a notice stating that denial of medical care to handicapped infants is prohibited by federal law, and including a "hotline" telephone number that persons having knowledge of such cases could call to report violations.[19] On April 14, 1983, these regulations were declared invalid by a federal district court because of the arbitrary procedure by which they were adopted.[20]

New regulations were proposed in July 1983, and this time the procedural niceties found lacking by the federal district court were observed. The regulations became final on January 12, 1984, and were very similar in content to the old regulations.[21] The new regulations were struck down by a different federal district court, this time on the merits rather than for procedural reasons.[22] The district court's decision was summarily upheld by the Second Circuit Court of Appeals.[23]

In *Bowen v. American Hospital Association*[24] the Supreme Court upheld the district court's ruling holding the regulations invalid. To be valid, regulations should be rationally related to the statutory purpose, which in this case is to prevent discrimination against handicapped persons. No instances were shown, however, of refusal of hospitals to treat handicapped newborns where parents had consented to treatment. The regulations, then, were directed toward instances in which parents had failed to consent to treatment. In those cases, however, the Court said, the hospitals refused treatment because the parents had not consented to treatment. Even the government conceded on appeal that in the absence of parental consent, a hospital has no statutory duty to provide treatment. The regulations were invalid, then, because they were addressed to nonexistent discrimination.

In October 1984 Congress enacted Public Law 98-457 amending the Child Abuse Prevention and Treatment Act.[25] The president signed the legislation and new regulations were issued pursuant to it, becoming final on April 15, 1985. Under the new regulations, effective October 1985, states are required to have procedures allowing intervention by state officials to prevent infants being denied needed medical treatment. Medical treatment can be withheld in only three instances: when the infant is in an irreversible coma, where death will occur quickly whether or not the infant is treated, or where the treatment itself is so extreme and the chance of life so remote that treatment would be inhumane.[26]

During the public furor and legal maneuverings surrounding the Infant Doe case in Indiana another case arose in New York. Baby Jane Doe was born on October 11, 1983, with a spina bifida condition similar to but perhaps more serious than that of the infant in the *Cicero* case discussed earlier. The parents declined to consent to proposed corrective surgery and elected to pursue a more conservative course of treatment. A third party, unrelated to the baby or the parents, sought and obtained appointment as the baby's guardian for the purpose of giving consent to surgery.

The trial court's decision was reversed by the appellate division because in its judgment this was not a case in which the child was being deprived of needed medical treatment in order to hasten death; to the contrary, the parents, on competent medical advice, had simply elected one course of treatment over another.[27] The New York Court of Appeals also reversed the trial court but for the different, procedural reason that under New York law only a child protective agency, or a person designated by the court, is authorized to seek intervention in a case of alleged child abuse or neglect. That was not the case here because the third-party intervenor had acted at his own behest.[28]

The New York case also ended up in federal court. The Department of Health and Human Services filed an action in federal district court seeking access to Baby Jane Doe's medical records under authority of section 504 of the Rehabilitation Act of 1973, ostensibly to determine the reasonableness of the medical judgment made in her case. In accord with the parents' wishes the hospital refused to turn over the records. The hospital's decision was upheld by the federal district court[29] and by the court of appeals in a decision on which the Supreme Court relied in *Bowen v. American Hospital Association*.[30]

Some state legislatures also have been responsive to widespread publicity about the Baby Doe cases. The Indiana legislature, for example, amended its statutes to include within the definition of a "child in need of services"

a handicapped child who is deprived of nutrition that is necessary to sustain life, or who is deprived of medical or surgical intervention that is necessary to remedy or ameliorate a life threatening medical condition, if the nutrition or medical or surgical intervention is generally provided to similarly situated handicapped or nonhandicapped children.[31]

Similarly, Louisiana enacted a rather comprehensive statutory scheme prohibiting withholding of "food or nutrients, water or oxygen" from newborn infants.[32] An exception is allowed under the statutes in the case of a permanently comatose infant whose parents, on the basis of competent medical advice, wish to terminate use of extraordinary life-support equipment.[33] This provision was upheld against constitutional attack in *In re P.V.W.*[34]

Far from moving toward a satisfactory solution, the Baby Doe controversy is just in its initial stages. Because these cases generate the most emotion and therefore the greatest controversy, perhaps in no other area of medical decision making for children is the division so sharply drawn between the competing interests of family autonomy and state concern for the welfare of children. Much has been and continues to be written on the subject.[35]

## The Alternative Therapy Cases

Recall the New York Appellate Division's decision in *Weber v. Stony Brook Hospital*,[36] in which the court upheld the parents' right to elect one course of treatment over another. In recent years two cases of the life-threatening genre have captured national attention as cases questioning the right of parents to elect an alternative, nontraditional course of treatment for a child's life-threatening illness. The cases were those of Joey Hofbauer in New York and Chad Green in Massachusetts.

Chad Green was diagnosed at age twenty months with acute lymphocytic leukemia. His doctors recommended a program of chemotherapy, and their prognosis was that with such therapy he had a substantial chance for a cure and a normal life. His parents refused to consent to the chemotherapy and instead expressed interest in pursuing a treatment program using laetrile. A trial judge ordered them to consent to the chemotherapy treatment, and this decision was upheld on appeal.[37] The appellate court did not view this as a case in which parents wished to elect one course of treatment over another but rather as one in which the parents, contrary to the child's best interests, were refusing traditional medical treatment with promise of success while proposing no alternative treatment "consistent with good medical practice."

When Chad was three years old his case was back in court again. His parents had petitioned for review and redetermination of the original order declaring him a child in need of care and protection. The trial court continued in effect the prior order and further ordered the parents to cease the laetrile treatments they had commenced since the prior court appearance.

By the time the case reached the appellate court, the parents had removed Chad from the state and taken him to Mexico for further laetrile treatments at a clinic there. Nevertheless, the court decided the case in the absence of parents and child. Once again the court upheld the trial court's order on the theory that the parents, against the overwhelming weight of medical evidence, were pursuing a course of treatment for their child that, aside from being useless, was actually dangerous. Because the parents had failed their child, the state had the authority to intervene in the child's best interests.[38]

Chad Green died in Mexico in October 1979, just short of his fourth birthday and only two months after the court's decision. When his parents returned to Massachusetts the following year, a trial court held them in contempt for removing Chad from the state but did not impose any punishment on them on the theory that they had suffered enough.[39]

The Massachusetts court that decided Chad Green's case was of the view that it was not a case of parental choice at all; the "choice" was between acceptable medical treatment and no treatment at all. Traditional medical treatment was acceptable; experimental treatment was ineffective and dangerous, therefore unacceptable. The New York court that decided Joey Hofbauer's case took a different approach.

Joey Hofbauer was diagnosed at age seven as having Hodgkin's disease. His doctor recommended traditional radiation therapy and chemotherapy. His parents, however, elected to pursue a course of nutritional or metabolic therapy, including injections of laetrile. They traveled to Jamaica for the initial treatment but eventually found a licensed physician in New York who used metabolic therapy. A petition was filed by the local child protection service agency seeking to have Joey declared a neglected child.

Medical testimony offered by both sides at the hearing was in sharp conflict. Physicians testifying for the agency advocated radiation and chemotherapy as the accepted treatment for Hodgkin's disease and denounced nutritional therapy as inadequate and ineffective. Doctors testifying for the parents, however, testified that they had used nutritional therapy in treating cancer patients and described it as beneficial and effective. The Hofbauers' physician testified that he used both traditional and nontraditional treatment with his patients and that he would not rule out traditional therapy if Joey's condition worsened under nutritional therapy. "Significantly," the appellate court later noted, Joey's father testified that he would allow Joey to be treated by traditional means if his physician recommended it.

Unlike in the Massachusetts case, the trial court here ruled in favor of the parents, and the appellate division unanimously affirmed the trial court's decision. When the case reached the New York Court of Appeals, the court narrowed the issue:

> [T]he issue presented for our determination is whether the parents of a child afflicted with Hodgkin's disease have failed to exercise a minimum degree of care in supplying their child with adequate medical care by entrusting the child's physical well-being to a duly licensed physician who advocates a treatment not widely embraced by the medical community.[40]

"What constitutes adequate medical care," the court stated, "cannot be judged in a vacuum free from external influences, but, rather, each case must be decided on its own particular facts."[41] On the facts in this case, the court affirmed the lower courts' conclusion that Joey was not a neglected child, that his parents were loving, caring parents looking out for his best interests.

Two principal factors seem to have guided the New York court's decision. First, the parents based their choice of treatment on competent medical advice:

> [A] parent, in making the sensitive decision as to how the child should be treated, may rely upon the recommendations and competency of the attending physician if he or she is duly licensed to practice medicine in this State, for "[i]f a physician is licensed by the State, he is recognized by the State as capable of exercising acceptable clinical judgment."[42]

Second, the particular mode of treatment chosen by the parents was not itself without credit or recognition:

> [T]he court's inquiry should be whether the parents, once having sought accredited medical assistance and having been made aware of the seriousness of their child's affliction and the possibility of cure if a certain mode of treatment is undertaken, have provided for their child *a treatment which is recommended by their physician and which has not been totally rejected by all responsible medical authority.*[43]

Joey Hofbauer died in 1980 at the age of ten. Following Joey's death his father told a reporter that Joey had been "a pioneer whose purpose was to establish the right of parents to make these decisions for their children and to keep Governor Carey and his faceless bureaucrats out of the family."[44]

Arguably, the New York court gave greater deference to parental authority than did the Massachusetts court, but it did so only as the facts of the case warranted such deference. In the *Hofbauer* case the parents had medical professionals on their side, and the mode of treatment they proposed to follow was, while unconventional, endorsed and used by those professionals. In contrast, in the Massachusetts case the parents were opposed by medical professional opinion, and the nontraditional therapy they proposed to follow was not shown in that case to be acceptable. Moreover, the parents did not propose following an alternative treatment program until the case was on appeal. Unlike the parents in the New York case, they remained adamant in their refusal to consent to traditional therapy.

The New York case was not a case in which the parents proposed some bizarre, esoteric, or mythical plan of treatment—for example, mud baths or a grapefruit diet, advocated by a witch doctor or even a faith healer. Had they done so, the court probably would have discredited their judgment and viewed the case as presenting a choice between acceptable treatment and no treatment at all. One might compare, for example, *State v. Hamilton*,[45] in which the court upheld a trial court's finding that a twelve-year-old child with a cancerous tumor in her leg was a neglected child because her parents had rejected medical treatment based on their belief that God alone can cure illness.[46]

## Non–Life-Threatening Cases

Despite their somewhat erratic approach in the Baby Doe and alternative treatment cases, courts as a rule readily have intervened in the family when a child's life was threatened and the parents refused needed medical treatment. A different story is seen, however, when the treatment is not life-saving but would enhance the quality of the child's life in some measure.

Recall the balancing approach of the court in *People ex rel. Wallace v. Labrenz:* the court weighed the slight risk entailed in the proposed surgical procedure against the very great risk of either death or permanent brain damage if the surgery were not performed. Those circumstances, the court concluded, overwhelmingly favored state intervention in the interest of preservation of life. When the balance tips the other way, however—that is, the medical procedure is risky and there is little or no risk of loss of life or serious injury in the absence of treatment—courts traditionally have been very reluctant to intervene in family decision making.

Examples of such reluctance abound. In *In re Hudson*[47] the Washington Supreme Court was called on to decide whether a parent's refusal to consent to amputation of her eleven-year-old daughter's arm constituted neglect under the statutes. The trial court had ordered amputation of the arm, which had grown much larger and longer than the other arm and had become quite useless. Although the condition was not life-threatening, the arm did place a strain on her heart and skeletal system and posed a threat to her general health. The mother thought the surgery too risky; doctors conceded that the surgery entailed a fair risk of loss of life. The appellate court reversed the trial court's order, deferring to natural parental authority to make such decisions without state interference, weighing the potential improvement in the quality of life with the surgery against the attendant risk of loss of life.

The New York Court of Appeals, faced with an identical issue in *In re Seiferth*,[48] likewise declined to order surgical correction of a fourteen-year-old boy's cleft palate and harelip condition. The court reached this decision by balancing the risks against the potential benefits. The boy's appearance and speech would have been improved by the surgery, and the only risk of mortality was the negligible one associated with use of anesthesia. On the other hand, the boy was opposed to the surgery, and the prospect of his failure to cooperate with speech therapists during the postoperative stage was very real. Moreover, no danger was inherent in postponing decision until the boy was older and more mature. On balance, the court concluded, the case for intervention against parental wishes (and the boy's) was too weak.

In *In re Green*[49] the Pennsylvania Supreme Court was confronted with a mother's refusal, on religious grounds, to consent to surgery necessary to correct her son's paralytic scoliosis (curvature of the spine). Her son's condition was so severe that he could not stand or walk. Without corrective surgery he faced the possibility of becoming bed-ridden. The surgery, however, was dangerous. The court stated the issue clearly:

> [T]he . . . question presented by this appeal is whether the state may interfere with a parent's control over his or her child in order to enhance the child's physical well-being when the child's life is in no immediate danger and when the state's intrusion conflicts with the parent's religious beliefs.[50]

The court found the life-threatening/non–life-threatening distinction a useful tool, particularly in a case invoking a claim of religious freedom:

> We are of the opinion that as between a parent and the state, the state does not have an interest of sufficient magnitude outweighing a parent's religious beliefs when the child's life is *not immediately imperiled* by his physical condition.[51]

The court clearly was reluctant to order the surgery over the mother's objection. The court reserved judgment on whether it would order the surgery over the mother's objection *if the boy desired surgery* because of the absence of information on what the boy's wishes were. The court remanded the case to trial court for a hearing to determine the boy's views. On remand, he opted not to have the surgery, and his decision was allowed to stand.[52]

In all three cases dissenting views were expressed. It is interesting that the keenest point of disagreement between the judges appears to be over whether it is the business of the state, acting through the courts, to intervene in the family to ensure not life itself but the quality of life. In *In re Hudson* the majority, critical of those (including everyone but the child's mother) who favored surgery, said that

> Implicit in their position is their opinion that it would be preferable that the child die instead of going through life handicapped by the enlarged, deformed left arm. That may be to some today the humane, and in the future it may be the generally accepted, view. However, we have not advanced or retrograded to the stage where, in the name of mercy, we may lawfully decide that one shall be deprived of life rather than continue to exist crippled or burdened with some abnormality. That right of decision is a prerogative of the Creator. . . .[53]

Just as vociferously the dissenters argued in *Hudson*:

> The welfare of Patricia Hudson demands that the operation be performed as ordered by the trial court. Patricia is entitled to be put into a condition where she can run and play, attend public school, and take part in school activities. She is entitled to a healthy body, to secure a good education, to take her place in American society, to grow up as a normal American girl, to get married, and to have a home and children. Without an operation all these are denied to her and she is condemned to travel along life's pathway a hopeless cripple, an object of pity dependent upon either private or public charity.[54]

The debate is interesting, we say, because it is precisely the debate seen in the Baby Doe cases. The only difference is that in the non–life-threatening cases, those who favor parental autonomy support a parent's decision favoring life over quality of life, whereas in the Baby Doe cases those favoring parental autonomy support a parent's decision in favor of quality of life against life itself. Of course, for those who favor parental autonomy over state protectionist intervention regardless of the kind of case, the choice is easy. But for the rest the life-threatening/non–life-threatening distinction—that, after all, separates the Baby Doe cases from these cases—looms very large indeed.

Some courts, in fact, have ruled in favor of state intervention in non–life-threatening cases, principally because the quality-of-life philosophy prevailed. An earlier example is *In re Sampson*,[55] in which the New York Court of Appeals affirmed the trial court's finding that a fifteen-year-old boy suffering from neurofibromatosis was neglected and its order requiring his mother to consent to corrective surgery.

Kevin Sampson had suffered from the disease since early childhood. The disease, seen by many in the movie *The Elephant Man*, caused a large growth to envelop one side of his face, making it approximately twice the size of the other side. The abnormal growth caused the cheek, eyelid, and ear on the affected side to droop.

Kevin's mother refused to consent to the surgery because of her religious objection to use of the blood transfusions it would require. The corrective surgery, which would improve Kevin's appearance but would not cure his disease, was a lengthy and dangerous process. Contrary to the typical life-threatening case, it was not the mother's refusal to consent to surgery but the surgery itself that was life-threatening.

Viewing this as an extreme case in which the boy was entitled to some semblance of a normal life (Kevin had not attended school in several years, so grotesque was his deformity) the court in effect cast aside the life-threatening/non–life-threatening distinction as outmoded. The appellate division criticized the life-threatening criterion as "a much too restricted approach." The court of appeals was so in accord with these views that it affirmed in a short per curiam opinion. Not a single judge dissented as the case moved through the entire court system in New York.

More recently, the California Court of Appeals upheld an award of guardianship in favor of two nonparents to make medical decisions on behalf of a twelve-year-old boy in a non–life-threatening case.[56] The boy, Phillip Becker, was a Down's syndrome child with a congenital heart defect requiring corrective surgery. Without surgical correction, his heart condition would deteriorate over a period of years to the point where his lungs would be unable to carry and oxygenate blood. Death would follow. His parents refused to consent to surgery because surgery of that type carried a 5 to 10 percent mortality rate, a risk they found unacceptable.

Phillip from birth had lived in a residential care facility. Yet his parents visited frequently and took Phillip out occasionally to restaurants and amusement parks, attempting under the circumstances to maintain as normal a relationship as possible. They preferred to have Phillip alive for a limited period of time than to face the risk that he might not survive the surgery.[57]

As in *Sampson,* the threat to life—at least the immediate threat—was not the parents' refusal to consent to corrective surgery but rather the surgery itself. Also as in *Sampson* the California court was concerned with assuring Phillip a certain quality of life, with the added prospect in this case of a longer life with the corrective surgery, assuming its success.

These two cases represent a significant move by the courts involved away from the traditional hands-off attitude of courts except in life-threatening cases. The life-threatening exception is best summarized in one of the cases mentioned earlier, *In re Green:*

> We are of the opinion that as between a parent and the state, the state
> does not have an interest of sufficient magnitude outweighing a parent's

religious beliefs when the child's life is *not immediately imperiled* by his physical condition.[58]

One could substitute "a parent's inherent authority to make decisions affecting the upbringing of the child" for "a parent's religious beliefs" and the result would be the same.[59] In contrast, the decisions of the New York and California courts do not focus on the "life-threatening" consideration but rather on the child's general welfare, a consideration that may prevail against a parent's claim of religious belief or inherent parental authority. As the trial court in *Sampson* put it,

> [T]his Court's authority to deal with the abused, neglected or physically handicapped child is not limited to "drastic situations" or to those which constitute a "present emergency," . . . the Court has a "wide discretion" to order medical or surgical care and treatment for an infant even over parental objection, if in the Court's judgment the child's health, safety or welfare requires it.[60]

Predictability and certainty, of course, favor the hands-off approach. Such a rule is easy to apply. If the child faces high risk of loss of life or permanent injury without medical treatment, the court may intervene. If such a risk is not present, the court may not intervene. In some cases, however, such a rule might prove to be too inflexible. When is that point reached? In a case like *Sampson*? In a case like *Phillip B.*? By what set of values should a judge decide that he knows better than the parents what is best for their child? Until some better theory comes along, courts are likely to continue vacillating between the hands-off approach and the ad hoc approach. If current concern for quality of life continues to grow, courts may, indeed, move more toward the *Sampson/Phillip B.* exercise of "wide discretion" in determining a child's best interests, although such an approach might be expected to be of less certain application than the hands-off approach.

## Children and Consent

An underlying assumption in the preceding cases was that children's interests were identified with parental interests—that is, the parents purported to be acting in the best interests of their children—and the issue was whether the state could intervene over parental objection. The conflict, therefore, was between parental authority and state authority.

Frequently, however, parents and their children are at odds over medical decision making affecting the child. The conflict, then, is between parent and child rather than between parent and state. This kind of conflict raises the question of when and under what circumstances the child, rather than the parent, ought to be able to make decisions for himself without undue interference from parents or the state.

An example of the latter kind of conflict is the abortion controversy. As indicated in the preceding chapter, a state cannot impose an absolute parental consent requirement in order for a child to obtain an abortion. Rather, a child must be afforded alternatives: either obtain parental consent or else go before a court to persuade the court that she is a mature minor capable of making decisions for herself or, even if she is immature, that the abortion would be in her best interests.[61] The Supreme Court has indicated, however, that parents have *some* role to play in such decision making; thus, a parental *notification* statute is permissible in order to promote communication between parents and children and communication of medical information between parents and physicians.[62]

Courts have been protective of a child's right to decide against abortion as well. In *In re Mary P.*,[63] for example, in which the mother of a fifteen-year-old girl sought to have her daughter declared a person in need of supervision because of her refusal to have an abortion, the court issued a protective order directing the mother not to interfere with her daughter's decision to carry the baby to term. In a similar case, an appellate court reversed a trial court's order that a sixteen-year-old girl submit to an abortion.[64]

Courts also have been supportive of a child's decision making with regard to family planning. In *Carey v. Population Services International*[65] the Supreme Court struck down a New York statute banning distribution of contraceptives to persons under age sixteen as an unwarranted state intrusion into the child's right of privacy—that is, her right to decide whether or not to beget a child.

On January 26, 1983, the Department of Health and Human Services implemented regulations requiring hospitals and clinics receiving federal funds to notify parents of the provision to any unemancipated minor of contraceptive drugs or devices available through any such program.[66] Popularly known as the "squeal rule," these regulations were struck down by two different federal district courts.[67] Subsequently, the squeal rule was withdrawn.[68]

In particular, the notion seems to have emerged and flourished in recent years that a mature minor ought to be able to make his or her own decisions regarding medical or surgical procedures. For example, the Supreme Court in *Bellotti v. Baird*[69] spoke of the opportunity a mature minor must be afforded to demonstrate that she is capable of deciding for herself whether to have an abortion. In other settings as well courts have accorded mature minors the "right" to make medical decisions, generally when (1) medical treatment was for the benefit of the minor and not a third party, (2) the minor was near majority (that is, age fifteen or older) and was of sufficient maturity to make an informed choice (that is, to understand the risks entailed in the proposed medical procedure), and (3) the medical procedure itself was not categorized as "major" or "serious."[70]

Legislatures, too, have given minors some measure of autonomy in medical decision making. Married minors typically are treated as adults and may give consent to furnishing of hospital, medical, or surgical care.[71] Sometimes a minor who is a parent of a child or who is pregnant may consent to medical treatment.[72] A minor serving in the armed forces generally may consent to treatment.[73] An emancipated minor—that is, a minor who is living separately from parents and is financially independent—may consent to treatment.[74] Moreover, if a minor has a statutory right to apply for a court decree of emancipation and has successfully done so, the effect of the decree is to accord the minor adult treatment, including capacity to consent to medical treatment.[75]

A minor who has a drug- or alcohol-related problem often can consent to medical care for the diagnosis or treatment of the problem.[76] Minors who have been exposed to a communicable disease required to be reported to public health authorities (such as venereal disease) often may consent to health care necessary to diagnose and treat such disease.[77]

In addition to most of the exceptions mentioned above, California law also provides that a minor age twelve or older deemed by the attending physician to be a mature minor may consent to mental health treatment or counseling on an outpatient basis if the minor presents a risk of serious physical or mental harm to himself or others without such treatment or is the alleged victim of incest or child abuse.[78] A minor age twelve or older alleged to be the victim of rape may consent to medical care related to the diagnosis or treatment of such condition,[79] and a minor of any age alleged to be the victim of sexual assault may give similar consent.[80] Finally, a minor age seventeen or older may give consent for a donation of blood.[81]

This does not purport to be an exhaustive list, but it is representative of the kinds of circumstances in which minors have limited capacity to consent to medical treatment. Generally, unless a state provides for one of these exceptions or others, or an emergency exists,[82] parents' consent is required.[83]

## Conclusion

To return for a moment to the observations of the changing concepts of life, liberty, and property mentioned at the beginning of this chapter,[84] our turn-of-the-century jurists observed that in the "modern" era the right to life had come to embrace the right to enjoy life—that is, the right to be let alone. Certainly at the present time, this concept of the right to life translates into claims that parents should be let alone to make medical decisions for their children without intrusion by the state and that children in some instances ought to be let alone to make medical decisions for themselves without interference from parents or the state.

The difficulty in this area, of course, is that such claims cannot be viewed in the abstract; inevitably such claims are tied to particular cases involving particular children—lives, if you will—with particular medical problems under a particular set of circumstances. Emotion enters into the picture as well, especially in the defective newborn cases, the non–life–threatening cases and cases involving abortions or birth control for children.

We seem to be in a period in which the trend is toward greater state involvement in the medical decision-making process. Courts are more willing now to intervene in family decision making with respect to non–life–threatening medical decisions, and legislatures and administrative agencies are proceeding with great urgency to draft rules governing medical decision making for defective newborns. On the other hand courts and legislatures seem to be fostering a greater role for children—mature minors, in particular—in making some medical decisions for themselves.

As mentioned earlier regarding medical decision making for newborns, we are not in the latter stages of coming to a resolution of the problem but rather are in the beginning stages of a debate that is likely to continue for years. Because it touches on the most basic human emotions and the social institution of the family, how this medico/legal/ethical dilemma will be resolved is unclear. Until the drama is played out, one can only speculate as to the eventual outcome. We have sought in this chapter to present the traditional views and the trends as we see them. The one general conclusion we have reached is that traditional views will continue to be tested, and with that testing likely will come change.

## Notes

1. Considerable debate exists over the extent to which Locke's political theories influenced the direction of eighteenth-century American political thought. For a detailed analysis of this issue, *see* LIFE, LIBERTY, AND PROPERTY: ESSAYS ON LOCKE'S POLITICAL IDEAS (G. Schochet ed. 1971). General works on Locke's political theories include J. DUNN, THE POLITICAL THOUGHT OF JOHN LOCKE (1969); J. GOUGH, JOHN LOCKE'S POLITICAL PHILOSOPHY (2d ed. 1973).

2. Source: SOURCES OF OUR LIBERTIES 311 (R. Perry ed. 1959).

3. *Id.* at 319.

4. *Id.* at 432.

5. From the Preamble to the Constitution of the United States. *Id.* at 408.

6. Warren & Brandeis, *The Right to Privacy*, 4 HARV. L. REV. 193 (1890). Copyright© 1890 by the Harvard Law Review Association. Reprinted with permission. In the preceding chapter the reader was exposed to constitutional protection of liberty and property interests in Ingraham v. Wright, 430 U.S. 651 (1977); Goss v. Lopez, 419 U.S. 565 (1975); Pierce v. Society of Sisters, 268 U.S. 510 (1925); Meyer v. Nebraska, 262 U.S. 390 (1923). Liberty and property interests are covered in greater detail in chapters 6 and 7, respectively.

7. The basics of the consent requirement, as well as the problems associated with consent by and for children, are discussed in Wadlington, *Minors and Health Care: The Age of Consent,* 11 Osgoode Hall L.J. 115 (1973).

8. 411 Ill. 618, 104 N.E.2d 769 (1952).

9. *Genesis* 9:4, *Leviticus* 17:14; *Acts* 15:20.

10. 411 Ill. at 624, 104 N.E.2d at 773.

11. *Id.* at 625, 104 N.E.2d at 773.

12. *See, e.g.,* Jehovah's Witnesses v. King County Hosp., 278 F. Supp. 488, 498–505 (W.D. Wash. 1967), *aff'd* 390 U.S. 598 (1968); Morrison v. State, 252 S.W.2d 97 (Mo. Ct. App. 1952); State v. Perricone, 37 N.J. 463, 181 A.2d 751 (1962).

13. 101 Misc. 2d 699, 421 N.Y.S.2d 965 (S. Ct., Bronx Co. 1979).

14. *Id.* at 701, 421 N.Y.S.2d at 967.

15. *Id.* at 702, 421 N.Y.S.2d at 968.

16. Washington Post, Apr. 17, 1982, at A1, col. 4.

17. 29 U.S.C.A. § 794. This section provides in part: "No otherwise qualified handicapped individual . . . shall, solely by reason of his handicap, be excluded from the participation in, be denied the benefits of, or be subjected to discrimination under any program or activity receiving Federal financial assistance."

18. H.H.S. News, May 18, 1982.

19. 48 Fed. Reg. 9630.

20. American Academy of Pediatrics v. Heckler, 561 F. Supp. 395 (D.D.C. 1983).

21. 49 Fed. Reg. 1622; 45 C.F.R. § 84.

22. American Hosp. Ass'n v. Heckler, 585 F. Supp. 541 (S.D.N.Y. 1984). The federal district court based its decision on the authority of the Second Circuit's decision in the second Baby Doe case, United States v. University Hosp., 729 F.2d 144 (2d Cir. 1984), discussed subsequently.

23. The Second Circuit's decision is unpublished.

24. 106 S. Ct. 2101 (1986).

25. 42 U.S.C.A. §§ 5101 *et. seq.*

26. 50 Fed. Reg. 14878; 45 C.F.R. § 1340.

27. Weber v. Stony Brook Hosp., 95 A.D.2d 587, 467 N.Y.S.2d 685 (1983).

28. Weber v. Stony Brook Hosp., 60 N.Y.2d 208, 456 N.E.2d 1186, 469 N.Y.S.2d 63 (1983).

29. United States v. University Hosp., 575 F. Supp. 607 (E.D.N.Y. 1983).

30. United States v. University Hosp., 729 F.2d 144 (2d Cir. 1984).

31. Ind. Code Ann. § 31-6-4-3(f).

32. La. Rev. Stat. Ann. § 40:1299.36.1–.3.

33. *Id.* § 40:1299.36.1(D).

34. 424 So. 2d 1015 (La. 1982). *Compare In re* L.H.R., 253 Ga. 439, 321 S.E.2d 716 (1984), in which the Georgia Supreme Court permitted removal of life-support apparatus from a comatose infant without any specific statutory authorization. Of course, the landmark case in this area is the New Jersey Supreme Court's decision allowing Karen Ann Quinlan's parents to authorize removal of her life-support systems. *In re* Quinlan, 70 N.J. 10, 355 A.2d 647 (1976).

35. For the reader desiring further clarification of the legal/medical/ethical issues involved in the Baby Doe cases, the following books and articles are suggested. Current works include R. Weir, Selective Nontreatment of Handicapped

NEWBORNS (1984); Editorial, *Baby Doe and Uncle Sam*, 309 NEW ENG. J. MED. 659 (1983); Ellis, *Letting Defective Babies Die: Who Decides*, 7 AM. J. L. & MED. 393 (1982). Some earlier works dealing with the dilemma before the current wave of litigation and attempted regulation include: Duff & Campbell, *Moral and Ethical Dilemmas in the Special-Care Nursery*, 289 NEW ENG. J. MED. 890 (1973); Goldstein, *Medical Care for the Child at Risk*, 86 YALE L.J. 645 (1977); Robertson, *Involuntary Euthanasia of Defective Newborns: A Legal Analysis*, 27 STAN. L. REV. 213 (1975); Shaw, *Dilemmas of "Informed Consent" in Children*, 289 NEW ENG. J. MED. 885 (1973). More general works on the subject include A. HOLDER, LEGAL ISSUES IN PEDIATRICS AND ADOLESCENT MEDICINE (2d ed. 1985); Baron, *Medicine and Human Rights: Emerging Substantive Standards and Procedural Protections for Medical Decision Making within the Family*, 17 FAM. L.Q. 1 (1983); Note, *Choosing for Children: Adjudicating Medical Care Disputes between Parents and the State*, 58 N.Y.U. L. REV. 157 (1983); Weithorn, *Developmental Factors and Competence to Make Informed Treatment Decisions*, in LEGAL REFORMS AFFECTING CHILD AND YOUTH SERVICES 85 (G. Melton ed. 1982).

36. *See* note 27 *supra* and accompanying text.

37. Custody of a Minor, 375 Mass. 733, 379 N.E.2d 1053 (1978).

38. Custody of a Minor, 378 Mass. 732, 393 N.E.2d 836 (1979).

39. N.Y. Times, Dec. 9, 1980, § 2, at 21, col. 1.

40. *In re* Hofbauer, 47 N.Y.2d 648, 652, 393 N.E.2d 1009, 1011, 419 N.Y.S.2d 936, 938 (1979).

41. *Id.* at 655, 393 N.E.2d at 1013, 419 N.Y.S.2d at 940.

42. *Id.*, 393 N.E.2d at 1014, 419 N.Y.S.2d at 940, *quoting from* Doe v. Bolton, 410 U.S. 179, 199 (1973).

43. *Id.* at 656, 393 N.E.2d at 1014, 419 N.Y.S.2d at 941 (emphasis added).

44. N.Y. Times, July 18, 1980, at D13, col. 5.

45. 657 S.W.2d 424 (Tenn. Ct. App. 1983).

46. The background of the case can be found in NEWSWEEK, Oct. 3, 1983, at 57.

47. 13 Wash. 2d 673, 126 P.2d 765 (1942).

48. 309 N.Y. 80, 127 N.E.2d 820 (1955).

49. 448 Pa. 338, 292 A.2d 387 (1972).

50. *Id.* at 345, 292 A.2d at 390.

51. *Id.* at 348, 292 A.2d at 392 (emphasis in original).

52. *In re* Green, 452 Pa. 373, 307 A.2d 279 (1973).

53. 13 Wash. 2d at 684, 126 P.2d at 771.

54. *Id.* at 733–34, 126 P.2d at 792. *Compare* the dissenting views of Judge Fuld in *In re* Seiferth, 309 N.Y. at 86–88, 127 N.E.2d at 823–24, and those of Judge Eagen in *In re* Green, 448 Pa. at 353–55, 292 A.2d at 394–95.

55. 29 N.Y.2d 900, 278 N.E.2d 918, 328 N.Y.S.2d 686 (1972). The best discussion of the case is found in the family court's opinion, *In re* Sampson, 65 Misc. 2d 658, 317 N.Y.S.2d 641 (Fam. Ct., Ulster Co. 1970), which was affirmed also by the appellate division, *In re* Sampson, 37 A.D.2d 668, 323 N.Y.S.2d 253 (1971).

56. *In re* Phillip B., 139 Cal. App. 3d 407, 188 Cal. Rptr. 781 (1983).

57. The Beckers' story was featured as a part of the My Turn series in *Newsweek* magazine following the California court's decision. NEWSWEEK, May 30, 1983, at 17.

58. 448 Pa. at 348, 292 A.2d at 392 (emphasis in original).

59. *See, e.g.,* Custody of a Minor, 378 Mass. 732, 393 N.E.2d 836 (1979); *In re* Hudson, 13 Wash. 2d 673, 126 P.2d 765 (1942).

60. 65 Misc. 2d at 671, 317 N.Y.S.2d at 657.

61. Bellotti v. Baird, 443 U.S. 622 (1979). The Supreme Court has reinforced this view in more recent decisions. City of Akron v. Akron Center for Reproductive Health, 462 U.S. 416 (1983); Planned Parenthood Ass'n v. Ashcroft, 462 U.S. 476 (1983).

62. H.L. v. Matheson, 450 U.S. 398 (1981).

63. 111 Misc. 2d 532, 444 N.Y.S.2d 545 (Fam. Ct., Queen's Co. 1981).

64. *In re* Smith, 16 Md. App. 209, 295 A.2d 238 (1972).

65. 431 U.S. 678 (1977).

66. 48 Fed. Reg. 3600 (formerly codified as 42 C.F.R. § 59.5(a) (12)).

67. Planned Parenthood Fed. of America v. Schweiker, 559 F. Supp. 658 (D.D.C.); *aff'd sub. nom.* Planned Parenthood Fed. of America v. Heckler, 712 F.2d 650 (D.C. Cir. 1983); New York v. Schweiker, 557 F. Supp. 354 (S.D.N.Y.), *aff'd sub. nom.* New York v. Heckler, 719 F.2d 1191 (2d Cir. 1983).

68. 49 Fed. Reg. 38118.

69. 443 U.S. 622 (1979).

70. Wadlington, *Minors and Health Care: The Age of Medical Consent,* 11 OSGOODE HALL L.J. 115, 117-20 (1973).

71. See, e.g., CAL. CIV. CODE § 25.6; MASS. GEN. LAWS ANN. ch. 112, § 12F; N.Y. PUB. HEALTH LAW § 2504(1)-(2).

72. *See, e.g.,* MASS. GEN. LAWS ANN. ch. 112, § 12F (except for abortion or sterilization); N.Y. PUB. HEALTH LAW § 2504(1)-(3); *see also* CAL. CIV. CODE § 34.5 (unmarried minor may consent to hospital, medical, or surgical care related to prevention or treatment of pregnancy, except for sterilization procedure).

73. *See, e.g.,* CAL. CIV. CODE § 25.7; MASS. GEN. LAWS ANN. ch. 112, § 12F (except for abortion or sterilization).

74. *See e.g.,* CAL. CIV. CODE § 34.6 (if age fifteen or older); MASS. GEN. LAWS ANN. ch. 112, § 12F (except for abortion or sterilization).

75. *See* the section on emancipation in chapter 3.

76. *See, e.g.,* CAL. CIV. CODE § 34.10(a) (if age twelve or older); MASS. GEN. LAWS ANN. ch. 112, § 12E (if age twelve or older; for drug-related problem only).

77. *See, e.g.,* CAL. CIV. CODE § 34.7 (if age twelve or older); MASS. GEN. LAWS ANN. ch. 112, § 12F (except for abortion or sterilization).

78. CAL. CIV. CODE § 25.9(a).

79. *Id.* § 34.8.

80. *Id.* § 34.9.

81. *Id.* § 25.5(a).

82. *See, e.g.,* MASS. GEN. LAWS ANN. ch. 112, § 12F; N.Y. PUB. HEALTH LAW § 2504(4).

83. *See, e.g.,* CAL. CIV. CODE § 25.8.

84. *See* note 6 *supra* and accompanying text.

# 6
# Liberty: Personal Freedom of Children

Concededly a statute or ordinance [regulating certain activities in the streets] applicable to adults or all persons generally, would be invalid. But the mere fact a state could not wholly prohibit this form of adult activity . . . does not mean it cannot do so for children. . . .

The state's authority over children's activities is broader than over like actions of adults. . . .

It is true children have rights . . . in the primary use of highways. But even in such use streets afford dangers for them not affecting adults. . . . What may be wholly permissible for adults therefore may not be so for children, either with or without their parents' presence.

—Justice Wiley B. Rutledge
*Prince v. Massachusetts*
321 U.S. 158, 167–69 (1944)

## Introduction

The previous chapter began with the observation of two distinguished jurists in 1890 that the concepts of life, liberty, and property had undergone considerable change since the English common law and since the early days of our republic. Of the concept of liberty, they noted that

in very early times, the law gave a remedy only for physical interference with life and property, for trespasses *vi et armis*. Then . . . liberty meant freedom from actual restraint. . . . Later, there came a recognition of man's spiritual nature, of his feelings and his intellect. Gradually the scope of these legal rights broadened; and now . . . the right to liberty secures the exercise of extensive civil privileges.[1]

After the turn of the century, the Supreme Court in *Meyer v. Nebraska*[2] gave an equally expansive meaning to the concept of liberty:

Without doubt, it denotes not merely freedom from bodily restraint, but also the right of the individual to contract, to engage in any of the common occupations of life, to acquire useful knowledge, to marry, establish a home and bring up children, to worship God according to the dictates of his own conscience, and, generally, to enjoy those privileges long recognized at common law as essential to the orderly pursuit of happiness by free men.[3]

The Court sought to strengthen its broad expression of individual freedom by outlining the limitations on state control over activities of the individual:

> The established doctrine is that this liberty may not be interfered with, under the guise of protecting the public interest, by legislative action which is arbitrary or without reasonable relation to some purpose within the competency of the state to effect. Determination by the legislature of what constitutes proper exercise of police power is not final or conclusive, but is subject to supervision by the courts.[4]

As if to confirm its supervisory role, the Court held unconstitutional a Nebraska statute prohibiting the teaching of foreign languages in school as an unreasonable infringement of the liberty interest protected by the due process clause. Teachers, the Court said, had a right to pursue their calling, children had a right to acquire knowledge, and parents had a right to control the education of their children.

The state's power, then, while considerable, is not without limits, and the courts are the final arbiters of whether those limits have been overreached. On the other hand, the individual's freedom is not limitless, either. This chapter will explore the concept of liberty in its traditional sense—that is, freedom from personal restraint—by examining attempts by states (or municipalities) to restrict individual freedom through imposition of curfews.

## Status Offenses and Criminal Misconduct

Our legal system limits a child's freedom in a number of ways. A child is often subject to state intervention for conduct that is unlawful only when engaged in by a child. Such conduct is known as a *status offense* (because of the offender's status as a child), a category of noncriminal misbehavior that includes, among other things, truancy from school, sexual misconduct, use of alcohol, and running away.[5]

Status offenses are not new. Early in our nation's history parents were given access to the legal system as a means of compelling appropriate behavior in their children.[6] An early ordinance of the Massachusetts colony provided that a child over age sixteen who struck or cursed his parent or a boy over age sixteen who would not obey his parent after being properly chastened should be put to death.[7] No evidence exists that any children of the Massachusetts colony suffered the ultimate penalty for such misconduct, but the old ordinance is itself evidence of the respect for absolute parental authority and the willingness of the legal system to enforce it.

Children are also subject to punishment for engaging in criminal conduct. In 1982 over 2 million arrests were made for serious crimes, which included about 666,000 juvenile arrests. Eight million arrests were made for other, less serious criminal offenses, of which about 1.2 million were juvenile arrests.[8]

## The State's Response: Curfews

Many state and local governments have attempted to deal with the problem of juvenile crime through the enaction of juvenile nocturnal curfews.[9] For example, at the close of the 1985–86 school year, the county commission in DeKalb County, Georgia (Metro Atlanta), enacted a midnight to 5:00 A.M. curfew for persons under age eighteen, in response to a perceived increase in youth crime.[10] Such curfews, the violation of which is a status offense, prohibit minors below a certain age from remaining in public areas within a given time frame. Agreement exists that, "absent a genuine emergency a curfew aimed at all citizens could not survive constitutional scrutiny."[11] On the other hand, curfews aimed specifically at children are often, but not always, deemed legally permissible.

### Origin

Like status offenses, curfews are not a recent phenomenon. It is thought that a general curfew was introduced in England by order of William the Conqueror. At 8:00 P.M. a town would ring a bell, signaling the citizens to extinguish all fires in their homes and to prepare for bed. Accordingly, the word *curfew* is derived from the French phrase *couvre feu*, meaning "to cover the fire." The curfew both helped prevent fires and encouraged gatherings of people to disperse. Evidence suggests that the same practice existed in France, Normandy, Spain, and other countries in Europe.[12]

Curfews directed exclusively at children gained prevalence in the United States during the late nineteenth century. In addition to protecting the community from juvenile crime and noncriminal mischief, two further motives justified the imposition of children's curfews: to protect children from harm beyond their control, such as accidents, and to reinforce parental authority.[13] Thus, state control over a child's nighttime behavior is consistent with the *parens patriae* philosophy by which the state seeks to protect the best interests of the child.[14]

## Emergency Curfews

As indicated earlier, under ordinary circumstances the state may not prevent a person from walking on public streets. Freedom of movement is one of the most important rights enjoyed by United States citizens. A city may regulate the use of its streets only if it does so in a way that does not interfere with the personal liberty of its residents.[15] As long as one is using the streets for a legitimate purpose, whether for business or pleasure, one can go wherever he pleases.[16] As one court explained: "One may have lawful business on the street even though he is there merely for exercise or recreation or any other proper purpose. . . . Officers of the law have no right to compel one to account for his actions merely because that person is on the streets at an unusual hour."[17] Thus, vagrancy ordinances and those prohibiting wandering about the streets and similar activities are seldom of much concern now, as they have for the most part been struck down.[18] The same is generally true of statutes that make it illegal to be in a public place unless able to give a satisfactory account of one's presence.[19]

But personal freedoms are not absolute. The liberty guaranteed by the due process clause of the Constitution implies an absence of arbitrary interference, not immunity from reasonable regulation. During an emergency, state and local governments may impose curfews on all of their citizens, adults and minors alike.[20] Riot curfews, for example, greatly infringe on individual rights, but they are usually upheld because of the extraordinary nature of the situation.[21] The constitutional standard to be applied when an ordinance is attacked as overly restrictive is one of reasonableness.

## Juvenile Curfews

Just as the right to personal freedom is not absolute, neither is the right of a parent to control his child an absolute right. When an issue regarding the child is viewed as critical to the public good, the state will step in and make decisions, at times even countermanding the wishes of the parents.[22] Thus, every state has a compulsory education law for minors under a certain age.[23] More controversial are the situations in which the state has been permitted to make medical decisions for the family when the child's life is in danger.[24]

Nonemergency nocturnal juvenile curfews, however, present greater constitutional problems than either the limited curfews enacted during emergencies or the governmental intervention compelled when a child's health is threatened. Courts have struggled with the question of the constitutional validity of juvenile curfews with varying results. Parental challenges to such curfews are usually based on the right of a parent to raise his family free from undue interference from the state. A child's legal challenges center largely on the alleged violation of his due process rights as protected by the Constitution. Although the Supreme Court has not defined the exact scope of the liberties that are protected by the due process clauses, the clauses clearly guarantee that each individual will have some degree of freedom of choice and action in all important personal matters.[25]

Children's constitutional rights, however, do not parallel those of adults. For example, the Supreme Court has refused to apply all the protections of a criminal trial to juvenile court hearings.[26] Also, obscenity is defined more broadly for minors than for adults.[27] Most important for purposes of juvenile curfews, the Court has said that some situations justify the placement of restraints on minors that would be unconstitutional if placed on adults.[28]

## Constitutionality of Juvenile Curfews

### The Vagueness and Overbreadth Doctrines

Two closely related doctrines must be understood before one can effectively analyze the case law involving juvenile curfew ordinances: the doctrine of void-for-vagueness and the doctrine of overbreadth. The doctrine of void-for-vagueness prohibits statutes that burden a constitutional right in terms that are so vague they leave a person without clear guidance as to the nature of the act for which he can be punished.[29] As the Supreme Court said in *Lanzetta v. New Jersey*,[30] "No one may be required at peril of life, liberty or property to speculate as to the meaning of penal statutes."[31] The Court held that a statute making gang membership a crime violated the defendant's due process rights.

The doctrine of overbreadth invalidates statutes that burden activities that are not constitutionally protected but that at the same time include within their scope activities that are protected under the Constitution.[32] Both doctrines have particular significance where freedoms that are protected by the first amendment are concerned.[33]

### Presence versus Remaining Statutes

Early state court decisions employed the doctrines of vagueness and overbreadth by distinguishing between two types of juvenile curfew ordinances: the presence type in which it was unlawful merely to be on a public street after a certain time, and the loitering or remaining type in which it was forbidden to loiter, congregate, or remain on a public street after a given hour. Statutes that proscribed presence in particular places were generally held unconstitutional based on vagueness or overbreadth or both; statutes interpreted to proscribe loitering or remaining were usually held constitutional.

In an 1898 case, *Ex parte McCarver*,[34] a Texas appellate court struck down a city curfew that prohibited people under age twenty-one from "being found" on the streets after 9:00 P.M. The only exceptions to the curfew were for children in the company of a parent or guardian and those "in search of a physician." The court found the ordinance to be an unconstitutionally overbroad invasion of personal liberties, noting that there were many reasons a young person might be away from home after curfew: "He may be at church or at some social gathering in the town, and yet when the curfew bell tolls, in the midst of a sermon or exhortation, he would be compelled to leave, and hie himself to his home, or, if at a social gathering, he must make his exit in haste."[35] In addition, the court viewed the curfew as a paternalistic attempt to usurp the functions of the family.

One must remember that when the *McCarver* case was decided in 1898, juvenile delinquency was not as great a public concern as it was to become later. Nor was the state as involved in parental decision making as it is today. The Texas court admitted that "it may be that there are some bad boys in our cities and towns whose parents don't properly control them,"[36] but it concluded that the freedoms of the many that were obedient outweighed society's problems with the few that were not.

In *People v. Walton*[37] a California court examined an ordinance prohibiting a child under age eighteen from "being and remaining" on a public street between 9:00 P.M. and 4:00 A.M. without a sheriff's permit or an adult companion. The word *remain* simplified the constitutional problems that faced the Texas court in *McCarver,* the California court said. According to the dictionary, remain meant "to stay behind while others withdraw; to tarry." Thus, the court said, the ordinance at issue applied only to those who were loitering and not to those in the process of going to and from places of legitimate activity. The statute was merely regulatory, not prohibitory.

In response to the defendant's contention that the age classification was unreasonable and arbitrary, the *Walton* court cited several valid statutes based on age, such as compulsory education laws, explaining that such legislation was necessary for the protection of the young. Unlike the Texas court in *McCarver,* the *Walton* court considered the curfew in question to be a necessary exercise of the state's authority under the doctrine of *parens patriae.*

Twelve years later, in *Alves v. Justice Court*,[38] a California appellate court held unconstitutional an ordinance making it unlawful for a child under age seventeen "to be in" any public street or place between 10:00 P.M. and 5:00 A.M. except when accompanied by a parent or guardian or when in the pursuit of some legitimate business, trade, or profession. Such a statute, said the court, proscribed presence rather than remaining and thus was impermissibly overbroad. The court cited both *McCarver* and *Walton,* finding the Texas decision, "antiquated as it may be," the more appropriate precedent.[39] As did the Texas court in *McCarver*, the *Alves* court described many forms of socially acceptable conduct that would be prohibited by the ordinance. The state, noted the court, may indeed enact legislation that interferes with the personal liberties of its citizens, but such legislation is always subject to a rule of reasonableness. A ban so broad as to prohibit mere presence has no substantial relationship to its purpose of controlling juveniles late at night.

The Maryland Court of Appeals in *Thistlewood v. Trial Magistrate*[40] affirmed a lower court's decision that an ordinance prohibiting persons under age twenty-one from "being found" on the streets of Ocean City between midnight and 6:00 A.M. on Labor Day weekend, when the resort town was visited by many minors, was not unreasonable or oppressive. The court extensively discussed the distinction between presence statutes and remaining statutes, determining that the ordinance in question—despite its language—forbade remaining on the streets rather than merely being on or traversing them. The court examined not only the prohibitory language itself but also the statute's preamble, which referred to "disorderly groups of minors." Such a reference, said the court, suggested that the aim of the ordinance was against the *congregating* of minors, as opposed to simply the presence of minors.

The *Thistlewood* court approached its review of the ordinance primarily as a substantive due process question, setting forth a three-part test: (1) Is there an evil? (2) Do the means selected to curb the evil have a real and substantial relation to the result sought? (3) If the answer to the first two inquiries is yes, do the means availed of unduly infringe or oppress fundamental rights of those restricted?[41] In other words, the court weighed the seriousness of the evil to be prevented and the need for the curfew to effectuate the cure against the seriousness of the invasion of the liberties of the persons restricted by the ordinance. Not surprisingly, the Ocean City ordinance easily met the requirements of the three-part test. Given that only four days out of the year were affected by the curfew, that the town grew several times its normal size during the four-day period, that the curfew's purpose was to prevent loitering, not presence, and finally, that minors were "peculiarly subject to regulation and control by the State," the court concluded that the statute was constitutionally valid.[42]

*City of Eastlake v. Ruggiero*[43] illustrates that even those ordinances that clearly proscribed presence were upheld if enough exceptions were included making it clear that the ordinance was not an absolute prohibition against presence. In *City of Eastlake* the curfew at issue restricted minors from "being upon" public streets or sidewalks during designated nighttime periods. Exceptions were made, however, for a minor accompanied by his parent, guardian, or responsible person over age twenty-one or a member of his family over age eighteen, or if the child had a "legitimate excuse." Thus, stated the Ohio Court of Appeals without further discussion, there was no curtailment of normal or necessary juvenile nighttime activities, and the ordinance was constitutionally valid.

The court's reasoning in *City of Eastlake* is unclear. Indeed, all curfew ordinances discussed thus far, whether presence or remaining types, exempted certain situations from the operation of the curfew. The most common exceptions have been for: (1) a minor accompanied by his parent, guardian, or other adult person having the legal care of the minor; (2) a minor engaged in lawful employment; (3) a minor on an emergency errand; and (4) a minor involved in school- or church-sponsored activities. Although the extent of the exceptions delineated in the *Eastlake* ordinance may have appeared to give it a more narrow impact, such an appearance was probably deceptive.

State courts continued to flounder with the distinction between presence and remaining. The California Court of Appeals in *In re Nancy C.*[44] upheld an ordinance proscribing a minor from "loitering, idling, wandering, strolling, or playing" in or on the public streets after 10:00 P.M., reasoning that despite its broad language, the words taken together and used in their ordinary sense prohibited tarrying and remaining in place and not merely being present. Moreover, applying the three-part test as first set forth in *Thistlewood*, the court found that the state's special interest in the protection of children and in the reduction of nocturnal juvenile crimes justified the ordinance's restrictions on the nighttime activities of minors.

Like the court in *City of Eastlake*, the *In re Nancy C.* decision noted with approval that the curfew excepted from its restrictions minors accompanied by parents or other persons having their custody, minors on emergency errands, and minors returning directly home from meetings or recreational activities. The exceptions, asserted the court, provided a police officer with clear guidelines by which to determine whether the minor was on the street for a lawful purpose. One must question the clarity of the guidelines, however; for example, who determines which activities are protected under the category of "recreational activities"? It is easy to imagine a situation in which a minor could be stopped and detained for doing something that he reasonably thought was legal. On the whole, *In re Nancy C.* appears to run counter to the doctrine of void-for-vagueness.[45]

In *W.J.W. v. State*[46] a Florida appellate court declared void for overbreadth a Pensacola juvenile curfew that prohibited anyone under the age of sixteen from "be[ing] in or upon any street . . . or other public place" or from "attend[ing] any public entertainment or amusement" during the hours between 11:00 P.M. and 5:00 A.M. Children accompanied by a parent or guardian or "regularly employed in a gainful occupation" were exempt from the provisions. Although the court recognized that the purpose of the ordinance was to control the activities of young people during the night, it nonetheless maintained that the "prohibition against the mere presence of a child under the age of sixteen . . . has [no] real relationship to the primary purpose of the statute."[47] Enforcement of the curfew, said the court, would make many activities unlawful that otherwise would be lawful.

## Movement away from the Presence/ Remaining Distinction

Most recent state court decisions have placed less weight on the distinction between presence and remaining. Nevertheless, to avoid a due process challenge, a curfew must be carefully drafted. The improper use of a word or phrase can render an ordinance unconstitutional. For example, in *City of Seattle v. Pullman*[48] the Washington Supreme Court struck down a curfew that made it illegal for minors to "loiter, idle, wander, or play" (the same words of prohibition as those found in the California case of *In re Nancy C.*) in public places between 10:00 P.M. and 5:00 A.M. The ordinance also prohibited anyone not the parent or guardian of the child, or anyone without the express consent of the parent or guardian, from accompanying a child that was violating the curfew. The defendant, a high school senior, was arrested at 4:30 A.M. as he was taking two minor females home from a party. The court found the ordinance unconstitutional on two grounds. First, its language was impermissibly vague; it did not precisely state the harmful activity from which the state sought to protect itself. Citing *City of Seattle v. Drew*[49] an earlier case in which the state supreme court struck down a Seattle ordinance making it a crime for a person to loiter under suspicious circumstances without giving a satisfactory account of his activities on demand of a police officer, the court reiterated that "the lay meaning of loitering cannot reasonably connote unlawful activity."[50] As in *Drew*, the words idle, loiter, and the like, when not qualified by ascertainable standards, simply did not imply any wrongdoing.

Second, the statute was an invalid exercise of the city's police power because it made no distinction between harmful conduct and conduct that was essentially innocent; that is, its language was overbroad. A person under eighteen years old, pointed out the court, could be arrested for standing on the sidewalk in front of his home at 10:01 P.M. Again quoting *Drew*, the court stated: "It is fundamental that no ordinance may unreasonably or unnecessarily interfere with a person's freedom, whether it be to move about or to stand still."[51] Moreover, the involvement of a minor should not change this result. The court refused to accept the reasoning that the state's interest in the protection of minors justified a prohibition on activity that was normally deemed lawful; rather, it focused on the minor's interference with the rights of others, finding none. Absent a showing of such an interference—of "bad conduct"—the language of the ordinance overstepped the boundaries of legitimate police power. Three justices dissented from the reversal of the defendant's conviction, basing much of their lengthy opinion on the proposition that the government has broader authority over children than it does over adults.

The same year, the Hawaii Supreme Court in *In re Doe*[52] agreed that an ordinance prohibiting persons under age eighteen from loitering in public places, with certain exceptions, was unconstitutionally vague and overbroad. The term *loitering*, said the court, was too imprecise to give proper notice as to what constitutes unlawful activity. In addition, it swept within its prohibition conduct that was otherwise lawful. The *Doe* court, unlike the majority in *City of Seattle v. Pullman*, did not simply dismiss the state's argument that a curfew aimed at juveniles was but one of many permissible distinctions between children and adults. The court acknowledged that children and adults are, and should be, at times treated differently under the law, but it stressed that when a constitutional protection is involved, the United States Supreme Court in *In re Gault*[53] has greatly circumscribed these distinctions. In *Gault* the Court said that a child facing the possibility of commitment in a state institution has a right to adequate and timely notice of the charges against him,[54] to have counsel present in his defense,[55] to enjoy the privilege against self-incrimination,[56] and to confront and cross-examine sworn witnesses.[57] Since *Gault*, continued the *Doe* court, the trend toward extending full constitutional protection to juveniles has not abated. Two justices strenuously dissented,[58] countering with the Supreme Court's declaration in *McKeiver v. Pennsylvania*:[59] "The Court . . . has not yet said that *all* rights constitutionally assured to an adult accused of crime also are to be enforced or made available to the juvenile."[60]

In *People v. Chambers*[61] the Illinois Supreme Court considered the constitutionality of a statute that made it unlawful for a person under eighteen years old to "be present at or upon" a public area without a parent or guardian during the hours of the curfew. The defendants contended that the curfew unconstitutionally restricted the first amendment rights of minors. On the contrary, responded the court, "the suggestion that those values are impaired by the restriction here involved seems to trivialize them."[62] Ignoring any distinction between presence and remaining, the court discussed at length the state's concern about juvenile crime, viewing the curfew as a legislative attempt to deal in a responsible manner with the problem. The law does not assume, said the court, that minor children have an unlimited right to choose their own associates or to decide when or where they will associate with them.

The *Chambers* court mentioned with approval the statute's sanction against a parent who knowingly permits his child to violate the curfew. Not only does it command the coopertion of the parent, but it "operate[s] indirectly to enlist cooperation from the child, who may be willing to risk getting into trouble himself, but unwilling to involve his parents in a violation of the law."[63] Thus, reasoned the court, the curfew actually strengthened parental control; it did not usurp it.

Several federal courts have contended with challenges to children's curfews. In *Bykofsky v. Borough of Middletown*[64] the first federal case to examine the constitutionality of a nocturnal juvenile curfew, a Pennsylvania district court upheld a narrowly drafted ordinance that contained a relatively high number of exceptions to its provisions. In addition to the exception for a juvenile accompanied by a parent, guardian, or authorized adult, the Middletown ordinance provided nine other exceptions: (1) when a minor was exercising first amendment rights and had submitted a signed writing to the sheriff's office specifying when, where, and how he or she would be out in public after the curfew hour; (2) when a "reasonable necessity" existed and the parents had first notified the police; (3) when the minor was on a sidewalk in front of his or her home; (4) when the minor was returning home from a school or religious activity and prior notice was given the police; (5) when authorized by a special individual permit from the mayor; (6) when authorized by a group permit; (7) when the minor had a current employment card signed by the chief of police; (8) when the minor was traveling in a motor vehicle with parental consent; and (9) when so ordered formally by the mayor. Moreover, the ordinance described in detail police enforcement procedures and the liability of parents who knowingly or negligently allowed their children to violate the curfew.[65]

A mother and her minor son filed suit, maintaining, among other grounds, that the ordinance was unconstitutionally vague, violated the due process right of freedom of movement, and encroached on parental rights.[66] The court found the curfew permissible in all respects. Although it agreed that the ordinance contained a few vague words and phrases, it reasoned that "while there must be definiteness and ascertainable standards so that [people] of common intelligence can apprehend the meaning of the ordinance, perfect precision is neither possible nor constitutionally required."[67] Rejecting the plaintiffs' contention that the ordinance violated due process, the court stressed the legitimate interests of Middletown that the curfew supported; it concluded that the interest of minors in being outside during the curfew hours was not nearly as important.[68] The court similarly balanced the state's interests against the rights of the parent, finding the state's interests overriding.[69]

The curfew exception requiring a minor to obtain prior approval before exercising first amendment rights, however, raises the issue of the constitutionality of a prior restraint of protected activity. Prior restraint of a first amendment freedom has long been considered to be more serious than subsequent punishment.[70] The courts have usually tolerated more prior restraint in situations involving obscenity, but even in such cases restraint is still suspect.[71] Nevertheless, the *Bykofsky* court dismissed the question of prior restraint with little discussion.

Significantly, the court refused to review in detail any of the previous state decisions examining the constitutionality of juvenile curfews, explaining that "the particular ordinances which were approved or rejected do not contain many features which might serve as significant points for distinguishing the valid from the invalid regulatory scheme."[72] The court also rejected outright the reasoning on which many state court decisions had relied that drew a line between remaining and presence. The court said that

> whether the statutory language of a curfew ordinance prohibits "remaining" or "being" on the streets is insignificant because "remain" and "to be" are generally given synonymous interpretations at the enforcement level for the obvious reason they have as a practical matter in the curfew context no intelligible difference in meaning, and a judicial determination on this ground as to the validity of an ordinance is mere semantics and untenable.[73]

The Second Circuit Court of Appeals in *Naprstek v. City of Norwich*[74] struck down a curfew ordinance that did not set forth a time at which the curfew terminated. The failure to provide an ending limit, said the court, made the ordinance unconstitutionally vague, as it subjected children and their parents (any parent permitting a curfew violation faced a $25 fine) to arbitrary, capricious, and erratic enforcement.

Finally, in *Johnson v. City of Opelousas*[75] a curfew ordinance exempting only those minors accompanied by a "parent, tutor or other reasonable adult" or those on an "emergency errand" failed to survive a constitutional challenge based on overbreadth. The Fifth Circuit reversed the finding of the district court that the curfew was constitutional, declaring that the lack of exceptions made the ordinance overbroad because minors were prevented from "attending associational activities such as religious or school meetings, organized dances, and theater and sporting events, when reasonable and direct travel to or from these activities has to be made during the curfew period."[76] The court cited *Bykofsky*, stating, "We express no opinion on [the] validity of curfew ordinances narrowly drawn to accomplish proper social objectives."[77] Nonetheless, the court indicated that even an ordinance providing a greater number of exceptions might have been found unconstitutional, for "less drastic means [than the nocturnal curfew] are available for achieving these goals [of decreasing juvenile crime]."[78]

## Daytime Regulations

Occasionally municipalities enact laws regulating the activities of minors during the daylight hours. Such measures usually are enacted to enforce the truancy laws. Like curfew ordinances they have been challenged as an unconstitutional burden on minors' freedom of movement.

In *In re Carpenter*[79] a minor challenged a municipal ordinance prohibiting, with certain exceptions, persons under age eighteen from being on the public streets during hours when their attendance was required at school. The court upheld the statute, citing the familiar refrain that a governmental body may restrict individual freedom only when the restriction bears a real and substantial relationship to a legitimate governmental interest (such as protection of health, safety, morals, or general welfare) and the restriction is not unreasonable or arbitrary. The court found such an interest in this case—namely, the interest in general welfare, if not public safety and morals, implicit in the school attendance requirement itself. If the school attendance requirement is itself constitutional, then an ordinance reasonably calculated to enforce it must be constitutional.

To the contrary, in *Aladdin's Castle v. City of Mesquite*[80] the Fifth Circuit Court of Appeals held unconstitutional a city ordinance prohibiting amusement center operators from allowing children under age seventeen to play coin-operated games unless accompanied by a parent or guardian. Rejecting the argument that the ordinance furthered the legitimate purpose of enforcing truancy laws, the court said that

> The decision to bar all people under seventeen years of age from all coin-operated amusement centers at all times is patently irrational. Barring young people from using coin-operated amusement devices at times and on days when school is closed simply bears no relation whatever to the city's alleged interest in eliminating truancy. The regulation instead evidences the city's disapproval of such centers in general or of Aladdin's owners in particular. Such disapproval may justify private action, such as the withholding of patronage, but mere disapproval is not enough constitutionally to justify bringing the full weight of the municipality's regulatory apparatus into play.[81]

On appeal to the Supreme Court, the Court remanded the case to the Fifth Circuit for a determination of whether its conclusion invalidating the age restriction was based on federal or state law.[82] On remand the Fifth Circuit let stand its decision that the age restriction was unconstitutional.[83]

## Conclusion

What emerges from the case law is a series of propositions whose validity now seems to be well recognized. First, the state's power to regulate the affairs of the individual is not absolute, as evidenced by *Meyer v. Nebraska*. Second, the individual's right to personal freedom is not absolute, either, for the freedom of the individual is subject to restraint through imposition of a curfew in riot or emergency situations. In the absence of the latter kind of exigency, however, the state cannot impose an outright ban on use of the streets by adults.

What, then, of children? Therein lies the third proposition—that is, that because of the peculiar vulnerability of children, the state may constitutionally regulate the movement of children to a greater degree than it may in the case of adults. Such regulation, however, must be reasonable. Even though courts seem to have abandoned the presence/remaining distinction, a state cannot, in the absence of an emergency, place a general ban on children being on the streets. Rather, any such regulation, as in the case of adults, must be "reasonable." In order to be reasonable, the regulation must be reasonably related to some legitimate state purpose.

In terms of what purposes are legitimate, perhaps the California Court of Appeals said it best in *In re Nancy C.*:[84]

> Commentators have suggested that "the interest of children in being abroad during the night hours is not nearly so important to the social, economic and healthful well-being of the community," as is free movement of adults. In addition, the community has a special interest in "the protection of children of immature years." Furthermore, the community has an interest in the reduction of juvenile nocturnal crime.[85]

## Notes

1. Warren & Brandeis, *The Right to Privacy,* 4 HARV. L. REV. 193 (1890). Copyright ©1890 by the Harvard Law Review Association. Reprinted with permission.

2. 262 U.S. 390 (1923).

3. *Id.* at 399.

4. *Id.* at 399–400.

5. L. SIEGEL & J. SENNA, JUVENILE DELINQUENCY 12 (1985) [hereinafter cited as L. SIEGEL & J. SENNA].

6. *See* W. WADLINGTON, C. WHITEBREAD & S. DAVIS, CHILDREN IN THE LEGAL SYSTEM 602 (1983).

7. *The General Laws and Liberties of the Massachusetts Colony (1672)* in JUVENILE OFFENDERS FOR A THOUSAND YEARS 318–19. (W. Sanders ed. 1970).

8. L. SIEGEL & J. SENNA, *supra* note 5, at 35.

9. Note, *Curfew Ordinances and the Control of Nocturnal Juvenile Crime,* 107 U. PA. L. REV. 66 (1958).

10. Atlanta Constitution, June 11, 1986, at 21A, col. 5. Enforcement of the curfew was later delayed, *id.,* June 12, 1986, at 65A, col. 1, and the curfew envventually was vetoed by the commission chairman because of his view that it was too broad and unenforceable, *id.,* June 20, 1986, at 3D, col. 1.

11. Bykofsky v. Borough of Middletown, 429 U.S. 964, 965 (1976) (Marshall, J., dissenting).

12. BLACK'S LAW DICTIONARY 457 (4th ed. 1951).

13. Note, *Juvenile Curfew Ordinances and the Constitution,* 76 MICH. L. REV. 109, 132 (1977).

14. *Parens patriae* literally means "parent of the country," referring to the sovereignty the state exercises over persons under disability, such as minors. BLACK'S LAW DICTIONARY 1269 (4th ed. 1951). The *parens patriae* concept was an underlying

rationale for the juvenile court movement at the turn of this century. *See* S. Davis, Rights of Juveniles: The Juvenile Justice System 1–2 (1986).

15. *See, e.g.,* City of St. Louis v. Gloner, 210 Mo. 502, 109 S.W. 30 (1908); Shuck v. Borough of Ligonier, 343 Pa. 265, 22 A.2d 735 (1941).

16. Beail v. District of Columbia, 82 A.2d 765, 767 (D.C. 1951).

17. *Id.* at 768.

18. *See, e.g.,* Papachristou v. City of Jacksonville, 405 U.S. 156 (1972); Palmer v. City of Euclid, 402 U.S. 544 (1971).

19. *See, e.g.,* Kolender v. Lawson, 461 U.S. 352 (1983).

20. *See, e.g.,* United States v. Chalk, 441 F.2d 1277 (4th Cir.), *cert. denied,* 404 U.S. 943 (1971); State v. Dobbins, 277 N.C. 484, 178 S.E.2d 449 (1971); Ervin v. State, 41 Wis. 2d 194, 163 N.W.2d 207 (1968).

21. *See* cases cited *supra* note 20.

22. *See, e.g.,* Prince v. Massachusetts, 321 U.S. 158 (1944), discussed in chapter 4. In *Prince* the Supreme Court upheld a state statute prohibiting minors from selling pamphlets on the streets, against parental (aunt acting as parent) claims that the statute violated the right of parental authority guaranteed by due process of law and the right of free exercise of religion guaranteed by the first amendment.

23. *See* Wisconsin v. Yoder, 406 U.S. 205 (1972), discussed in chapter 4.

24. *See generally* chapter 5.

25. *See* J. Nowak, R. Rotunda & J. Young, Constitutional Law 542–45 (2d ed. 1983) [hereinafter cited as J. Nowak, R. Rotunda & J. Young].

26. *See, e.g.,* McKeiver v. Pennsylvania, 403 U.S. 528 (1971) (right to jury trial not required in juvenile court proceedings).

27. *See, e.g.,* New York v. Ferber, 458 U.S. 747 (1982); Ginsberg v. New York, 390 U.S. 629 (1968).

28. *See, e.g.,* Prince v. Massachusetts, 321 U.S. 158 (1944); *see also* Bellotti v. Baird, 433 U.S. 622 (1979). The Court in *Bellotti* set forth three reasons explaining why a child can be restrained when an adult cannot: "the peculiar vulnerability of children; their inability to make critical decisions in an informed, mature manner; and the importance of the parental role in child rearing." 433 U.S. at 634.

29. J. Nowak, R. Rotunda & J. Young, *supra* note 25, at 872.

30. 306 U.S. 451 (1939).

31. *Id.* at 453.

32. J. Nowak, R. Rotunda & J. Young, *supra* note 25, at 868.

33. P. Kauper & F. Beytagh, Constitutional Law 1192 (5th ed. 1980).

34. 39 Tex. Crim. 448, 46 S.W. 936 (1898).

35. *Id.* at 452, 46 S.W. at 937.

36. *Id.*

37. 70 Cal. App. 2d Supp. 862, 161 P.2d 498 (Cal. App. Dep't Super. Ct. 1945).

38. 148 Cal. App. 2d 419, 306 P.2d 601 (1957).

39. *Id.* at 423, 306 P.2d at 604.

40. 236 Md. 548, 204 A.2d 688 (1964).

41. *Id.* at 556, 204 A.2d at 693.

42. *Id.* at 557, 204 A.2d at 694.

43. 7 Ohio App. 2d 212, 220 N.E.2d 126 (1966).

44. 28 Cal. App. 3d 747, 105 Cal. Rptr. 113 (1972).

45. Note, *Nonemergency Curfews and the Liberty Interests of Minors*, 12 FORDHAM URB. L.J. 513, 545–46 n.144 (1984).

46. 356 So. 2d 48 (Fla. Dist. Ct. App. 1978).

47. *Id.* at 50.

48. 82 Wash. 2d 794, 514 P.2d 1059 (1973).

49. 70 Wash. 2d 405, 423 P.2d 522 (1967).

50. 82 Wash. 2d at 798, 514 P.2d at 1062.

51. *Id.* at 800, 514 P.2d at 1063.

52. 54 Hawaii 647, 513 P.2d 1385 (1973).

53. 387 U.S. 1 (1967).

54. *Id.* at 33.

55. *Id.* at 41.

56. *Id.* at 55.

57. *Id.* at 57.

58. 54 Hawaii at 653, 513 P.2d at 1389–90.

59. 403 U.S. 528 (1970).

60. *Id.* at 533.

61. 66 Ill. 2d 36, 360 N.E.2d 55 (1976).

62. *Id.* at 41, 360 N.E.2d at 57.

63. *Id.* at 42–43, 360 N.E.2d at 58.

64. 401 F. Supp. 1242 (M.D. Pa.), *aff'd mem.*, 535 F.2d 1245 (3d Cir. 1975), *cert. denied*, 429 U.S. 964 (1976).

65. 401 F. Supp. at 1269–71.

66. *Id.* at 1248.

67. *Id.* at 1253.

68. *Id.* at 1256.

69. *Id.* at 1262–64.

70. J. NOWAK, R. ROTUNDA & J. YOUNG, *supra* note 25, at 1021–22.

71. *Id.* at 1021.

72. 401 F. Supp. at 1245–46 n.1.

73. *Id.* at 1252.

74. 545 F.2d 815 (2d Cir. 1976).

75. 658 F.2d 1065 (5th Cir. 1981), *rev'g* 488 F. Supp. 433 (W.D. La. 1980).

76. *Id.* at 1072.

77. *Id.*

78. *Id.* at 1074.

79. 31 Ohio App. 2d 184, 287 N.E.2d 399 (1972).

80. 630 F.2d 1029 (5th Cir. 1980).

81. *Id.* at 1039–40.

82. City of Mesquite v. Aladdin's Castle, 455 U.S. 283 (1982).

83. Aladdin's Castle v. City of Mesquite, 713 F.2d 137 (5th Cir. 1983). This time the Supreme Court declined further review of the case, City of Mesquite v. Aladdin's Castle, 464 U.S. 927 (1983).

84. 28 Cal. App. 3d 747, 105 Cal. Rptr. 113 (1972).

85. *Id.* at 755, 105 Cal. Rptr. at 119.

# 7

# Property: Protected Entitlements of Children

> The Fourteenth Amendment's procedural protection of property is a safeguard of the security of interests that a person has already acquired in specific benefits. These interests—property interests—may take many forms. . . .
>
> Certain attributes of "property" interests protected by procedural due process emerge from [our earlier] decisions. To have a property interest in a benefit, a person clearly must have more than an abstract need or desire for it. He must have more than a unilateral expectation of it. He must, instead, have a legitimate claim of entitlement to it.
>
> —Justice Potter Stewart
> *Board of Regents v. Roth*
> 408 U.S. 564, 576-77 (1972)

## The Changing Concept of Property

The preceding two chapters have opened with references to constitutional and other guarantees of the rights to life, liberty, and property. The authors of the 1890 article previously quoted included property rights among those changing in nature and scope over the years:

> [I]n very early times, the law gave a remedy only for physical interference with life and property, for trespasses *vi et armis*. Then . . . the right to property secured to the individual his lands and his cattle. Later, there came a recognition of man's spiritual nature, of his feelings and his intellect. Gradually the scope of these legal rights broadened; . . . the term "property" has grown to comprise every form of possession—intangible, as well as tangible.[1]

Several points of reference come to mind when one contemplates the scope of children's property interests. One is a child's right (that is, capacity) to own and dispose of property,[2] although such capacity is not a part of the constitutional concept of property as envisioned by the 1890 commentators or the courts. One also thinks of a case such as *Goss v. Lopez*,[3] in which the Supreme Court held that where a state creates a right to public education by statute, a child acquires a constitutionally protected property interest in a free public education that cannot be deprived without due process of law—that is, notice and a hearing.[4]

The modern concept of what constitutes a property interest entitled to constitutional protection is traced to two Supreme Court decisions decided in relatively recent years—*Board of Regents v. Roth*[5] and *Perry v. Sindermann*.[6] Both cases involved judicial review of administrative decisions not to renew the contracts of nontenured college professors. In both cases the Court's concept of a constitutionally protected property interest was that it must involve something more than "an abstract need or desire" or "a unilateral expectation"; rather, it must entail "a legitimate claim of entitlement."[7] The Court further pointed out that such interests "are not created by the Constitution" but "are created and their dimensions . . . defined by existing rules or understandings that stem from an independent source such as state law."[8]

In other words, in any given case one does not look to the Constitution in order to determine whether a property right is implicated. Rather, one looks outside the Constitution—such as to state law—to determine whether a property right has been created. If the state has created such a property right, then the individual is entitled to constitutional protection of that property right. The state, having created the property right, may not take it away without *procedural* due process of law (namely, without notice and a hearing).

The facts in *Roth* were that the teacher had been employed under a one-year contract without tenure, and midway during his first year of employment he was notified that he would not be rehired for the following year. He alleged that he was denied a property (as well as a liberty) interest without due process of law—that is, without a right to be heard.

The Court developed a two-step test to be employed in any case alleging deprivation of a property interest in violation of due process of law: (1) determination of whether a property interest is implicated and (2) if a property interest is found to be implicated, determination of what process is due. In the *Roth* case the Court determined that no property interest was at stake because all the untenured teacher possessed was "an abstract concern in being rehired." No state law or university policy "secured his interest in re-employment or . . . created any legitimate claim to it." Because no property interest was implicated, he was not entitled to a right to a hearing.[9]

In *Perry v. Sindermann* the teacher was also untenured. Here, however, he had been employed in the state system for ten years in an unbroken series of one-year renewable contracts. Under these circumstances the Court was of the view that he possessed more than a "unilateral expectancy" of continued employment because the college, through its published policies, had led him to believe that he would be rehired as long as his teaching was satisfactory and he got along with his fellow teachers and superiors. This sort of understanding, the Court said, amounted to *de facto* tenure (tenure

in fact), which is the kind of entitlement that qualifies as a property interest. Therefore, before being unilaterally dismissed he was entitled to a
hearing at which he would be given the reasons for his nonretention and an
opportunity to respond to them.[10]

Thus, the key to decision in these cases was not whether the teachers
involved had tenure explicitly or not. Rather, the key was whether there
was a bilateral understanding between the parties sufficient to give rise to a
reasonable expectation on the employee's part of continued receipt of a
benefit. As the Court in *Perry* put it:

> We have made clear . . . that "property" interests subject to procedural
> due process protection are not limited by a few rigid, technical forms.
> Rather, "property" denotes a broad range of interests that are secured by
> "existing rules or understandings." A person's interest in a benefit is a
> "property" interest for due process purposes if there are such rules or
> mutually explicit understandings that support his claim of entitlement to
> the benefit and that he may invoke at a hearing.[11]

## The Concept of Property for Children

The first and certainly the most well-known opportunity for the Supreme
Court to apply these principles to children occurred in *Goss v. Lopez*.[12] In
*Goss* students at a high school in Columbus, Ohio, were suspended from
school for alleged disciplinary violations without notice or a hearing. Relying on the two-step approach of *Roth*, the Court first inquired whether a
property interest was implicated in the case. The Court noted that Ohio
was not constitutionally obliged to provide a public education for its children, but it nevertheless had done so and also had required their attendance
at school. Because of such action, the Court said, the state was "constrained
to recognize a student's legitimate entitlement to a public education as a
property interest . . . protected by the Due Process Clause . . . which may
not be taken away for misconduct without adherence to the minimum
procedures required by that Clause."[13]

Having decided that a property right created by the state is entitled to
constitutional protection, the Court then turned to the second step of its
analysis, determining what process is due. The "minimum procedures"
required in connection with a suspension of ten days or less include "oral
or written notice of the charges against him and, if he desires them, an
explanation of the evidence the authorities have and an opportunity to
present his side of the story."[14] Such rudimentary protections as notice and
a hearing, the Court said, "will provide a meaningful hedge against erroneous action."[15]

In such informal hearings, students generally are not entitled to representation by counsel, the right to confront and cross-examine witnesses against them, or the right to call witnesses of their own.[16] The Court went on to add, however, that

> Longer suspensions or expulsions for the remainder of the school term, or permanently, may require more formal procedures. Nor do we put aside the possibility that in unusual situations, although involving only a short suspension, something more than the rudimentary procedures will be required.[17]

## Further Refinement of Property in the School Setting

Subsequently, the Court decided another case that, while not involving children, nevertheless spoke of the same issue raised in *Goss v. Lopez* and had implications for academic decision making in the public school context. In *Board of Curators v. Horowitz*[18] a medical student who had been dismissed from medical school brought suit against the governing board of the university, alleging that she had not been accorded procedural due process prior to her dismissal. She did not claim that she had been unconstitutionally deprived of a property interest but rather a liberty interest.[19]

The Supreme Court found it unnecessary to decide whether the respondent had been deprived of a liberty interest or any other kind of constitutionally protected interest because it concluded that in any event she was afforded all the process due her under the fourteenth amendment. She was fully informed of the faculty's dissatisfaction with her clinical progress, and her status was carefully and deliberately evaluated several times prior to the ultimate decision resulting in her dismissal. More important, Justice Rehnquist, speaking for the Court, had this to say about the difference between disciplinary as opposed to academic evaluations:

> Since the issue first arose 50 years ago, state and lower federal courts have recognized that there are distinct differences between decisions to suspend or dismiss a student for disciplinary purposes and similar actions taken for academic reasons which may call for hearings in connection with the former but not the latter. . . .
>
> Academic evaluations of a student, in contrast to disciplinary determinations, bear little resemblance to the judicial and administrative fact-finding proceedings to which we have traditionally attached a full hearing requirement. In *Goss*, the school's decision to suspend the students rested on factual conclusions that the individual students had participated in demonstrations that had disrupted classes, attacked a police officer, or caused physical damage to school property. The requirement of a hearing,

where the student could present his side of the factual issue, could under such circumstances "provide a meaningful hedge against erroneous action." The decision to dismiss respondent, by comparison, rested on the academic judgment of school officials that she did not have the necessary clinical ability to perform adequately as a medical doctor and was making insufficient progress toward that goal. Such a judgment is by its nature more subjective and evaluative than the typical factual questions presented in the average disciplinary decision. Like the decision of an individual professor as to the proper grade for a student in his course, the determination whether to dismiss a student for academic reasons requires an expert evaluation of cumulative information and is not readily adapted to the procedural tools of judicial or administrative decisionmaking.

Under such circumstances, we decline to ignore the historic judgment of educators and thereby formalize the academic dismissal process by requiring a hearing. The educational process is not by nature adversary; instead it centers around a continuing relationship between faculty and students, "one in which the teacher must occupy many roles—educator, advisor, friend, and, at times, parent substitute." This is especially true as one advances through the varying regimes of the educational system, and the instruction becomes both more individualized and more specialized. In *Goss*, this Court concluded that the value of some form of hearing in a disciplinary context outweighs any resulting harm to the academic environment. Influencing this conclusion was clearly the belief that disciplinary proceedings, in which the teacher must decide whether to punish a student for disruptive or insubordinate behavior, may automatically bring an adversary flavor to the normal student-teacher relationship. The same conclusion does not follow in the academic context. We decline to further enlarge the judicial presence in the academic community and thereby risk deterioration of many beneficial aspects of the faculty-student relationship.[20]

Beginning at the time *Board of Curators v. Horowitz* was decided, Justice Rehnquist has questioned the value of the adversary process to "the maintenance of a good society" in certain cases, particularly those where continuing, ongoing relationships are involved.[21] The kinds of cases to which he refers are those involving an institution, such as the family,[22] where litigation may result in irreparable harm to the institution itself.[23] In such cases we must decide, Justice Rehnquist says, whether "the game is . . . worth the candle."[24] The same might be said of the school as an institution and of the ongoing faculty/student relationship of which Justice Rehnquist spoke in *Horowitz*.

## Attendance, Participation, or Membership

The vast majority of cases in which a property interest is asserted are cases arising in the school or education context. Many of these involve a claim of a right to attend a particular school, to participate in a particular educational program at school, or to belong to a particular organization or group at school.

A common fact pattern, for example, is one in which a family with school-age children moves from one school district to another district, and the children desire to continue attending their old school. In one such case,[25] the parents were told that in order for their children to continue to attend the same school, they would have to pay tuition. When the parents refused, the children were dismissed from school. The court held that the children, at the time of their dismissal, had no constitutionally protected property interest in attending their old school; therefore, the principal's action in dismissing them was not subject to due process requirements.

The court questioned what the purpose of a predismissal hearing would have been because it was undisputed that the family had, in fact, moved out of the district. Their reason for moving was irrelevant.

In a case[26] with similar facts, the court took a somewhat different approach, although the result was the same. The court focused less on whether there was a protected property interest and more on whether the parties were afforded due process, concluding that they were. The parents were given notice and an adequate opportunity to respond and to correct any mistakes of fact. The court observed: "That is not to say, however, that the school officials involved did everything that they could have done to aid the students more completely, but that is not what the Due Process Clause requires. We find only that the minimum requirements were complied with."[27]

In still another attendance case,[28] a five-year-old child initially admitted to a kindergarten class in the fall was denied admission for the spring based on his disruptive behavior during the fall and the results of psychological testing. The school offered homebound instruction as an alternative. The parents refused and filed suit.

Under Pennsylvania law, school districts are required to provide public education for every child between the ages of six and twenty-one. The court held that under state law, a child under the age of six has no constitutionally protected property interest in attending public school. Moreover, the school district's offer of homebound instruction demonstrated it was not acting in an arbitrary or capricious manner, nor did it show an abuse of discretion.

Occasionally the issue is not over admission to or attendance at school but rather participation in a particular educational program. For example, in one case[29] two elementary school students who were evaluated for but not admitted to a program for gifted students brought suit alleging a property right in a free public education "appropriate to their needs." The court observed that the right to a free public education created by state law does not confer on each student the right to a particular level or quality of education; it merely imposes on the state the obligation to furnish a state-wide system of public education. Therefore, the court held, the plaintiffs had no property interest in participating in the gifted program.[30]

In similar fashion, membership in an organization is sometimes asserted as a protected property interest. In one case,[31] for example, a student was academically eligible for membership in the National Honor Society, but based on anonymous evaluations from teachers, he was not elected to membership. His father filed suit, alleging that the practice of utilizing anonymous evaluations was unfair and denied his son due process of law. The court, however, held that membership in the National Honor Society is not a property interest entitling a student to due process of law. Other courts have held likewise.[32]

## Grading and Evaluation

Due process analysis does not always take the form of an inquiry into whether notice and a hearing are required. It sometimes simply inquires into whether procedures employed are fair or are fairly administered.

In one case,[33] for example, students who had failed a proficiency examination required for graduation from high school filed suit to enjoin its continued use on the ground, among others, that the test denied them due process of law in that they were tested on material in which they had not received instruction. The court observed that where the state had created a system of free public education and required attendance, students had an expectation that if they attended school for the required number of years and passed required courses, they would receive a diploma. This expectation, the court said, is a property interest within the meaning of the Constitution.

Having created a property interest under state law, the state could not deprive students of this property interest without due process of law. The requirement that students take and pass a functional literacy test was denial of due process of law if the test covered material not taught to the students. Such a test would not be "fair." Although the state may condition graduation on a passing score on the test, the test itself must be a fair test. The court therefore remanded the case to the trial court for a determination of whether the test covered material not taught. On remand, the federal district court found the test to be fair in that it covered only what had been taught in the state's public schools.[34] This time the appellate court affirmed the lower court's decision.[35]

In a case[36] reminiscent of *Board of Curators v. Horowitz*, a medical student was dismissed from a combined undergraduate/medical degree program when he failed part of the examination given by the National

Board of Medical Examiners. The university's practice had been to allow students who initially failed to pass the examination to retake it and to remain in school while awaiting the results of the retest. The court of appeals held that in light of the university's practice, the student had an expectation that he would be allowed to retake the test and to remain in school, and this expectation amounted to a property interest; the university's action in arbitrarily dismissing him from school denied him this property interest.[37]

The Supreme Court, however, reversed.[38] The Court assumed, without deciding, that the student had a constitutionally protected property interest in continued enrollment free from arbitrary action by the university. Even so, the Court held, no due process violation occurred because the university did not act arbitrarily or unfairly. The Court stated: "The record unmistakably demonstrates . . . that the faculty's decision was made conscientiously and with careful deliberation, based on an evaluation of the entirety of Ewing's academic career."[39] Citing *Board of Curators v. Horowitz*, the Court continued:

> When judges are asked to review the substance of a genuinely academic decision, such as this one, they should show great respect for the faculty's professional judgment. Plainly, they may not override it unless it is such a substantial departure from accepted academic norms as to demonstrate that the person or committee responsible did not actually exercise professional judgment.[40]

In another case[41] alleging unfair grading practices, high school students brought a class action suit challenging the school board's policy of imposing academic sanctions on students for nonattendance (course credit was withheld from any student missing more than twenty-four classes in a year-long course). The students maintained that their rights were violated by a system that based grades on anything other than academic performance. Although the court hinted that the students possessed a protected property interest in a fairly administered grading system, it held there had been no infringement of a property interest in this case. Specifically, the evidence failed to show that the policy, which was universally known to students, was applied in an arbitrary or capricious way.

## Athletics

Most of the cases raising claims of property interests in the school setting are cases involving interscholastic and intercollegiate sports. The typical fact pattern is that a high school or college athlete is ruled ineligible to play by the appropriate governing authority, usually because of an age or residency requirement or because of academic difficulty or even improper conduct. The athlete or his parents then file a suit claiming, among other grounds perhaps, that the athlete has a constitutionally protected property interest in playing football, basketball, hockey, or whatever sport is at issue.

As a general proposition, the courts have held that participation in interscholastic or intercollegiate sports is not a constitutionally protected property interest.[42] Courts have declined to read *Goss v. Lopez* as establishing a property interest in participation in any extracurricular activity.[43] The cases that follow, dealing with particular kinds of eligibility requirements, are particularly informative.

**No Pass/No Play.** A requirement that has attracted a great deal of attention recently is the so-called no pass/no play rule—that is, in order for an athlete to participate in interscholastic sports he must maintain a certain academic average. Grades below that average will result in the student's being declared ineligible to participate.

Texas, for example, has a statute that requires a student to maintain a 70 average (on a 100-point scale) in all classes in order to remain eligible for participation in extracurricular activities.[44] Parents of some students filed a suit to enjoin enforcement of the no pass/no play rule. The Texas Supreme Court, however, ruled that students do not have a constitutionally protected property interest in participation in extracurricular activities.[45] Underscoring the importance of this decision is the fact that the United States Supreme Court dismissed the appeal because of want of a substantial federal question,[46] likely indicating the Court's view that in light of the overwhelming weight of the case law, the issue is settled that students do not possess a constitutionally protected property interest in their participation in extracurricular activities.

To illustrate the breadth of the no pass/no play rule, the West Virginia State Board of Education has a rule requiring students to maintain a 2.0 overall average (on a 4.0 scale) in order to be eligible for participation in nonacademic extracurricular activities.[47] *Nonacademic extracurricular activity* is defined generally as including student government, service as a class officer, student publications, drama and music productions, debate competitions, interscholastic athletics, and cheerleading.

This no pass/no play rule came under fire in a case[48] in which the local school board had imposed an additional requirement that students receive passing grades in all courses in order to maintain eligibility for participation in extracurricular activities. The West Virginia court, however, held that participation in interscholastic athletics is not a property interest entitling students to due process protection.[49]

**Residence.** High school athletic governing bodies typically have rules that require students to attend (that is, play for) the school in the district in which the student athlete lives, and if the student transfers to another district, he is ineligible to participate in sports at the new school for a stated period of time. The purpose of such a rule is obviously to discourage competition among schools for athletes by penalizing moves that are athletically motivated.

In Pennsylvania, for example, the Pennsylvania Interscholastic Athletic Association has a rule that allows the PIAA to ban from participation in interscholastic sports a student transferring from one district to another where the PIAA determines the transfer is athletically motivated.[50] A student challenged enforcement of the rule, alleging that the association's action in declaring him ineligible to play basketball interfered with his right to a complete public education. In a familiar refrain, the court found no property interest in participation in interscholastic athletics.[51] The court did add, however, that its decision "does not mean that the PIAA is free to act capriciously, arbitrarily or in a discriminatory manner."[52]

In a similar case[53] another court held that student athletes had no property interest in playing hockey. Thus, the action of school officials in dismissing them from the hockey team because they were suspected of having obtained guardianships solely to enable them to play on the same team, did not violate any constitutionally protected right of theirs.

In Louisiana the applicable rule provides that a student who transfers to another district is ineligible to participate in interscholastic athletics for a period of one year.[54] In response to a challenge to the rule, the court held that participation in interscholastic athletics does not fall within the ambit of due process protection. In language reflective of that in *Board of Regents v. Roth*, the court said, "A student's interest in participating in a single year of interscholastic athletics amounts to a mere expectation rather than a constitutionally protected claim of entitlement."[55]

**Age.** In a Texas case,[56] football players sought to enjoin enforcement of a rule that barred any student attaining his nineteenth birthday on or before the first day of September preceding a league contest from participation in that or any subsequent contest. The court held that the players had no property interest in alleged injury to their prospective careers in college football or prospects for scholarships, arising from their ineligibility to participate in playoff games or to be seen by college scouts. In the absence of any protected property interest, due process protections were inapplicable.[57]

### Discipline

In cases involving discipline as opposed to academic decision making, the courts have followed the dictates of *Goss v. Lopez*, although that does not always mean that a due process violation has occurred. *Goss v. Lopez*, after all, contained some exceptions.

For example, in one case[58] the court held that no constitutionally protected property interest was at stake in a school board's practice of temporarily suspending bus routes because of students' violation of rules and regulations. Even though the state provided a right to free bus transportation, temporary suspension as a means of controlling vandalism and disruption and avoiding safety hazards was a *de minimis* deprivation of rights that did not invoke application of constitutional due process safeguards. Temporary suspension only caused temporary inconvenience, not loss of educational opportunities or other significant injury as in *Goss v. Lopez*.

In still another case[59] the court followed *Goss v. Lopez*, but because one of the sanctions imposed against the student was a four-month suspension from participation in after-school extracurricular activities, the court addressed the question of whether lengthy suspension (as opposed to the ten-day suspension in *Goss v. Lopez*) required further due process protections than those required in *Goss v. Lopez*.

The court said, as most do, that there is no property interest in participation in extracurricular activities as such. Such participation, however, is a part of the total educational experience, in which one does have a property interest under *Goss v. Lopez*. Still, the court said, each component does not give rise to a separate property interest:[60]

[T]he property interest in education created by the state is participation in the entire process. The *myriad activities* which combine to form that educational process *cannot be dissected to create hundreds of separate property rights*, each cognizable under the Constitution. Otherwise, removal from a particular class, dismissal from an athletic team, a club or any extracurricular activity, would each require ultimate satisfaction of procedural due process (emphasis added).[61]

The court goes on to say:

Since there is not a property interest in each separate component of the "educational process," denial of the opportunity to participate in merely one or several extracurricular activities would not give rise to a right to due process. However, *total exclusion* from participation in that part of the educational process designated as extracurricular activities for a *lengthy period of time* could, depending upon the particular circumstances, be sufficient deprivation to implicate due process.[62]

In this case, however, the student was not excluded from *all* participation in extracurricular activities, only those taking place after school. Moreover, he was accorded the minimal protections required by due process of law.

## Conclusion

To return for the moment to Justice Rehnquist's concern that use of litigation to resolve disputes involving an institution such as the school or the family might cause irreparable harm to the institution itself,[63] two examples might suffice to illustrate the point. One is a lawsuit that arose out of the disputed result in a football game, appropriate here because much of this chapter has dwelled on property rights of students in the school context, particularly in sports. The second concerns a lawsuit that arose out of a dispute within a family over whether a teenaged daughter would accompany the rest of her family on an extended trip, appropriate here because the case expands the principles discussed in this chapter to lengths perhaps not imagined.

In the first example, to set the stage, the occasion was a football game between two Georgia high school teams, R.L. Osborne and Lithia Springs, to determine which team would advance to the playoffs. With seven minutes and one second remaining in the game, the score was seven to six in favor of Osborne. Osborne had the ball on its own forty-seven-yard line with a fourth down and twenty-one yards to go for a first down. Osborne elected to punt, but a roughing-the-kicker penalty was called on Lithia Springs. In assessing the fifteen-yard penalty, the referee placed the ball on the Lithia Springs thirty-eight-yard line and erroneously signaled that it was fourth down and six yards to go.

The applicable rules clearly state that the penalty of roughing the kicker is fifteen yards and an automatic first down. There was some dispute as to whether the Osborne coaches protested the erroneous call before the ball was put in play at the Lithia Springs thirty-eight-yard line.

In any event, Osborne again punted. After receiving the punt, Lithia Springs put the ball in play, moved down the field and scored a field goal, making the score nine to seven in favor of Lithia Springs. Now behind by two points with time running out, Osborne elected to pass when they received the ball again. Lithia Springs intercepted the errant pass and scored a touchdown. After a successful extra point try, the score was Lithia Springs over Osborne, sixteen to seven, which was the final score.

The Osborne coaches protested the game through administrative channels, but their protest and appeal were unsuccessful, apparently on the ground that they had not protested the bad call immediately, before the ball was put back into play. Parents of Osborne players then filed suit against the Georgia High School Association. The trial court ruled that the parents had a property right in the game of football being played by the rules and that they and their sons were denied the right when the rules were not correctly applied. The court ordered the two teams to meet on a subsequent date to resume play with the ball in Osborne's possession at the Lithia

Springs thirty-eight-yard line, with a first down and ten to go, and that the clock be set at seven minutes and one second remaining in the game.

In reversing the trial court, the court relied on an earlier decision[64] in which it had held that a high school football player had no right to participate in interscholastic athletics and had no protectable property interest that would give rise to a due process claim.[65] The court went on to add: "We now go further and hold that courts of equity in this state are without authority to review decisions of football referees because those decisions do not present judicial controversies."[66]

The second example is furnished by Professor Lawrence Friedman of the Stanford University Law School and is attributed to Professor Michael Wald of the same school. Professor Friedman tells it best:

> In 1972, a fourteen-year-old girl sued her parents in a juvenile court in Minnesota. The family had three daughters and a lifetime dream. They owned a forty-foot boat, and on that boat they intended to cruise out through the Great Lakes into the big world. The girls would, of course, go along; mother and father would educate them "through an approved correspondence system." The date of the trip grew near. The father sold his business; the mother quit her job. They planned to be gone at least a year—maybe two, maybe three.
>
> Lee Anne, the oldest daughter (fourteen), was the fly in the ointment. She had a new set of friends; they meant a lot to her. The idea of the trip was "anathema." She wanted to stay behind with her friends. Her parents, on the other hand, disapproved of her crowd. They worried about her behavior in general. They insisted she break off with her friends and come on the trip. The daughter refused, and brought the matter to the court. The judge heard both sides and reached out for a compromise: Lee Anne would stay behind, but in the care of an aunt.[67]

Both these examples are notable not for the solutions they offer, but for the profound questions they raise. Should courts rule on decisions by referees made in high school football games? Should they rule on the eligibility of students to play in athletic events or to participate in extracurricular activities generally or to belong to a school organization? Should they resolve disputes between parents and their children over where the family will go on its vacation or what foods the children will or will not eat or the hour by which a child must be home from a date?

In *Board of Curators v. Horowitz*, and more recently in *Regents of the University of Michigan v. Ewing*,[68] the Supreme Court was reluctant to enter into the uncharted waters of academic decision making, traditionally characterized by a highly subjective, discretionary process.[69] Despite its pronouncements in *Board of Regents v. Roth, Perry v. Sinderman*, and *Goss v. Lopez*, there is a point beyond which the Court is unwilling to go.

Perhaps as Justice Rehnquist has indicated,[70] it is unwilling to traverse the bounds of discision making in which ongoing relationships are affected, perhaps to their detriment.

The difficulty, of course, is that once the courts have resolved the dispute between the parties—whether they be irate parents opposed to school or athletic officials or parents versus their own children—the parties will have to go on living or working together in their usual relationship. Their usual relationship, however, may have been adversely affected by the bitterness of the dispute carried out in an adversarial arena.

This is not to say that parents should have no recourse at all against school boards or athletic associations or for that matter that children should have no recourse against their parents. What it says is that the adversary process is not an appropriate means by which to resolve such disputes, except in extreme cases.[71] Rather, such disputes should be worked out within the institution—school or family—itself, or if that is not possible, through alternative means of dispute resolution, such as mediation or arbitration, and using a disinterested third party as a mediator or arbitrator.

## Notes

1. Warren & Brandeis, *The Right to Privacy*, 4 HARV. L. REV. 193 (1890). Copyright © 1890 by the Harvard Law Review Association. Reprinted with permission.

2. A child's capacity to make a testamentary disposition of property was covered in chapter 3, in connection with other attitudes of private law toward children.

3. 419 U.S. 565 (1975). Goss v. Lopez was discussed in chapter 4, in connection with other children's cases decided by the United States Supreme Court.

4. The right to education, in a much broader sense than it is discussed in this chapter, is the subject of chapter 8.

5. 408 U.S. 564 (1972).

6. 408 U.S. 593 (1972).

7. 408 U.S. at 577.

8. *Id.*

9. *Id.* at 578.

10. *Id.* at 599–600, 603.

11. *Id.* at 601. For an intellectual rationale of the Supreme Court's concept of property in *Roth* and *Perry*, *see* Simon, *Liberty and Property in the Supreme Court: A Defense of* Roth *and* Perry, 71 CAL. L. REV. 146 (1983).

12. For an in-depth account of the *Goss v. Lopez* decision, including the factual background of the case, profiles of the parties, lawyers, and judges involved, the decision itself, implications of the decision, and an assessment of the case in terms of the value of test-case litigation as a means of protecting children's welfare, *see* R. MNOOKIN, IN THE INTEREST OF CHILDREN 450–508 (1985).

13. 419 U.S. at 574.

14. *Id.* at 581.

15. *Id.* at 583.

16. *Id.*

17. *Id.* at 584.

18. 435 U.S. 78 (1978).

19. The concept of liberty was covered in the preceding chapter as well as some of the cases covered in chapter 4.

20. 435 U.S. at 87, 89–90.

21. Rehnquist, *The Adversary Society: Keynote Address of the Third Annual Baron de Hirsch Meyer Lecture Series*, 33 U. MIAMI L. REV. 1, 2, 14–15 (1978).

22. *Id.* at 8–9.

23. *Id.* at 2.

24. *Id.* at 16. A response to Justice Rehnquist's views and a defense of the adversary process is found in Tribe, *Seven Pluralist Fallacies: In Defense of the Adversary Process—A Reply to Justice Rehnquist*, 33 U. MIAMI L. REV. 43 (1978).

25. Daniels v. Morris, 746 F.2d 271 (5th Cir. 1984).

26. Horton v. Marshall Pub. Schools, 589 F. Supp. 95 (W.D. Ark. 1984).

27. *Id.* at 103.

28. Goldsmith v. Lower Moreland School Dist., 75 Pa. Commw. 288, 461 A.2d 1341 (1983).

29. Lisa H. v. State Bd. of Educ., 67 Pa. Commw. 350, 447 A.2d 669 (1982), *aff'd*, 502 Pa. 613, 467 A.2d 1127 (1983).

30. *Cf.* Board of Educ. v. Rowley, 458 U.S. 176 (1982) (deaf student not entitled to a sign-language interpreter because a "free appropriate education" was satisfied by personalized instruction with adequate support services).

31. Price v. Young, 580 F. Supp. 1 (E.D. Ark. 1983).

32. Karnstein v. Pewaukee School Bd., 557 F. Supp. 565 (E.D. Wis. 1983).

33. Debra P. v. Turlington, 644 F.2d 397 (5th Cir. 1981).

34. Debra P. v. Turlington, 564 F. Supp. 177 (M.D. Fla. 1983).

35. Debra P. v. Turlington, 730 F.2d 1405 (11th Cir. 1984).

36. Regents of the Univ. of Mich. v. Ewing, 106 S. Ct. 507 (1985).

37. Ewing v. Board of Regents, 742 F.2d 913 (6th Cir. 1984).

38. Regents of the Univ. of Mich. v. Ewing, 106 S. Ct. 507 (1985).

39. *Id.* at 513.

40. *Id.*

41. Campbell v. Board of Educ., 193 Conn. 93, 475 A.2d 289 (1984).

42. *See, e.g.*, Albach v. Odle, 531 F.2d 983 (10th Cir. 1976); Parish v. National Collegiate Athletic Ass'n, 506 F.2d 1028 (5th Cir. 1975); National Collegiate Athletic Ass'n v. Gillard, 352 So. 2d 1072 (Miss. 1977); *see also* Regents of University of Minnesota v. National Collegiate Athletic Ass'n, 560 F.2d 352 (8th Cir.), *cert. dismissed*, 434 U.S. 978 (1977) (assuming, without deciding, that such a property interest exists, the procedures employed were within the minimum required by due process). *Contra*, Behagen v. Intercollegiate Conf. of Faculty Reps., 346 F. Supp. 602 (D. Minn. 1972) (college basketball player had a property interest in practicing and playing with team, until such time as hearing could be held, because of the possibility of a remunerative career in professional basketball and because basketball was an integral part of the student athlete's educational experience).

43. *See especially* Albach v. Odle, 531 F.2d 983 (10th Cir. 1976).

44. TEX. EDUC. CODE ANN. § 21.920(b).

45. Spring Branch Indep. School Dist. v. Stamos, 695 S.W.2d 556 (Tex. 1985).

46. Stamos v. Spring Branch Indep. School Dist., 106 S. Ct. 1170 (1986).

47. The rule is set forth and discussed in Bailey v. Truby, 321 S.E.2d 302 (W. Va. 1984).

48. Bailey v. Truby, 321 S.E.2d 302 (W. Va. 1984).

49. Cases *pro* and *con* are cited at 321 S.E.2d at 314-15. The court also quotes from J. WEISTART & C. LOWELL, THE LAW OF SPORTS (1979), which is an excellent treatise on the subject generally.

50. The rule is set forth and discussed by Pennsylvania Interscholastic Athletic Ass'n v. Greater Johnstown School Dist., 76 Pa. Commw. 65, 463 A.2d 1198 (1983).

51. Pennsylvania Interscholastic Athletic Ass'n v. Greater Johnstown School Dist., 76 Pa. Commw. 65, 463 A.2d 1198 (1983).

52. *Id.* at 73, 463 A.2d at 1202.

53. Hebert v. Ventetuolo, 638 F.2d 5 (1st Cir. 1981).

54. The rule is set forth and discussed in Walsh v. Louisiana High School Athletic Ass'n, 616 F.2d 152 (5th Cir. 1980).

55. *Id.* at 159.

56. Blue v. University Interscholastic League, 503 F. Supp. 1030 (N.D. Tex. 1980).

57. *Accord*, Smith v. Crim, 240 Ga. 390, 240 S.E.2d 884 (1977).

58. Rose v. Nashua Bd. of Educ., 679 F.2d 279 (1st Cir. 1982).

59. Pegram v. Nelson, 469 F. Supp. 1134 (M.D.N.C. 1979).

60. *Id.* at 1139, citing Albach v. Odle, mentioned earlier in this chapter, *see* notes 42 & 43 *supra*.

61. *Id.*, quoting from Dallam v. Cumberland Valley School Dist., 391 F. Supp. 358, 361 (M.D. Pa. 1975).

62. *Id.* at 1140.

63. *See* notes 21-24 *supra* and accompanying text.

64. Smith v. Crim, 240 Ga. 390, 240 S.E.2d 884 (1977).

65. Georgia High School Ass'n v. Waddell, 248 Ga. 542, 285 S.E.2d 7 (1981).

66. *Id.* at 543, 285 S.E.2d at 9.

67. Friedman, *The Six Million Dollar Man: Litigation and Rights Consciousness in Modern America*, 39 MD. L. REV. 661, 667 (1980). As reported by Professor Friedman, the case is *In re* Lee Anne G. (4th Dist. Juv. Div. Mn., Aug. 11, 1972).

68. 106 S. Ct. 507 (1985).

69. *See* the excerpt from Justice Rehnquist's opinion for the Court in *Board of Curators v. Horowitz*, quoted near the beginning of this chapter.

70. *See* notes 21-24 *supra* and accompanying text.

71. As examples of "extreme cases," refer to the material on medical decision making for children in chapter 5 and the material on neglect and abuse in chapter 9.

# 8
# The Right to an Education

Public education is not a "right" granted to individuals by the Constitution. But neither is it merely some governmental "benefit" indistinguishable from other forms of social welfare legislation. Both the importance of education in maintaining our basic institutions, and the lasting impact of its deprivation on the life of the child, mark the distinction. The "American people have always regarded education and [the] acquisition of knowledge as matters of supreme importance." We have recognized "the public schools as a most vital civic institution for the preservation of a democratic system of government," and as the primary vehicle for transmitting "the values on which our society rests." "[A]s . . . pointed out early in our history, . . . some degree of education is necessary to prepare citizens to participate effectively and intelligently in our open political system if we are to preserve freedom and independence." . . . In addition, education provides the basic tools by which individuals might lead economically productive lives to the benefit of us all. In sum, education has a fundamental role in maintaining the fabric of our society.

—Justice William J. Brennan
*Plyler v. Doe*
457 U.S. 202, 221 (1982)

## The Nature of the Right to Receive Instruction

*Equality*

Equality has been the central theme of school law since at least 1954.[1] The concept of equality in educational opportunity flows not from constitutional language about education or schooling, but rather from the more general constitutional provisions about equal protection or equal treatment under the law; thus, neither education nor the right to education is mentioned in the United States Constitution, whereas other fundamental principles are.[2] The concept of equality in education, therefore, originated as

This chapter is based largely on J. HOGAN, THE SCHOOLS, THE COURTS, AND THE PUBLIC INTEREST (2d ed. 1985) Copyright ©1985 by D.C. Heath and Company. Parts of it are reproduced or paraphrased here with permission.

judge-made law, derived by the courts from the equal protection clause of the fourteenth amendment and applied by them to the schools; the first cases involved racial discrimination in the schools.[3]

The absence of specific constitutional guidance is also found in the states.[4] In California, for example, the concept of equality in educational opportunity is drawn not from the constitutional language about education itself,[5] but from the more general provisions of the state constitution that require equal treatment for all persons through "uniform general laws"[6] and the prohibition against the granting of special "privileges and immunities."[7] The California Supreme Court has held that these provisions of the state constitution are "substantially equivalent" to the fourteenth amendment of the federal Constitution and has defined education as a "fundamental interest."[8]

In making the connection between the general constitutional provisions about equality and the responsibility of the state to provide all of its children with a "general educational opportunity," the courts, beginning about 1950, have referred to the great public interest served by schooling today.[9] Thus, in 1954 the Supreme Court in *Brown v. Board of Education*[10] established the precept that has been adopted wholeheartedly by federal and state courts in most education cases decided since—namely, that the public interest is broadly served by education:

> Today, education is perhaps the most important function of state and local governments. Compulsory school attendance laws and the great expenditures for education both demonstrate our recognition of the importance of education to our democratic society.[11]

The public benefits of education were also noted: "It is required in the performance of our most basic public responsibilities, even service in the armed forces. It is the very function of good citizenship."[12]

This precept has been embellished on by other courts. Thus, education is a "priceless commodity" and a "fundamental right of every citizen,"[13] a "basic personal right."[14] It is "vital and, indeed, basic to civilized society,"[15] so fundamental as to be "fittingly considered the cornerstone of a vibrant and viable republican form of democracy."[16] This theme of abiding respect for the vital role of education in our society has been echoed in numerous other decisions of the courts, but it reached its pinnacle in *Serrano v. Priest*,[17] wherein the Supreme Court of California declared: "We are convinced that the distinctive and priceless function of education in our society warrants, indeed, compels our treatment of it as a 'fundamental interest.'"[18]

At that high point, however, the precept was shot down by the Supreme Court of the United States in *San Antonio Independent School District v. Rodriguez*:[19] "the importance of a service performed by the State does not determine whether it must be regarded as fundamental for purposes of examination under the Equal Protection Clause."[20] Without detracting in any way from the grave significance of education to the individual and to society and affirming that, in the context of racial discrimination, *Brown v. Board of Education* "has lost none of its vitality with the passage of time," the Supreme Court declared: "Education, of course, is not among the rights afforded explicit protection under our Federal Constitution. Nor do we find any basis for saying it is implicitly so protected."[21] Education, *per se*, is not a federal matter;[22] it was one of the powers left to the states, or to the people, when the Constitution was adopted. The states are thus, constitutionally, the custodians of the public interest in maintaining a public school system that, at a minimum, provides "each child with an opportunity to acquire the basic minimum skills necessary for the enjoyment of the rights of speech and of full participation in the political process."[23] According to *Rodriguez*, the public interest is not served when the federal courts intervene in a school matter that does not involve infringement of a legitimate constitutional right.

## State Control over Education

Education traditionally has been viewed as exclusively a state and local matter, subject to periodic review by the courts, particularly the Supreme Court, to assure that education policies and practices developed at the state and local level meet federal constitutional standards and requirements.[24] Some of these Supreme Court decisions have already been discussed earlier in this book.

In *Meyer v. Nebraska*,[25] for example, the Supreme Court invalidated a Nebraska statute prohibiting the teaching of foreign languages in schools. In *Pierce v. Society of Sisters*[26] the Court, while recognizing that states could probably require children to attend some school, held unconstitutional an Oregon statute requiring children to attend *public* school. In *Tinker v. Des Moines Independent Community School District*[27] the Court held unconstitutional a local school board ban on the wearing of black armbands to protest the Vietnam war, as violative of students' first amendment freedom of expression.

In *Wisconsin v. Yoder*[28] the Court, while again affirming the authority of states generally to compel school attendance, held Wisconsin's compulsory attendance statute unconstitutional to the extent it required attendance of Amish children beyond the eighth grade. The Court held enforcement of the statute violative of their first amendment freedom of religion without any overriding state interest being furthered by enforcement of the attendance law.

To these cases could also be added *Goss v. Lopez*[29] and *Ingraham v. Wright*, [30] as well as the *Brown v. Board of Education*[31] desegregation case itself and, more recently, the school finance case, *San Antonio Independent School District v. Rodriguez*.[32]

Compulsory school attendance laws are an example of state control over public education, and they are universal in all states.[33] A state has authority to compel school attendance in the absence of any infringement of a protected constitutional right, such as freedom of religion.[34] The Supreme Court in *Wisconsin v. Yoder* recognized the state's "paramount responsibility" to educate its citizens, an obligation that empowers states "to impose reasonable regulations for the control and duration of basic education." At the same time, however, the Court emphasized the fact that a state's interest in universal education "is not totally free from a balancing process when it impinges on fundamental rights and interests."[35]

Some exceptions are generally recognized in compulsory attendance statutes—such as attendance at a private school that meets minimum education requirements set by the state for public schools and participation in alternative instruction where the child is unable to attend school because of a physical or mental disability.[36] In *Wisconsin v. Yoder* the Court itself created an additional exception to compulsory attendance where it unreasonably interferes with a genuinely held religious belief.

The *Yoder* exception appears to be a very narrow one, applicable perhaps only to the Amish. Other religious groups have had little success in challenging compulsory attendance laws, usually because the teachers at their private schools have not been certified by the state or their educational program does not meet reasonable state requirements.[37] Furthermore, the Court in *Yoder* indicated that a free exercise of religion claim must be firmly rooted in a sincerely held religious belief, as opposed to philosophical or social beliefs. In *In re McMillan*[38] a North Carolina appellate court refused to allow a *Yoder* exception for American Indian children. The parents claimed that the decision to keep their children home from school was based on failure of the school system to present adequate instruction in American Indian culture, and that their sincerely held cultural beliefs, like religious beliefs, were entitled to constitutional protection.

An exception to compulsory school attendance is often allowed for adequate home instruction, which may be a separate exception or may fall within the private school exception. Some states require that instruction be given by a "competent" or "qualified" person;[40] most simply require that home instruction be the equivalent of that offered in the public schools.[41] Emphasis is on the "adequacy" of home instruction. The outcome of court decisions has varied, depending on whether parents have met the burden of showing that home instruction is the equal of that obtainable in the public schools in terms of instruction in the required subjects, number of hours of instruction per day, number of days of instruction per year, record keeping, adequacy of library materials, and the like.[42]

Another exception to compulsory attendance—actually an exemption because no alternative to public education, such as attendance at a private school, is required—sometimes is allowed in the case of a child emancipated by marriage. In *In re Rogers*[43] a New York court allowed an exemption for a fifteen-year-old girl who had been lawfully married since age fourteen, even though marriage was not an exception or exemption under the compulsory attendance law. Comparing this case with the vaccination cases,[44] the court found it "ludicrous" that a child who had not been vaccinated could be excluded but that attendance of a married fifteen-year-old girl with other, unmarried fifteen-year-old children could be compelled. Occasionally, however, marriage is not recognized as an exception or exemption.[45]

Two common threads seem to run through the caselaw dealing with compulsory school attendance. First, regardless of what sort of claim is raised by the individual, courts are concerned with asserting the state's interest in maintaining an educated citizenry, and this interest usually prevails absent some overriding right of parents entitled to constitutional protection. Second, courts and legislatures alike are concerned with the presence of an adequate alternative to public education. The universality, and to a degree the inflexibility, of compulsory school attendance laws suggests a need for increased flexibility in both available alternatives and sanctions for noncompliance.[46]

In *In re Peters*,[47] for example, a North Carolina appellate court reversed an adjudication of delinquency of a fifteen-year-old boy based on his truancy. The court observed:

> Eddie obviously is a child who should be afforded some technical training where he can use his hands and develop his aptitudes along that line and have some motivation. He obviously does not take to book learning. Forcing him into a classical schoolroom introduces a disruptive element which is not good for the school, the teachers, the other students and likewise is not good for Eddie.[48]

A number of states offer vocational education as an alternative to traditional classroom instruction for children who are so inclined.[49]

## Eligibility to Receive a Free Public Education

There are many barriers to free access to a public education, and the courts have sought to dismantle most of them, including those based on race, wealth, sex, residence, national origin, and intelligence. Although there may not be a constitutional right to education as such, if it is provided by the state at all, it must be provided to all on an equal basis.[50] It may not be denied for any of the reasons just mentioned. This is the essence of the constitutional right to equal protection of the laws. Following is a discussion of some of the barriers to free access to public education, on the basis of which free access may not be denied.

## Race or Color

Today a public education may not be denied on account of a person's race or color, but that was not always true. The "separate but equal" doctrine sanctioning a system of segregated schools for blacks and whites was approved as early as 1849,[51] and received the Supreme Court's blessing as late as 1896.[52] That changed, of course, with the Supreme Court's momentous desegregation decision in *Brown v. Board of Education* in 1954.

In the name of securing compliance with the *Brown* decision, courts have exercised broad control over the organization, administration, and programs of the public schools, including the power to reopen schools closed by local school districts to avoid desegregation and the power to prohibit the closing of schools for the same reason; the power to order state taxation for support of schools; the power to order assignment of pupils and teachers to specific schools to achieve racial balance and to order special remedial programs; the power to order studies made of school district desegregation plans, involving the hiring of additional personnel and mandating that the costs thereof be paid by the state board of education; and the power to order busing to achieve racial balance.[53]

Some states, most notably California, have taken steps to alleviate racial imbalance in schools regardless of whether the imbalance is *de jure* (by operation of law—that is, intentionally caused) or *de facto* (in fact). The landmark California decision on school desegregation is *Jackson v. Pasadena City School District*,[54] wherein the California Supreme Court held that (on the basis of state law) *de facto* racial segregation in the public schools of the state is "an evil" and that school boards should take affirmative steps to eliminate racial imbalance, however created. The court said that

> it should be pointed out that even in the absence of gerrymandering or other affirmative discriminatory conduct by a school board, a student under some circumstances would be entitled to relief where, by reason of residential segregation, substantial racial imbalance exists in his school.[55]

The court noted that as long as large numbers of blacks live in segregated areas, school authorities will face the difficult situation of providing them with the kind of education to which they are entitled, since "[r]esidential segregation is in itself an evil which tends to frustrate the youth in the area and to cause antisocial attitudes and behavior."[56] Further:

> Where such segregation exists, it is not enough for a school board to refrain from affirmative discriminatory conduct. . . . The right to an equal opportunity for education and the harmful consequences of segretion require that school boards take steps, *insofar as reasonably feasible*, to alleviate racial imbalance in schools regardless of its cause.[57]

This statement has been quoted and reaffirmed many times since as the law as it stands today in California.[58] However, not all state and federal courts accept the California doctrine that school districts have an affirmative duty to eliminate racial imbalance in the schools.[59]

In *Winston-Salem/Forsyth County Board of Education v. Scott*[60] Chief Justice Burger referred to the school board's apparent misunderstanding—that it was *required* to achieve a fixed racial balance that reflected the total composition of the school district—as "disturbing":

> If we were to read the holding of the District Court to require, as a matter of substantive constitutional right, any particular degree of racial imbalance or mixing, *that approach would be disapproved and we would be obliged to reverse*. The constitutional command to desegregate schools does not mean that every school in every community must always reflect the racial composition of the school system as a whole.[61]

The determination of racial balance is an "obvious and necessary starting point" for courts to decide whether in fact any violation exists.

## Age

States typically provide age requirements for school admission and a maximum age requirement for free school attendance.[62] A minimum age of six as a requirement for school admission is not uncommon. The maximum age is sometimes determined by the number of years a student has been in the school system, usually twelve. Such age requirements, established by the legislature as part of an overall plan to allocate limited financial resources, are given great deference by the courts.[63]

For example, in *Hammond v. Marx*[64] a federal district court upheld a constitutional challenge to Maine's requirement that, in order to be admitted to first grade, a child must be or become six years of age on or before October 15 of the school year. The child in question was born on December 19, 1967, and in August of 1973 he sought to enroll in the first grade. He was informed that he did not meet the age requirement since he was sixty-five days short of his sixth birthday. His father insisted that his son was precocious and that he be given a readiness test. The school system refused, and the father brought suit challenging the age requirement on due process and equal protection grounds.

The court first established as the appropriate standard of review the rational basis test—that is, whether a reasonable basis exists for the statutory scheme. The court upheld the statute because it was the product of careful thought and planning, reflecting the conclusions that (1) "a significant correlation exists between chronological age and school readiness and that very few underage children are in fact ready to begin school"; (2) the cost of administering a readiness test to each student was $70 in 1960; (3) a dearth of qualified examiners exists; and (4) reliability of test results for school readiness is not clearly established.[65] The court concurred in the legislative judgment that the six-year minimum age requirement reasonably reflects the readiness of children for first grade. For similar reasons the court upheld the statute against the due process challenge.

### Residence or National Origin

School systems typically have rules requiring students to attend school in the district in which they reside, at least for purposes of attending public school tuition-free. If the family moves to another district, the child must attend school in the new district or else pay tuition at the school in the former district. These residence requirements have generally been upheld by the courts.[66]

On the other hand, in *Plyer v. Doe*[67] the Supreme Court held unconstitutional a Texas statute withholding from school districts any funds for the education of undocumented alien children and authorizing school districts to deny enrollment to such children. The statute was held in violation of the equal protection clause, which provides that no state shall "deny to any person within its jurisdiction the equal protection of the laws."[68] Even aliens illegally in the country are "persons" within the meaning of the equal protection clause.

Such discrimination is not rational, the Court said, unless it furthers a substantial state interest, and the Court found no such interest being served here. The Court rejected arguments that the prohibition was an effective means of furthering the state's interest in (1) preserving its limited resources for education of its lawful residents; (2) stemming the tide of illegal immigration into the state; (3) maintaining an unburdened ability to provide high quality public education; or (4) avoiding investment in children less likely than others to remain in the state and put thier education to productive social or political use in the state.[69]

### Sex

Discrimination in admission requirements based on sex violates the equal protection clause of the fourteenth amendment. In *Berkelman v. San Francisco*

*United School District,*[70] for example, the court struck down, on equal protection grounds, the school district's policy requiring a higher academic standard for girls than for boys for admission to a college preparatory public high school.

Lowell High School each year accepted those applicants whose prior academic performance placed them in the top 15 percent of the middle school graduates in the district. Girls, however, were required to have a 3.25 average (later a 3.50 average) to be admitted, whereas boys were only required to have a 3.0 average (later a 3.25 average) for admission. The school district defended this policy by claiming it was necessary to maintain an equal ratio of boys to girls.

The court applied a stricter test than the rational basis test, requiring that in cases of alleged sex discrimination, a statute to be valid must *substantially* further some legitimate governmental objective.[71] No evidence was offered in this case to show that a sexual balance furthered any valid educational goal. Therefore, the discriminatory admissions policy violated equal protection of the laws.[72] The court also indicated that had these courses been offered in each high school rather than a separate high school, and had the same admission standards been applied, this practice would have been unlawful under Title IX of the Education Amendments of 1972.[73]

## Pregnancy

The assertion was made earlier in this chapter that a married minor may claim an exemption from the compulsory attendance law.[74] In converse, if she desires to attend school she certainly has a right to do so. Suppose, however, that she is pregnant, and the school district denies her admission for that reason. In *Shull v. Columbus Municipal Separate School District*[75] the court held that a school district's denial of admission to an unwed mother, solely for the reason that she was an unwed mother, was a denial of equal protection of the laws.[76] The court indicated that the school board could hold a due process hearing[77] to determine whether the girl was "so lacking in moral character that her presence in the public school would taint the education of other students."[78] Absent such a showing, however, the girl was entitled to admission.

## Health

Throughout this chapter the point has been made that if a state is going to deprive a person of his life, liberty, or property, (1) the state must have a valid objective, and (2) the means used must be reasonably (or sometimes *substantially*) calculated to achieve that objective. The courts have consistently held, for example, that the state may require school-age children to submit to vaccination before attending school.[79] The state's objective is clear: to provide for the general health and well-being of school children. If children are to remain in reasonably good health and attend school regularly, they require immunization from common diseases. This is a valid objective, and vaccination is a means reasonably calculated to achieve the objective.[80]

In *Avard v. Dupuis*[81] the court held unconstitutionally vague a law giving local school boards complete discretionary authority to grant a religious exemption from the vaccination requirement. The plaintiff had applied for but been denied an exemption for his son and brought suit seeking to have the law declared unconstitutional and to have his son readmitted to school. The court, while holding the religious exemption unconstitutional, let the vaccination requirement itself stand; therefore, the student was not reinstated without evidence of vaccination.

Also, for valid health reasons a school may exclude unsanitary or obscenely or scantily clad students from school.[82] However, a school regulation prohibiting the wearing of dungarees was held unconstitutional in the absence of any showing that the prohibition was reasonably related to a valid educational purpose (that is, health).[83]

## Testing, Grades, and Evaluation

**Competency Tests for Graduation.** A competency test is a standardized test designed to determine whether a student has reached a prescribed level of proficiency in one or more basic skills.[84] Such tests are used in some states as functional literacy tests that students must pass to receive a high school diploma.

In *Debra P. v. Turlington*[85] students claimed such a test was racially discriminatory because the failure rate among black students was much higher than that among white students. The federal district court first acknowledged that since the minority children had spent their initial years of schooling in segregated, inferior schools, requiring them to take the same test as white children who had benefitted from superior schools was a violation of equal protection of the laws. An injunction was issued prohibiting the use of the test for four years to remedy the discrimination. The case was appealed,[86] and on remand from the Fifth Circuit Court of Appeals the district court found that the disproportionate failure rate among blacks was not causally linked to the present effects of past segregation. The test was found "instructionally valid" and therefore constitutional.[87]

To the contrary, in *Anderson v. Banks*[88] a federal district court imposed an injunction against such a test on equal protection grounds (because of early segregated education) and in addition found the test to be violative of Title VI of the Civil Rights Act of 1964[89] and the Equal Educational Opportunities Act of 1974.[90]

The competency test movement has surged and since ebbed, but more challenges to such testing might be expected.[91]

**Achievement and Aptitude Tests for Placement.** Courts have questioned other uses of achievement tests and scholastic aptitude tests[92] in the schools. A number of cases have challenged the constitutionality of such tests when they are used for pupil placement purposes. Although such tests may be used for student placement, they must be shown to contain no bias against any cultural, racial, or ethnic group.[93]

Courts in the South have held that assignment to classes on the basis of achievement test scores is not permissible if its effect is to resegregate students. In *Singleton v. Jackson Municipal Separate School District*[94] the Fifth Circuit held that testing in any event could not be used for assignment purposes until unitary schools had been established. "Heterogeneous, racially integrated classes" were ordered by the court in *Moses v. Washington Parish School Board*,[95] which involved standardized ability and achievement tests administered to students in a recently desegregated school. Assignments of students were to eleven levels (instead of six grades) on the basis of their test scores, and within each level the students were grouped homogeneously into sections. The basis of the grouping was the students' scores in reading but not in mathematics and science. The court said that black students, subjected to such testing for the first time, were put at a disadvantage by being tested in reading alone, in which they tended to score lower than in mathematics and science.[96]

*Lemon v. Bossier Parish School Board*[97] held that a school district that had operated as a unitary system for only one semester could not assign students to schools within the district on the basis of achievement test scores. Citing *Singleton*,[98] the Fifth Circuit said that

> In *Singleton* we made it clear that regardless of the innate validity of testing, it could not be used until a school district had been established as a unitary system. We think at a minimum this means that the district in question must have for several years operated as a unitary system.[99]

**Intelligence Tests for Placement.** Two recent cases have dealt with the issue of intelligence testing for the placement of black children in classes for educable mentally retarded (EMR) students. In *Larry P. v. Riles*[100] a federal district court ruled that intelligence (IQ) tests are discriminatory toward blacks and could no longer be used for educational placement in California. The court granted a preliminary injunction against such future testing, which was upheld on appeal.[101] The district court later issued a permanent injunction against the use of IQ testing for EMR placement,[102] which judgment was also upheld.[103]

In *Parents in Action on Special Education v. Hannon*[104] another federal distict court found that nine items on three IQ tests were culturally biased, but held that when used in conjunction with other criteria, the tests could be used for educational placement of black children in the Chicago public schools. The court acknowledged the similarity of the case to the *Larry P.* case but stated that

> Judge Peckham's lengthy and scholarly opinion is largely devoted to the question of what legal consequences flow from a finding of racial bias in the tests. There is relatively little analysis of the threshold question of whether test bias in fact exists, and Judge Peckham even remarked that the cultural bias of the tests . . . "is hardly disputed in this litigation. . . ."[105]

Unwilling to assume cultural bias in the tests, the court undertook a three-week, item-by-item analysis of each of the three tests—the Stanford-Binet, the Wechsler Intelligence Scale of Children (WISC), and the Wechsler Intelligence Scale for Children Revised (WISC-R). Having identified a total of nine items on the three tests as racially biased, the court concluded that the possibility of the items causing a child to be placed improperly in an EMR class was practically nonexistent. Therefore, the court ruled in favor of the defendants and allowed continued use of IQ testing in the placement of children in EMR classes in Chicago public schools.

Low IQ test scores, low achievement test scores, and language deficiencies were cited in *Serna v. Portales Municipal Schools*[106] to show that Hispanic students were denied equal educational opportunity because the school system's educational programs were tailored for middle-class Anglo children without regard for the "educational needs" of Spanish-speaking children. The court rejected arguments that the "special needs" of the children were not the result of "state action" and that financial considerations made expansion of bilingual/bicultural programs impossible.[107]

**Tracking Systems.** In *Hobson v. Hansen*[108] a federal district court invalidated the "track system" then being used in the public schools in Washington, D.C. Scores on aptitude tests were employed to assign students to the various tracks. The court's opinion looked in detail at the use and misuse of tests, the accuracy of test measurements, and misjudgments and "under-education" resulting from use of test scores for student placement purposes. The court found that

> The track system as used in the District's public schools is a form of ability grouping in which students are divided in separate, self-contained curricula or tracks ranging from "Basic" for the slow student to "Honors" for the gifted.
>
> The aptitude tests used to assign children to the various tracks are standardized primarily on white middle-class children. Since these tests do not relate to the Negro and disadvantaged child, track assignment based on

such tests relegates Negro and disadvantaged children to the lower tracks from which, because of the reduced curricula and the absence of adequate remedial and compensatory education, as well as continued inappropriate testing, the chance of escape is remote.

Education in the lower tracks is geared to . . . the "blue collar" student. Thus such children, so stigmatized by inappropriate aptitude testing procedures, are denied equal opportunity to obtain the white collar education available to the white and more affluent children.[109]

Consequently, the defendants were permanently enjoined from operating the track system in the District of Columbia.[110]

Tracking must be reduced to the minimum required for a sound education. Fast learners may move ahead, while slow learners may move at their own pace. Thus, fast learner and slow learner sections are proper if no racial discrimination is involved.[111]

**Grades.** In chapter 7 of this book student challenges to academic grading practices were discussed. For example, in *Campbell v. Board of Education*,[112] high school students challenged the school board's policy of imposing academic sanctions on students for nonattendance (course credit was withheld for any student missing more than twenty-four classes in a year-long course). The Court held that there had been no infringement of the students' property interest in a fairly administered grading system because the evidence failed to show that the policy, which was universally known to students, was applied in an arbitrary or capricious way.[113]

**Educational Malpractice.** A number of students recently have sought to establish a tort action for what has come to be known as educational malpractice, but in the cases decided thus far school authorities have been held not accountable for the students' failure to attain basic academic skills.

In *Peter W. v. San Francisco Unified School District*,[114] for example, an eighteen-year-old with a history of "social promotion" alleged the schools had been negligent in failing to provide him with adequate instruction in the basic skills and nevertheless had promoted him knowing that he had not achieved the level of proficiency required to prepare him for the next level of instruction. He sought damages based on his inability to obtain gainful employment and costs incurred for remedial tutoring. His claim was dismissed, however, for two reasons: the absence of a basis for a teacher's duty to educate students successfully and the fact that other, non–school-related factors affect the attainment of literacy in the schools.

On similar facts, the New York Court of Appeals reached an identical result in *Donohue v. Copiague Union Free School District*.[115] The New

York court was of the view that as a matter of policy courts should not entertain such claims:

> To entertain a cause of action for "educational malpractice" would require the courts not merely to make judgments as to the validity of broad educational policies—a course we have unalteringly eschewed in the past—but, more importantly, to sit in review of the day-to-day implementation of these policies. Recognition . . . of this cause of action would constitute blatant interference with the responsibility for the administration of the public school system lodged by Constitution and statute in school administrative agencies.[116]

The *Donohue* rationale has been applied in subsequent cases,[117] indicating the difficulty courts are experiencing in dealing with alleged negligence in the educational process.[118]

### Bilingualism and Biculturalism

Although English is the basic language used for instruction in the public schools, bilingual instruction is authorized if the school board finds that it would be advantageous to the students. In *Lau v. Nichols*[119] the Supreme Court held that failure of the San Francisco school system to provide needed Engligh-language instruction to Chinese students who did not speak English violated section 601 of the Civil Rights Act of 1964,[120] which bans discrimination based on race, color, or national origin in any program receiving federal funds, as well as implementing regulations of the Department of Health, Education, and Welfare.[121] On the other hand, if the school system has adopted measures to cure language deficiencies of non–English-speaking students, students are not entitled to bilingual instructors.[122]

Recently, some suits have been filed alleging both cultural and socioeconomic bias in testing. For example, alleged white Anglo cultural and linguistic bias in IQ tests was an issue in *Serna v. Portales Municipal Schools.*[123] The federal district court, however, did not rule that the tests themselves were biased; it ruled only that deficiencies having been shown as a result of the tests, the school district had an obligation to enlarge its program of services and support to Spanish-speaking children.

In *Diana v. State Board of Education*[124] the court was concerned with cultural bias in standardized tests that were used to place Diana and eight other children in special education classes for mildly retarded children. The tests, it was alleged, were biased against Mexican-American students because they were standardized on white, middle-class norms and were inappropriate because they relied on verbal aptitude in English rather than Spanish.[125] The case was settled out of court.

## Mental or Physical Handicap

Under the Education for All Handicapped Children Act of 1975,[126] popularly known as Public Law 94-142, handicapped children are entitled to a "free appropriate education" in the "least restrictive environment." Handicapped child under the act includes those who are mentally retarded, hard of hearing, deaf, speech or language impaired, visually handicapped, seriously emotionally disturbed, orthopedically impaired, or other health impaired or who have a specific learning disability.[127]

The act envisions each handicapped child's being provided with an individualized plan of instruction. It places a number of specific requirements regarding placement alternatives and special schools or instruction on those states deciding to adhere to the act in order to qualify for certain federal funding. States are required to make available certain "support services," "medical services," or "related services" in order to provide handicapped children a "free appropriate education."

An eight-year-old girl in Texas suffered from spina bifida, a congenital condition that left her with orthopedic and speech impairments and a neurogenic bladder, which prevented her from emptying her bladder voluntarily. As a result, she had to be catheterized every three or four hours to avoid injury to her kidneys. This was accomplished by a procedure known as clean intermittent catheterization (CIC), a procedure that can be performed in a few minutes by a lay person with as little as an hour's training. In *Irving Independent School District v. Tatro*[128] the Supreme Court held that CIC is a "related service" required to be provided by the school district as a part of the child's right to a "free appropriate education" under the Education for All Handicapped Children Act.

In another case a seven-year-old multihandicapped student suffered from an inability to control his body temperature. The school proposed to furnish him an air-conditioned plexiglass cubicle within the regular classroom. The boy and his parents, however, went to court asking for an air-conditioned classroom so the boy could interact fully with his classmates. In *Espino v. Besteiro*[129] the federal district court issued a preliminary injunction requiring the school to provide a fully air-conditioned classroom under the mandate of the act.

On the other hand, in *Board of Education v. Rowley*[130] the Supreme Court rejected the claim of parents of a deaf child that the act required the state to furnish a qualified sign-language interpreter for all of the child's academic classes. Justice Rehnquist, writing for the Court, explained that the standard imposed on states by the act is not "to maximize the potential of each handicapped child commensurate with the opportunity provided non-handicapped children" but instead "to identify and evaluate handicapped children, and to provide them with access to a free public education."[131]

Other legislation also may require states to accommodate the special needs of handicapped children. The spina bifida condition of a West Virginia child left her with a minor physical impairment that included incontinence of the bowels and a noticeable limp. The school board refused to admit her to a regular kindergarten classroom, and her parents filed suit. In *Hairston v. Drosick*[132] the federal district court held that exclusion of the child from the regular classroom in public school in the absence of a valid educational reason was a violation of Title V of the Rehabilitation Act of 1973,[133] which prohibits discrimination against and denial of benefits to handicapped persons in any program receiving federal funds. The court also held that removal of the child from the regular classroom without notice or a hearing was a denial of due process of law.[134]

## Religion and Education

### State Authority to Control Nonpublic Education

The authority of the state over education versus the right of parents to select a nonpublic school, religious or military, for their children was litigated in 1925 in *Pierce v. Society of Sisters*.[135] The Oregon Compulsory Education Act, which required parents of children between the ages of eight and sixteen years to send them to public schools only, was declared an unreasonable interference with the right of parents to direct the upbringing of their children. To choose between a public education or an education at a nonpublic school (religious or otherwise) for their children was described as a "fundamental liberty" of parents under the Constitution's fourteenth amendment. Said the Court, there is no "general power of the State to standardize its children by forcing them to accept instruction from public teachers only."[136] This 1925 landmark case established the law on this subject.

In 1972 a clear conflict between religious belief and the Wisconsin compulsory school attendance law arose in the case of *Wisconsin v. Yoder*[137] where it was decided that the first and fourteenth amendments prevent a state from compelling Amish parents to cause their children who have graduated from eighth grade to attend formal public or private high school to age sixteen. The Court thus further limited the state's control over education, saying that

a state's interest in universal education . . . is not totally free from a balancing process when it impinges on fundamental rights and interests, such as those specifically protected by the Free Exercise Clause of the First Amendment, and the traditional interest of parents with respect to the religious upbringing of their children.[138]

The Amish were found to have "amply supported their claim"—namely, that enforcement of the compulsory formal education requirement after the eighth grade "would gravely endanger if not destroy the free exercise of their religious beliefs." The evidence showed that the Amish provide continuing informal vocational education to their children that is designed to prepare them for life in the rural Amish community.[139] This decision was a major addition to the law affecting the rights of parents and of the states regarding the education of children.

## Textbooks

A very early case, *Cochran v. Louisiana State Board of Education*,[140] challenged the constitutionality of a state statute providing free textbooks to school children. A Louisiana law authorized the use of public funds to purchase schoolbooks. It also directed the state board of education to provide the books to "school children free of cost to such children." The Supreme Court held that the law was not a violation of the state constitution nor of the fourteenth amendment to the federal Constitution. The plaintiffs contended that the purpose of the law was to aid private, religious, sectarian, and other schools not embraced in the public education system by furnishing free textbooks to the children attending such schools. This was answered by a quotation from the decision of the state supreme court:

> One may scan the acts in vain to ascertain where any money is appropriated for the purchase of school books for the use of any church, private, sectarian or even public school. The appropriations were made for the specific purpose of purchasing school books for the use of the school children of the state, free of cost to them.[141]

The "child benefit theory" was then recognized in this case as formulated by the state court:

> It was for their benefit and the resulting benefit to the state that the appropriations were made. True, these children attend some school, public or private, the latter, sectarian or non-sectarian, and that the books are to be furnished them for their use, free of cost, whichever they attend. The schools however are not the beneficiaries of these appropriations. They obtain nothing from them, nor are they relieved of a single obligation, because of them. The school children and the state alone are the beneficiaries.[142]

The Supreme Court thus adopted the Louisiana Supreme Court's statement of the child benefit theory and concluded its opinion, by Chief Justice Hughes, as follows:

> [W]e can not doubt that the taxing power of the State is exerted for a public purpose. The legislation does not segregate private schools, or their pupils, as its beneficiaries or attempt to interfere with any matters of exclusively private concern. Its interest is education, broadly; its method comprehensive. Individual interests are aided only as the common interest is safeguarded.[143]

This case was followed in 1968 by *Board of Education v. Allen*,[144] wherein local school boards sought to obtain a declaration from the state courts that New York's Education Law, requiring local public school authorities to lend textbooks free of charge to all students in grades seven through twelve, including those in private schools, violated the federal and state constitutions. The state court of appeals said that the law was a benefit to all school children, without regard to the type of school they attended, and that the law was "completely neutral with respect to religion." The Supreme Court likewise held that the New York law did not violate the establishment clause nor the free exercise clause of the first amendment. The Court noted that the express purpose of the law was the furtherance of educational opportunities for the young and that "the law merely [made] available to all children the benefits of a general program to lend school books free of charge." It said that the financial benefit is "to parents and children, not to schools," and it found no evidence that religious books had been loaned.[145] Thus, the child benefit theory was perpetuated.

*Meek v. Pittenger*[146] involved two Pennsylvania laws that authorized the state to provide directly to all children enrolled in nonpublic elementary and secondary schools "auxiliary services" and the loans of textbooks acceptable for use in the public schools. The acts also provided for the loan directly to such nonpublic schools of "instructional material and equipment, useful to the education" of nonpublic school children. The auxiliary services included testing, counseling, psychological services, speech and hearing therapy, related services for exceptional, remedial, or educationally disadvantaged students, "and such other secular, neutral, nonideological services as are of benefit to nonpublic school children" and are provided to those in the public schools. The instructional materials included periodicals, photographs, maps, charts, recordings, and films. The equipment included projectors, recorders, and laboratory paraphernalia.

The Court held that all of the provisions except the textbook loan provisions violated the establishment clause of the first amendment as made applicable to the states by the fourteenth amendment. The textbook loan provisions were constitutional since they "merely [made] available to all children the benefits of a general program to lend school books free of charge" and the "financial benefit is to the parents and children, not to schools."[147]

There are limitations on this theory, however. In *Norwood v. Harrison*[148] the Supreme Court held that textbooks purchased by the state and loaned to students in both public and private schools, without reference to whether any private school discriminates on the basis of race, is prohibited. In reversing a three-judge district court that had sustained the validity of a Mississippi statutory program whereby textbooks were purchased by the state and loaned to the schools, the Court said:

> In *Pierce*, the Court affirmed the right of private schools to exist and to operate. . . . [However], a State's special interest in elevating the quality of education in both public and private schools does not mean that the State must grant aid to private schools without regard to constitutionally mandated standards forbidding state-supported discrimination.[149]

The Court went on to notice that the establishment clause permits a greater degree of state assistance to sectarian schools than may be given to private schools that engage in discriminatory practices. It said that "[f]ree textbooks, like tuition grants directed to private school students, are a form of financial assistance inuring to the benefit of the private schools themselves."[150]

Four years later, in *Wolman v. Walter*[151] an Ohio statute came under challenge because it provided for the loan to nonpublic students of textbooks, standardized tests and scoring services, speech and hearing diagnostic services, specialized therapeutic, guidance, and remedial services, instructional materials and equipment, and field trip transportation and services. The district court held the statute constitutional in all respects. On appeal, however, the Supreme Court held that those portions of the statute providing nonpublic school students with textbooks, standardized tests and scoring, diagnostic services, and therapeutic and remedial services were constitutional. Those portions of the statute relating to instructional materials and equipment and field trip services were unconstitutional. The textbook loan system was described as strikingly similar to the systems approved in *Board of Education v. Allen* and *Meek v. Pittenger*, which were followed.

## Transportation

In 1947 the Supreme Court affirmed the constitutionality of busing nonpublic school students in *Everson v. Board of Education*.[152] A New Jersey statute authorized local school districts to make contracts for the transportation of children to schools "other than private schools operated for profit." A taxpayer challenged a board resolution authorizing the reimbursement of parents for fares paid for the transportation by public carrier of children attending public and Catholic schools. (No question was raised regarding whether the exclusion of private schools operated for profit denied them equal protection of the laws.) The Supreme Court held that the expenditure of tax money as thus authorized was for a public purpose and did not violate the due process clause of the fourteenth amendment nor any provisions of the first amendment (establishment clause) made applicable to the states by the fourteenth amendment.

Thus, along with the lending of textbooks to nonpublic schools, transportation was sanctioned by the Court as not being a violation of any provisions of the federal Constitution.

### Public Funds for Nonpublic Schools

Most of the cases involving the expenditure of public funds for nonpublic education have arisen in states in the East—for example, New York, Rhode Island, Pennsylvania, and New Jersey. In 1971 Rhode Island and Pennsylvania statutes providing public funds for nonpublic schools were struck down in *Lemon v. Kurtzman*.[153] The Rhode Island statute provided for a 15 percent salary supplement to be paid by the state to teachers in nonpublic schools that were mostly Roman Catholic affiliated. The Pennsylvania statute authorized the state to "purchase" certain "secular educational services" from the nonpublic schools, thus reimbursing them directly for such things as teachers' salaries, textbooks, and instructional materials. Most of the 20 percent of the students in nonpublic schools were in schools affiliated with the Roman Catholic Church.

The Court held both statutes unconstitutional under the religion clauses of the first amendment, saying that they involved excessive entanglement between the government and religion. The tests for such entanglement were set out as follows, with the Court saying that every analysis in this area must begin with consideration of the cumulative criteria developed by the Court over many years:

> First, the statute must have a secular legislative purpose; second, its principal or primary effect must be one that neither advances nor inhibits religion; finally, the statute must not foster "an excessive government entanglement with religion."[154]

In the Rhode Island case, the entanglement arose because of the religious activity and purpose of the church-affiliated schools, which would require "continuing state surveillance" to ensure that the statutory restrictions were obeyed. The entanglement in the Pennsylvania case arose from the "restrictions and surveillance" necessary to ensure that teachers play a strictly nonideological role and the state supervision of accounting procedures.

In a subsequent decision in the same case,[155] the Court held that Pennsylvania could reimburse the sectarian nonpublic schools for services performed before the 1971 decision invalidating the state statute. Recognizing that "statutory or even judge-made rules of law are hard facts on which people must rely in making decisions and in shaping their conduct,"[156] the Court noted that the schools had relied in "good faith" on the statute that had invited the contract and had authorized the reimbursement.[157]

In *Levitt v. Committee for Public Education and Religious Liberty*[158] the Court held as an impermissible aid to religion violative of the establishment clause of the first amendment a New York statute authorizing the state to reimburse nonpublic schools for services in connection with the administration, grading, compiling, and reporting of the results of tests and examinations, as required by state law. It said that the statute provided no means to ensure that "internally prepared" tests were free of religious instruction.

Following this decision, the New York legislature enacted a new statute, which, unlike the earlier version of the law, provided a means by which the state funds appropriated for the administration, grading, and reporting of the results of the tests would be audited, thus assuring that the actual costs reimbursed covered only secular services. The district court upheld this statute, and the Supreme Court, in *Committee for Public Education and Religious Liberty v. Regan*,[159] held that the statute was now constitutional under the first and fourteenth amendments.

In *Committee for Public Education and Religious Liberty v. Nyquist*[160] a New York law that provided for aid to nonpublic schools in the form of (1) maintenance and repair grants, (2) tuition reimbursement grants, and (3) income tax benefits for parents was held by the Supreme Court in all respects to have the primary effect of advancing religion and offending the establishment clause of the first amendment. The Court said that "the propriety of a legislature's purpose may not immunize from further scrutiny a law which either has a primary effect that advances religion, or which fosters excessive entanglements between Church and State."[161]

A Pennsylvania statute providing for reimbursement of tuition paid by parents who send their children to nonpublic schools was declared unconstitutional under the establishment clause of the first amendment in *Sloan v. Lemon*.[162] The statute had the impermissible effect of advancing religion and the Court saw no constitutional difference between this Pennsylvania scheme and the New York tuition reimbursement program declared unconstitutional in *Nyquist*. There was no indication in the statute of possible separate treatment of parents sending their children to sectarian schools and those sending their children to nonsectarian, nonpublic schools. Said the Court:

> [W]e have been shown no reason to upset the District Court's conclusion that aid to the nonsectarian school could not be severed from aid to the sectarian. . . . Even if [it] were clearly severable, valid aid to nonpublic,

nonsectarian schools would provide no lever for aid to their sectarian counterparts. The Equal Protection Clause has never been regarded as a bludgeon with which to compel a state to violate other provisions of the Constitution. Having held that tuition reimbursements for the benefit of sectarian schools violate the Establishment Clause, nothing in the Equal Protection Clause will suffice to revive that program.[163]

In *Mueller v. Allen*,[164] decided in 1983, however, the Supreme Court upheld a state scheme allowing parents of nonpublic school children to deduct tuition payments from their state income taxes.

## Release Time for Religious Instruction

The first case on the subject of release time to come before the Supreme Court, *Illinois ex rel McCollum v. Board of Education*,[165] held that a release time program whereby students were released to attend religious instruction in public school classrooms located on the school campus, violated the first amendment. With the permission of the local board of education, religious teachers were employed (with the approval and supervision of the superintendent of public schools) by a private religious group, including representatives of Catholic, Protestant, and Jewish faiths, to give religious instruction in the public school buildings once each week. On their parents' request, pupils were released from class for this religious instruction, but other pupils were not released from their public school duties. Said the Court:

> Pupils compelled by law to go to school for secular education are released in part from their legal duty upon the condition that they attend the religious classes. This is beyond all question a utilization of the tax-established and tax-supported public school system to aid religious groups to spread their faith. And it falls squarely under the ban of the First Amendment (made applicable to the States by the Fourteenth) as we interpreted it in *Everson v. Board of Education*.[166]

Four years later, however, in *Zorach v. Clauson*,[167] a New York statute providing for release of public school pupils to attend religious classes given off school property was held constitutional. The New York statutory scheme, said the Court, neither prohibited the free exercise of religion nor sought to establish religion within the meaning of the first amendment. Also, the Court found no evidence in the record to support a conclusion that the system involved the use of coercion to get public school students into religious classrooms. The Court distinguished *McCollum:* "This 'released time' program involves neither religious instruction in public school classrooms nor the expenditure of public funds. All costs, including the application blanks, are paid by the religious organizations."[168]

In 1981, in *Widmar v. Vincent,*[169] the Court held that a state university rule forbidding use of public school facilities by registered student groups for religious services was a violation of the first amendment. The Court conceded the state's duty to avoid any action that might violate the first amendment's prohibition against establishment of religion, but it thought that an "equal access" policy did not offend that prohibition and also met the three-pronged test set forth in *Lemon v. Kurtzman*. Having created a forum open generally to student groups, the university could not deny equal access to certain religious groups.

### Prayer and Bible Reading

A New York school district, acting under state law, directed the school district's principals to cause the following prayer to be said aloud by each class in the presence of a teacher at the beginning of each school day: "Almighty God, we acknowledge our dependence upon Thee, and we beg Thy blessings upon us, our parents, our teachers and our country." Students who wished to do so could remain silent or even leave the room while the prayer was being recited. This daily procedure was adopted on the recommendation of the State Board of Regents for New York. In *Engle v. Vitale*[170] the Court held the New York state-sponsored program of nondenominational prayer in public schools unconstitutional.

In 1963 this decision was followed by *School District v. Schempp,*[171] wherein a Pennsylvania law requiring, and a City of Baltimore rule permitting, Bible verses to be read, without comment, at the opening of the public school day were held violative of the establishment clause of the first amendment. The Court said that

> we find that the states are requiring the selection and reading at the opening of the school day of verses from the Holy Bible and the recitation of the Lord's Prayer by the students in unison. These exercises are prescribed as part of the curricular activities of students who are required by law to attend school. They are held in the school buildings under the supervision and with the participation of teachers employed in those schools. . . . We agree with the trial court's finding as to the religious character of the exercises. Given that finding, the exercises and the law requiring them are in violation of the Establishment Clause.[172]

The following year, in *Chamberlin v. Dade County Board of Public Instruction,*[173] prayer and devotional Bible reading in Florida public schools, pursuant to a state statute, were held unconstitutional, the Court citing its decision in the *Schempp* case.

More recently, a Kentucky statute requiring the posting of a copy of the Ten Commandments, purchased with private contributions, on the wall of each public school classroom in the state was said to have no secular legislative purpose. It was therefore held unconstitutional in *Stone v. Graham*[174] as a violation of the establishment clause of the first amendment. At the bottom of each display, in small print, were these words: "The secular application of the Ten Commandments is clearly seen in its adoption as the fundamental legal code of Western Civilization and the Common Law of the United States." The Court said that

> Under this Court's rulings . . . such an "avowed" secular purpose is not sufficient to avoid conflict with the First Amendment. . . .
>
> The pre-eminent purpose for posting the Ten Commandments on schoolroom walls is plainly religious in nature. . . .
>
> . . . Posting of religious texts on the wall serves no . . . educational function.[175]

Also, the fact that the posted copies were financed by voluntary private contributions was immaterial because they were posted under the auspices of the legislature. Nor did the Court find it significant that the Ten Commandments were merely posted rather than read aloud because "'it is no defense to urge that the religious practices here may be relatively minor encroachments on the First Amendment.'"[176]

The Court referred to the three-part test for determining whether a challenged state statute is permissible under the establishment clause, as enunciated in *Lemon v. Kurtzman:*

1st. The statute must have a secular legislative purpose;
2nd. Its principal or primary effect must be one that neither advances nor inhibits religion;
3rd. The statute must not foster an excessive government entanglement with religion.[177]

If a statute violates any of these three principles, it must be struck down. The Supreme Court concluded that the Kentucky statute violated the first principle, in that it had no secular legislative purpose, and it was therefore unconstitutional. To induce school children "to read, meditate upon, perhaps to venerate and obey the Commandments" was not a permissible state objective under the first amendment's establishment clause.

Most recently, a case involving two Alabama laws reached the Supreme Court. One law authorized teachers in the public schools to lead participating students in reciting a specific nondenominational prayer that began, "Almighty God, you alone are our God. We acknowledge you as the creator and supreme judge of the world." The second law allowed public school teachers to begin the school day with a brief period of silence for meditation or silent prayer.

The federal district court held both laws constitutional, arguing that the Supreme Court's precedents on school prayer were incorrect.[178] The Eleventh Circuit Court of Appeals reversed, holding both laws unconstitutional.[179] The Supreme Court summarily affirmed the Eleventh Circuit's ruling that the law respecting prayer recitations was unconstitutional but agreed to hear the appeal on the "moment of silence" law.[180]

In *Wallace v. Jaffree*[181] the Court held that the moment of silence statute was a law respecting the establishment of religion and therefore was unconstitutional. Adhering to its three-part analysis set forth in *Lemon v. Kurtzman,* the Court held that the Alabama law lacked a "secular legislative purpose." Rather, the Court concluded that the record showed a clear religious purpose—namely, to return voluntary prayer to the public schools, a purpose prohibited under its prior decisions discussed here.

## Notes

1. Brown v. Board of Educ., 347 U.S. 483 (1954) (landmark case declaring segregated schools to be a denial of equal protection of the laws).
2. San Antonio Indep. School Dist. v. Rodriguez, 411 U.S. 1, 35–36 (1973); *cf.* Stock v. Texas Catholic Interscholastic League, 364 F. Supp. 362 (N.D. Tex. 1973). *See generally* F. STIMPSON, THE LAW OF THE FEDERAL AND STATE CONSTITUTIONS OF THE UNITED STATES, WITH AN HISTORICAL STUDY OF THEIR PRINCIPLES, A CHRONOLOGICAL TABLE OF ENGLISH SOCIAL LEGISLATION, AND A COMPARATIVE DIGEST OF THE CONSTITUTIONS OF THE FORTY-SIX STATES 141 (1908) [hereinafter referred to as F. STIMPSON].
3. The debate about equality—not about the substance of the claims for equality but about the form they should take—is found in a series of articles. Westen, *The Empty Idea of Equality,* 95 HARV. L. REV. 537 (1982) (argues that *equality* is an empty vessel with no substantive moral content of its own and that as a form of discourse it ought to be abolished); Greenawalt, *How Empty Is the Idea of Equality?,* 83 COLUM. L. REV. 1167 (1983) (Greenawalt's reply); Westen, *To Lure the Tarantula from Its Hole,* 83 COLUM. L. REV. 1187 (1983) (Westen's rebuttal, in which he urges replacement of arguments about equalities and inequalities with arguments about "the prescriptive standards of measure that the equalities and inequalities logically presuppose").
4. F. STIMPSON, *supra* note 2, at 140.
5. CAL CONST. art. IX.
6. *Id.* art. IV, § 16(a).
7. *Id.* art. I, § 7(b).
8. Serrano v. Priest, 5 Cal. 3d 584, 487 P.2d 1241, 96 Cal. Rptr. 601 (1971). Other courts have not been so eager to follow this lead. The United States Supreme Court rejected it in San Antonio Indep. School Dist. v. Rodriguez, 411 U.S. 1 (1973). The Michigan Supreme Court, after initially deciding that education was a fundamental right, changed its mind following the Supreme Court's decision in *Rodriguez* and vacated its earlier decision. Milliken v. Green, 389 Mich. 1, 203 N.W.2d 457

(1972), *vacated*, 390 Mich. 389, 212 N.W.2d 711 (1973). The New Jersey courts were equally uncertain about the impact of *Rodriguez* on their earlier expression of education as a fundamental right. *See* Robinson v. Cahill, 118 N.J. Super 223, 287 A.2d 187 (1972), *modified*, 62 N.J. 473, 303 A.2d 273 (1973).

9. Actually, education serves not only the public interest but also individual interests and social interests. *See* R. POUND, OUTLINES OF LECTURES ON JURISPRUDENCE 96–97 (5th ed. 1943); J. HOGAN, THE SCHOOLS, THE COURTS, AND THE PUBLIC INTEREST 45–69 (1985) [hereinafter cited as J. HOGAN].

10. 347 U.S. 483 (1954).

11. *Id.* at 493.

12. *Id.*

13. Sullivan v. Houston Indep. School Dist., 333 F. Supp. 1149, 1172 (S.D. Tex. 1971).

14. Ordway v. Hargraves, 323 F. Supp. 1155, 1158 (D. Mass. 1971).

15. Dixon v. Alabama State Bd. of Educ., 294 F.2d 150, 157 (5th Cir. 1961).

16. Hosier v. Evans, 314 F. Supp. 316, 319 (D.V.I. 1970).

17. 5 Cal. 3d 584, 487 P.2d 1241, 96 Cal. Rptr. 601 (1971).

18. *Id.* at 608–09, 487 P.2d at 1258, 96 Cal. Rptr. at 618.

19. 411 U.S. 1 (1973).

20. *Id.* at 30.

21. *Id.* at 35.

22. Violations of rights secured by the Constitution, whether they occur on a school campus or elsewhere, are, of course, a federal matter in which courts may legitimately intervene.

23. 411 U.S. at 37.

24. J. HOGAN, *supra* note 9, at 9–10.

25. 262 U.S. 390 (1923).

26. 268 U.S. 510 (1925).

27. 393 U.S. 503 (1969).

28. 406 U.S. 205 (1972).

29. 419 U.S. 565 (1975). Goss v. Lopez was discussed in chapters 4, 6, and 7.

30. 430 U.S. 651 (1977). Ingraham v. Wright was discussed in chapter 4.

31. 347 U.S. 483 (1954).

32. 411 U.S. 1 (1973).

33. Mississippi, after repealing its compulsory school attendance law in 1956 as a response to the Supreme Court's desegregation in 1954, enacted a new statute in 1977, making such statutes universal among the fifty states and the District of Columbia.

34. *See* Wisconsin v. Yoder, 406 U.S. 205 (1972); Pierce v. Society of Sisters, 268 U.S. 510 (1925).

35. 406 U.S. at 214.

36. *See, e.g.,* ILL. ANN. STAT. ch. 122, § 26-1.

37. *See, e.g.,* Duro v. District Attorney, 712 F.2d 96 (4th Cir. 1983), *cert. denied,* 465 U.S. 1006 (1984); State v. Shaver, 294 N.W.2d 883 (N.D. 1980).

38. 30 N.C App. 235, 226 S.E.2d 693 (1976).

39. *See, e.g.,* COLO. REV. STAT. ANN. § 22-33-104(2)(i).

40. *See, e.g.,* S.D. COMP. LAWS ANN. § 13-27-3.

41. *See, e.g.,* N.Y. EDUC. LAW § 3204(2).

42. *Compare In re* Falk, 110 Misc. 2d 104, 441 N.Y.S.2d 785 (Fam. Ct., Lewis Co. 1981) (home instruction adequate), *with In re* Thomas H., 78 Misc. 2d 412, 357 N.Y.S.2d 384 (Fam. Ct., Yates Co. 1974).

43. 36 Misc. 2d 680, 234 N.Y.S.2d 172 (Fam. Ct., Schuyler Co. 1962).

44. *See* the discussion of vaccination as a permissible health regulation later in this chapter.

45. *See, e.g.,* 56 Op. Cal. Att'y Gen. 111 (1973).

46. W. Wadlington, C. Whitebread & S. Davis, Children in the Legal System 112 (1983).

47. 14 N.C. App. 426, 188 S.E.2d 619 (1972).

48. *Id.* at 430, 188 S.E.2d at 621.

49. *See, e.g.,* 24 Pa. Cons. Stat. Ann. § 13-1327.

50. *See, e.g.,* Brown v. Board of Educ., 347 U.S. 483 (1954); Stanton v. Sequoia Union High School Dist., 408 F. Supp. 502 (N.D. Cal. 1976).

51. Roberts v. City of Boston, 59 Mass. (5 Cush.) 198 (1849).

52. Plessy v. Ferguson, 163 U.S. 537 (1896).

53. These cases, the prodigy of the *Brown* decision, are discussed in J. Hogan, *supra* note 9, at 24–31.

54. 59 Cal. 2d 876, 382 P.2d 878, 31 Cal. Rptr. 606 (1963).

55. *Id.* at 881, 382 P.2d at 881, 31 Cal. Rptr. at 609.

56. *Id.,* 382 P.2d at 881, 31 Cal. Rptr. at 609.

57. *Id.* at 881, 382 P.2d at 881–82, 31 Cal. Rptr. at 609–10 (emphasis added); *see also* San Francisco Unified School Dist. v. Johnson, 3 Cal. 3d 937, 479 P.2d 669, 92 Cal. Rptr. 309 (1971).

58. Sometimes, however, court's efforts to alleviate racial imbalance (such as through busing or pupil reassignment) are frustrated. *See, e.g.,* Crawford v. Board of Educ., 458 U.S. 527 (1982) (containing a summary of the Los Angeles school litigation). *But see* Washington v. Seattle School Dist. No. 1, 458 U.S. 457 (1982) (state constitutional amendment designed to thwart court-ordered busing to achieve racial imbalance in schools, held unconstitutional).

59. The majority of courts reject the asserted affirmative duty to remedy *de facto* segregation; notable decisions are those of the Second Circuit, Sixth Circuit, Seventh Circuit, and Tenth Circuit. Other federal district courts, however, have asserted this affirmative duty in the District of Columbia, Massachusetts, Michigan, and New York.

60. 404 U.S. 1221 (1971) (opinion in chambers).

61. *Id.* at 1228, *quoting from* Swann v. Charlotte-Mecklenburg Bd. of Educ., 402 U.S. 1, 24 (1971).

62. *See, e.g.,* Cal. Educ. Code §§ 48200, 48210.

63. *See, e.g.,* Hammond v. Marx, 406 F. Supp. 853 (D. Me. 1975).

64. 406 F. Supp. 853 (D. Me. 1975).

65. *Id.* at 856–57.

66. *See, e.g.,* Daniels v. Morris, 746 F.2d 271 (5th Cir. 1984); Horton v. Marshall Pub. Schools, 589 F. Supp. 95 (W.D. Ark. 1984). Both cases are discussed in chapter 7.

67. 457 U.S. 202 (1982).

68. U.S. Const. amend. XIV, § 1.

69. 457 U.S. at 227–30.

70. 501 F.2d 1264 (9th Cir. 1974).

71. Sex is not a suspect classification calling for application of the strictest scrutiny. Nor is it relegated, however, to the least demanding scrutiny, the rational basis test. Rather, it calls for the intermediate level of scrutiny used by the court in *Berkelman.* Frontiero v. Richardson, 411 U.S. 677 (1973); Reed v. Reed, 404 U.S. 71 (1971).

72. *Accord,* Bray v. Lee, 337 F. Supp. 934 (D. Mass. 1972). *Compare* Williams v. McNair, 316 F. Supp. 134 (D.S.C. 1970) (statute limiting enrollment in college to females not a denial of equal protection where men had option of attending all-male or coeducational colleges in the state), *with* Kirsten v. Rector of the Univ. of Va., 309 F. Supp. 184 (E.D. Va. 1970) (exclusion of women from university was denial of equal protection where courses offered at the university were not offered elsewhere in the state and where women were denied opportunity to attend state's largest, most prestigious, most well-known university).

73. 20 U.S.C.A. § 1681.

74. *See* notes 44–46 *supra* and accompanying text.

75. 338 F. Supp. 1376 (N.D. Miss. 1972).

76. *Accord,* Ordway v. Hargraves, 323 F. Supp. 1155 (D. Mass. 1971).

77. *See* Goss v. Lopez, 419 U.S. 565 (1975), discussed in chapters 4, 6, and 7.

78. 338 F. Supp. at 1377.

79. *See, e.g.,* Zucht v. King, 260 U.S. 174 (1922).

80. In *In re* Elwell, 55 Misc. 2d 252, 284 N.Y.S.2d 924 (Fam. Ct., Dutchess Co. 1967), for example, a state law requiring school children to be immunized against poliomyelitis was upheld.

81. 376 F. Supp. 479 (D. N.H. 1974).

82. *See* Bannister v. Paradis, 316 F. Supp. 185 (D.N.H. 1970) (dictum).

83. *Id.*

84. Logar, *Minimum Competency Testing in Schools: Legislative Action and Judicial Review,* 13 J.L. & EDUC. 35 (1984) [hereinafter cited as Logar]; *see generally* McClung, *Competency Testing Programs: Legal and Educational Issues,* 47 FORDHAM L. REV. 651 (1979).

85. 474 F. Supp. 244 (M.D. Fla. 1979).

86. Debra P. v. Turlington, 644 F.2d 397 (5th Cir. 1981).

87. Debra P. v. Turlington, 564 F. Supp. 177 (M.D. Fla. 1983), *aff'd,* 730 F.2d 1405 (11th Cir. 1984). *See* Sandlin v. Johnson, 643 F.2d 1027 (4th Cir. 1981) (failure to promote a student to a higher grade because of failure to complete requisite level of Ginn Reading Series is not impermissible).

88. 520 F. Supp. 472 (S.D. Ga. 1981), *app. dismissed sub. nom.* Johnson v. Sikes, 730 F.2d 644 (5th Cir. 1984).

89. 42 U.S.C.A. §§ 2000d *et seq.*

90. 20 U.S.C.A. §§ 1701 *et seq.*

91. Logar, *supra* note 85, at 49.

92. Achievement tests are used for competency testing and preregistration skills assessment. They attempt to identify persons through assessment of their skills. Whereas achievement tests are used to measure what has been learned, aptitude tests are used to predict future performance. J. HOGAN, *supra* note 9, at 97–98.

93. *See generally* Arvizu v. Waco Indep. School Dist., 373 F. Supp. 1264, 1271 (W.D. Tex. 1973), *rev'd in part on other grounds,* 495 F.2d 499 (5th Cir. 1974).

94. 419 F.2d 1211 (5th Cir.), *rev'd in part on other grounds sub nom.* Carter v. West Feliciana Parish School Bd., 396 U.S. 290 (1970).

95. 330 F. Supp. 1340 (E.D. La. 1971), *aff'd*, 456 F.2d 1285 (5th Cir.), *cert. denied*, 409 U.S. 1013 (1972).

96. *Id.* at 1343.

97. 444 F.2d 1400 (5th Cir. 1971).

98. *See* note 96 *supra.*

99. 444 F.2d at 1401.

100. 343 F. Supp. 1306 (N.D. Cal. 1972).

101. 502 F.2d 963 (9th Cir. 1974) (per curiam).

102. 495 F. Supp. 926 (N.D. Cal. 1979). The case and the issues it presents are discussed in Note, *Racial Discrimination in IQ Testing—Larry P.* v. Riles, 29 DePaul L. Rev. 1193 (1980).

103. 52 U.S.L.W. 2456 (9th Cir. 1984).

104. 506 F. Supp. 831 (N.D. Ill. 1980).

105. *Id.* at 882.

106. 351 F. Supp. 1279 (D.N.M. 1972).

107. *See* Lau v. Nichols, 414 U.S. 563 (1974), discussed subsequently in this chapter in connection with bilingual instruction.

108. 269 F. Supp. 401 (D.D.C. 1967).

109. *Id.* at 406–07.

110. On appeal the District of Columbia Circuit allowed a group of parents "to appeal those provisions of the decree which curtail the freedom of the school board to exercise its discretion in deciding upon educational policy" but in the end affirmed the district court's abolition of the track system. Smuck v. Hobson, 408 F.2d 175 (D.C. Cir. 1969). *See also* Anderson v. Banks, 520 F. Supp. 472 (S.D. Ga. 1981), *appeal dismissed sub nom.* Johnson v. Sikes, 730 F.2d 644 (5th Cir. 1984). *See generally* H. Horowitz & K. Karst, Law, Lawyers and Social Change 505–06 (1969).

111. Swann v. Charlotte-Mecklenburg Bd. of Educ., 300 F. Supp. 1358, 1367 (W.D.N.C. 1969).

112. 193 Conn. 93, 475 A.2d 289 (1984).

113. *Contra*, 58 Op. Cal. Att'y Gen. 575 (1975) (impermissible to reduce a student's course credit because of low grades caused by his absences).

114. 60 Cal. App. 3d 814, 131 Cal. Rptr. 854 (1976).

115. 47 N.Y.2d 440, 391 N.E.2d 1352, 418 N.Y.S.2d 375 (1979).

116. *Id.* at 444–45, 391 N.E.2d at 1354, 418 N.Y.S.2d at 378. *Compare* the similar views of Justice Rehnquist as set forth in his opinion in Board of Curators v. Horowitz, 435 U.S. 78, 87, 89–90 (1978), and in the excerpt from his article mentioned in chapter 7 *supra*, Rehnquist, *The Adversary Society: Keynote Address of the Third Annual Baron de Hirsch Meyer Lecture Series*, 33 U. Miami L. Rev. 1, 2, 14–15 (1978).

117. *See, e.g.*, Hunter v. Board of Educ., 47 Md. App. 709, 425 A.2d 681 (1981); Helm v. Professional Children's School, 103 Misc. 2d 1053, 431 N.Y.S.2d 246 (Sup. Ct. App. Term 1980) (private school); Hoffman v. Board of Educ., 49 N.Y.2d 121, 400 N.E.2d 317, 424 N.Y.S.2d 376 (1979) (improper placement of child in class for children with retarded mental development).

118. A discussion of the issues is found in Funston, *Educational Malpractice: A Cause of Action in Search of a Theory*, 18 San Diego L. Rev. 743 (1981).

119. 414 U.S. 563 (1974).

120. 42 U.S.C.A. § 2000d.

121. 33 Fed. Reg. 4956; 35 Fed. Reg. 11595; 45 C.F.R. §§ 80.3(b)(1)–(2), 80.5(b).

122. Guadalupe Organization, Inc. v. Tempe Elementary School Dist., 587 F.2d 1022 (9th Cir. 1978).

123. 351 F. Supp. 1279 (D. N.M. 1972), *aff'd,* 499 F.2d 1147 (9th Cir. 1974).

124. 3 Clearinghouse Rev. 271 (Feb. 1970).

125. *Cf.* Hoffman v. Board of Educ., 49 N.Y.2d 121, 400 N.E.2d 317, 424 N.Y.S.2d 376 (1979).

126. 20 U.S.C.A. §§ 1401–1461.

127. *Id.* § 1401(1).

128. 468 U.S. 883 (1984).

129. 520 F. Supp. 905 (S.D. Tex. 1981).

130. 458 U.S. 176 (1982).

131. *Id.* at 200.

132. 423 F. Supp. 180 (S.D.W. Va. 1976).

133. 29 U.S.C.A. § 794.

134. *See* Goss v. Lopez, 419 U.S. 565 (1975), discussed in chapters 4, 6, and 7.

135. 268 U.S. 510 (1925).

136. *Id.* at 535.

137. 406 U.S. 205 (1972).

138. *Id.* at 214.

139. *Id.* at 222–29.

140. 281 U.S. 370 (1930).

141. *Id.* at 374, *quoting from* Bordon v. Louisiana State Bd. of Educ., 168 La. 1006, 1020, 123 So. 655, 660 (1929).

142. *Id.* at 374–75.

143. *Id.* at 375.

144. 392 U.S. 236 (1968).

145. *Id.* at 243–45.

146. 421 U.S. 349 (1975).

147. *Id.* at 360, 362.

148. 413 U.S. 455 (1973).

149. *Id.* at 462–63.

150. *Id.* at 463–64.

151. 433 U.S. 229 (1977).

152. 330 U.S. 1 (1947).

153. 403 U.S. 602 (1971).

154. *Id.* at 612–13.

155. Lemon v. Kurtzman, 411 U.S. 192 (1973).

156. *Id.* at 199.

157. *Id.* at 203–07.

158. 413 U.S. 472 (1973).

159. 444 U.S. 646 (1980).

160. 413 U.S. 756 (1973).

161. *Id.* at 774. *See also* Bob Jones U. v. United States, 461 U.S. 574 (1983) (IRS denial of tax-exempt status to schools that discriminate on the basis of race does not violate the first amendment).

162. 413 U.S. 825 (1973).

163. *Id.* at 834.

164. 463 U.S. 388 (1983).

165. 333 U.S. 203 (1948).

166. *Id.* at 209–10.

167. 343 U.S. 306 (1952).

168. *Id.* at 308–09.

169. 454 U.S. 263 (1981).

170. 370 U.S. 421 (1962).

171. 374 U.S. 203 (1963).

172. *Id.* at 223.

173. 377 U.S. 402 (1964) (per curiam).

174. 449 U.S. 39 (1980) (per curiam).

175. *Id.* at 41–42.

176. *Id.* at 42, *quoting from* School Dist. v. Schempp, 374 U.S. 203, 225 (1963).

177. 449 U.S. at 40, *quoting from* Lemon v. Kurtzman, 403 U.S. 602, 612–13 (1971).

178. Jaffree v. Board of School Comm'rs, 554 F. Supp. 1104 (S.D. Ala. 1983).

179. Jaffree v. Wallace, 705 F.2d 1526 (11th Cir. 1983).

180. Wallace v. Jaffree, 466 U.S. 924 (1984).

181. 105 S. Ct. 2479 (1985).

# 9

# Protection of Children
# from Inadequate Parenting

> [T]he function of the court must be to pursue the transcendent goal of addressing the most pernicious social ailment which afflicts our society, family abuse, and more specifically, child abuse. . . .
>
> This court has pursued a policy in child homicide cases of developing rules which ultimately will assist in protecting the innocent victims of child abuse. . . . [N]o apology is necessary for this policy. Because of the manifest need to protect the most helpless members of our society from violence on the part of others, the policy is both necessary and proper.
>
> —Judge Richard V. Thomas
> *Goldade v. State* 674 P.2d 721, 725, 727
> (Wyo. 1983)

## Changing Criteria: Family Autonomy or Increased Intervention?

Chapter 5 in part focused on the question of when the state might appropriately intervene in family affairs under circumstances that few people would characterize as neglect. Thus, cases were reviewed there in which courts approved of state intervention where parents, for religious and other reasons, refused to consent to surgery for children in both life-threatening and non–life-threatening circumstances.

Most of those cases were brought to court on allegations that the children involved were neglected, even if in a narrow, technical sense. In fact, many of the courts acknowledged that the children were not otherwise neglected, and their parents provided them with love, nurturing, and the basic necessities of life. Yet they were alleged to be neglected, mainly because the courts were powerless to act without an adjudication of neglect, followed by temporary removal of custody from the parents and an award of custody to a guardian authorized to consent to surgery.

The gist of the discussion in chapter 5 was that such cases presented close questions, from moral, medical, legal as well as ethical perspectives. On the other hand, one might expect to find general agreement respecting the need for state intervention in more typical kinds of neglect cases—that is, where children are being denied necessary care and supervision essential to their physical, mental, and emotional well-being—and certainly in cases of abuse. In truth, however, considerable debate exists over the issue of whether the state should intervene at the current or an even greater level or families rather should be accorded more autonomy than they currently possess—that is, should be "let alone."

A number of professionals and other commentators have advocated narrowing the scope of state intervention on the theory that children are more apt to be harmed than helped by official action.[1] Two of the most influential works in recent years are *Beyond the Best Interests of the Child*, a 1973 publication by Joseph Goldstein, Anna Freud, and Albert Solnit, and the *Juvenile Justice Standards Relating to Abuse and Neglect*, a model proposed in 1977 by the Institute of Judicial Administration and the American Bar Association.

In their book, Goldstein, Freud, and Solnit criticized the legal community for devoting too much concern to the physical well-being of children while failing to tend to their psychological well-being. In particular, they advocated the value of continuity, the notion that the deepest need children have is the need for continuing relationships and that such relationships should be continued at all costs, except in the most extreme cases. The continuity concept—also expressed as psychological parenthood—was further refined in a 1979 book by the same authors, *Before the Best Interests of the Child*. Their views have been criticized even by advocates of increased family autonomy as perhaps too extreme, carrying the goal of continuity too far, not allowing for intervention in some cases in which separation of parent and child would be appropriate.[2]

Courts traditionally have been concerned with parental conduct and conditions in the home, resulting in intervention and even removal of children from the home in many cases where the courts, in their subjective view, simply disagreed with or disapproved of the parents' lifestyles or child-rearing methods.[3] In contrast, the philosophy advocated by the *Juvenile Justice Standards Relating to Abuse and Neglect* is one favoring parental autonomy and focusing on specific harms to children rather than parental conduct or conditions in the home as such.[4] Thus, removal of a child from the home is authorized only where

1.  the child has suffered or is about to suffer physical harm causing or about to cause disfigurement, impairing of bodily functioning or similar serious physical injury, and the harm is inflicted nonaccidentally by a parent;

2.  the child has suffered or is about to suffer physical harm of the kind described above as a result of conditions created by a parent or because of inadequate parental supervision;

3. the child presently is suffering serious emotional harm, evidenced by severe anxiety, depression, withdrawal or wilful aggressive behavior toward himself or others, and the parents are unwilling to seek treatment;

4. the child has been sexually abused by a parent or other member of the household (an alternative would require that the child be seriously harmed physically or emotionally by such act);

5. the child is in need of medical treatment for a condition that threatens loss of life, disfigurement or impairment of bodily functions, and the parents are unwilling to seek or consent to such treatment; or

6. the child is engaging in delinquent behavior fostered or encouraged by a parent.[5]

The extent of disagreement over the appropriate level of state intervention is illustrated by the fact that the volume on *Standards Relating to Abuse and Neglect* was one of only three volumes in the entire set of the proposed *Standards* (twenty-three volumes in all) *not* approved by the American Bar Association in 1980. The ABA's dissatisfaction stemmed largely from disagreement with the basic noninterventionist philosophy of the proposed *Standards* and differences of opinion over definition of terms such as *neglect, dependency, abuse,* and *endangering.* The two concerns are related because as these terms are defined so is the level of intervention determined.

With the possible exception of the medical decision-making cases, few issues generate as much public concern for the plight of children as does the matter of child maltreatment. Child maltreatment is a social phenomenon, but it also gives rise to a number of legal consequences. Three sets of observations are presented here: (1) those concerned with defining *child maltreatment,* (2) those concerned with measuring the amount of child maltreatment, and (3) those concerned with legal issues arising in the prosecution of child abuse cases. All three are related, and all three are necessary to an understanding of how children, parents, and the state interact in this important area.

## Definition of Child Maltreatment

Depending on the form it takes, child maltreatment might be the basis for a civil action to remove custody of the child from the parents or the basis for a criminal action against the alleged abuser. In the former, emphasis is on protection of the child, in the latter on punishment of the offender. A civil action for removal of custody can be brought for either abuse or neglect, whereas criminal prosecution typically is sought, if at all, only in cases of abuse.

The definitions of abuse and neglect might be found in the juvenile court code, the criminal code, or a special child abuse reporting statute, and they might be found together or separately. In any event, conceptually the two are different and for purposes of definition are treated differently at first. In the subsequent section of this chapter, however, dealing with measuring the incidence of child maltreatment, they are combined. In the final section, dealing with evidentiary problems in presenting maltreatment cases in court, the cases are almost exclusively abuse cases because the evidentiary problems discussed have arisen in such cases.

### Neglect and Dependency

Frequently, a single designation is used in statutes to describe a child who has no living parent or has been abandoned, abused, or neglected or lacks adequate parental care or supervision. Such a child may be classified as a *dependent child,*[6] a *deprived child,*[7] or a *neglected child.*[8]

Occasionally, two designations are used—*neglected* and *dependent*—and different meanings attach to each. The *neglect* designation usually implies some degree of parental fault—that is, the parents have failed to provide adequate food, shelter, clothing, or supervision. The *dependency* designation typically implies the absence of parental fault—such as the child has no living parent. Thus, under North Carolina statutes, a *neglected juvenile* is defined as one who lacks proper parental care and supervision or who has been abandoned,[9] and a *dependent juvenile* as one who is without a parent or other person responsible for his care or whose parent or custodian is unable to provide proper care and supervision.[10]

Typically, judges must make dependency or neglect determinations in situations calling for exercise of a great deal of subjective judgment. In California, for example, a child can be adjudged dependent if he "is in need of proper and effective parental care or control" or if he lacks "a suitable place of abode" or his home "is an unfit place."[11] Obviously, such determinations depend on the subjective judgment of the observer as formed by his values and experiences.

Occasionally claims are raised that such statutory descriptions are so loosely worded and so open to subjective evaluation that they are unconstitutionally vague. These challenges have had mixed results in the courts. In a South Dakota case,[12] for example, the court held valid a statute defining a neglected child as one who is "subjected . . . to mistreatment or abuse," who "lacks proper parental care" or "whose environment is injurious to his welfare." Such descriptions, the court said, are capable of commonly understood meanings.

On the other hand, a federal district court held unconstitutionally vague a statute that defined a neglected child as "any child, who, while under sixteen years of age . . . has no proper parental care or guardianship or whose home, by reason of neglect, cruelty, or depravity, on the part of his parent or parents, guardian or other person in whose care he may be, is an unfit or improper place for such child."[13] The circumstances in the case were that the child, a white child, was declared to be neglected on the basis that his mother, also white, was living with a black man in a black neighborhood.

Similar vagueness claims have been raised against other kinds of descriptive statutes dealing with children—such as those describing "children in need of supervision," that is, runaways, truants, children who will not mind their parents, children "seriously endangered by their surroundings," children "in danger of leading an idle, dissolute, lewd, or immoral life," or children "habitually so deporting themselves as to injure or endanger the morals or health of themselves or others." With few exceptions such statutes have been upheld.[14] The vagueness objection has been claimed with respect to child abuse statutes as well, as discussed in the following subsection.

*Abuse*

Abuse[15] sometimes is included in the definition of neglect or dependency and sometimes is placed in a category of its own. However categorized, abuse characteristically lacks a universally accepted definition. In a pioneering article[16] written over twenty years ago, Dr. Henry Kempe and his associates introduced the term *battered child syndrome* to describe "a clinical condition in young children who have received serious physical abuse, generally from a parent or foster parent."[17] Obvious reference to *battered* children and *serious physical abuse* denotes a concept of abuse including only physical trauma with physical manifestations.

The year following publication of Dr. Kempe's article, Dr. Vincent Fontana and his associates published an article[18] in which they maintained the designation *battered child* was too narrow, that there were additional harms suffered by children that should be included in a broader clinical category. They coined the label *maltreatment syndrome*.

Doctors Kempe and Fontana were not the first to realize that child abuse, however defined, existed,[19] but they were the first to call popular attention to an insidious phenomenon. Since appearance of their articles in the early 1960s, when very little had been written on the problem of child abuse, a virtual flood of medical literature on the subject has appeared.[20] As a result of revelations of the occurrence and incidence of child abuse, legislatures in all fifty states enacted child abuse reporting laws during a four-year period in the mid-1960s.[21]

Most statutes share certain categorical features—such as provisions stating the persons who must report and the agency to whom reports must be made, as well as provisions granting civil immunity to persons reporting in good faith and waiving the spousal and physician/patient privileges in such cases. The statutes vary considerably in detail, however, particularly in their definitions of what constitutes abuse.

In addition to Dr. Kempe's litany of physical abuse,[22] most modern statutes include an ever-expanding description of other kinds of abuse, an expansion that gives a new and changing meaning to the definition of abuse from year to year. A number of statutes, for example, provide that excessive corporal punishment constitutes abuse.[23]

At first glance one might suppose excessive corporal punishment to be simply another kind of physical abuse and therefore not a kind of harm to be categorized separately.[24] Special mention of excessive corporal punishment was prompted, no doubt, in response to claims that what was alleged to be abuse was nothing more than normal discipline. At common law parents could impose reasonable discipline on their children without civil or criminal liability, but if the disciplinary measures taken were excessive or "outrageous" then the parents lost their privilege and were subject to civil or criminal penalties otherwise applicable. The purpose of the recent legislation seems to have been to codify the common law view.[25]

Probably the most hotly litigated issue in excessive corporal punishment cases centers on the difficulty in determining what constitutes normal discipline, which parents and others traditionally have been allowed to impose on children,[26] and what constitutes *excessive* discipline amounting to abuse. A number of statutes have been attacked on vagueness grounds, but for the most part they have been upheld.[27]

Many statutes also include sexual abuse within the general definition of *abuse*,[28] quite obviously because, unless the act results in physical harm, it otherwise does not constitute abuse.[29]

The Maryland Code further defines *sexual abuse* as

> any act that involves sexual molestation or exploitation of a child by a parent or other [custodian].
>
> "Sexual abuse" includes, but is not limited to:
>
> a. Incest, rape, or sexual offense in any degree;
> b. Sodomy; and
> c. Unnatural or perverted sexual practices.[30]

Maryland's inclusion of sexual exploitation in its definition of *sexual abuse* is representative of a further trend in expansion of the definition of *abuse*. Florida's statute, for example, defines *harm* as including sexual abuse and further defines *sexual abuse* to include sexual exploitation for pornographic purposes or prostitution.[31]

Most states also make sexual exploitation of children a criminal offense.[32] New York's statute, which prohibits knowing promotion of a sexual performance by a child under age sixteen through distribution of material depicting such a performance,[33] was upheld by the Supreme Court in *New York v. Ferber*,[34] a decision that should give added impetus to inclusion of sexual exploitation in child abuse statutes.

Finally, a number of states have included emotional or psychological abuse within the general definition of *abuse*.[35] Wyoming's statute, for example, defines *mental injury* as "an injury to the psychological capacity or emotional stability of a child as evidenced by an observable or substantial impairment in his ability to function within a normal range of performance and behavior with due regard to his culture."[36] The same definitional difficulty seen earlier with *excessive corporal punishment* is seen here as well.[37]

As with neglect and dependency, as a state defines *abuse*, so it in part determines both the incidence of reported abuse in that state and, as a matter of policy, the desired level of intervention by the state in the lives of families. Perhaps an example will suffice. Suppose states *A* and *B* share identical demographic characteristics in terms of total population, number of families, family size, and the like. Further suppose that state *A* defines *abuse* only in terms of physical abuse, whereas state *B* defines *abuse* to include not only physical abuse but as well emotional abuse, sexual abuse and exploitation, and excessive corporal punishment.

It is readily apparent that even if in fact the same kind of behavior occurs in both states, state *B* will have a statistically more significant abuse problem than state *A*, solely as a result of the difference in how *abuse* is defined in the two states. Equally obviously, by adopting such a broad definition of *abuse* state *B* has made a policy decision favoring increased state intervention in the lives of families as its answer to the continuing debate over the role the state should play in regulating family behavior.

To an extent the issue of the preferred level of state intervention is related to the issue of how abuse is to be defined because by giving *abuse* a very broad definition a state might be expressing a preference for increased intervention. The two are not necessarily related, however. A state, for example, could define *abuse* in its broadest sense but still express a policy favoring less rather than more intervention. The latter approach is taken, for example, in the *Juvenile Justice Standards Relating to Abuse and Neglect*.[38] In either event, how a state defines *abuse* and what level of intervention it prefers as a matter of policy are major factors in measuring how much abuse goes on.

## Determining the Incidence of Abuse

Although measurement methodology has improved over the years since the first reporting statutes were enacted in the mid-1960s, accurate measurement of the incidence of abuse continues to pose difficulties. A recent summary of the major measurement research over the last twenty years revealed incidence estimates ranging from a few hundred to upwards of 2½ to 4 million cases per year.[39] The summary concluded that because of the many difficulties in obtaining accurate data of the national incidence of child abuse and neglect, not much confidence could be placed in even the most recent (at that time) studies producing estimates ranging from 40,000 to almost 2 million cases per year.[40] Two of the major obstacles to accurate measurement are differences from state to state in information collecting procedures and the lack of a uniform definition of abuse.[41]

Two reports completed since publication of the above summary have contributed significantly to knowledge of the incidence of child abuse in this country. Their methodologies differ greatly, but their estimates of the national incidence of child abuse are fairly proximate.

The first report,[42] issued in 1979 and revised in November 1981, is the latest in a series conducted annually since 1976 by the American Humane Association for the National Center on Child Abuse and Neglect. These reports are based on cases actually reported by official state reporting agencies. The report summarizes information submitted by all fifty states, the District of Columbia, and three U.S. territories, Guam, Puerto Rico, and the Virgin Islands. In addition, thirty-one states and two territories furnished individual case data enabling analysts to report two separate figures: (1) numbers of cases according to type of report—abuse or neglect—and (2) numbers of cases according to type of maltreatment.

For reporting purposes *abuse* is defined as any "intentional, nonaccidental injury, harm, or sexual abuse inflicted on a child."[43] *Neglect* is defined as "the responsible caretaker's nonprovision of care essential to a child, such as food, clothing, shelter, medical attention, education, or supervision."[44]

Employing these reporting categories and a methodology based on cases actually reported to official agencies, the report states that the number of incidents of abuse and neglect in all fifty states, the District of Columbia, and the three territories for 1979 was 711,142.[45] Because all the reporting states did not furnish individual case data, this total could not be subdivided into separate categories for abuse and neglect nor subdivided according to type of maltreatment.

Of the total of 711,142 cases of abuse and neglect, 296,321 cases, or 42 percent of the total cases reported, were reported by the group of thirty-one states and two territories furnishing individual case data.[46] Of the 296,321 cases reported by this group, 62,014 were reported as cases of abuse, 116,484 were reported as cases of neglect, 43,577 were reported as cases involving both abuse and neglect, and the remaining 74,244 cases were reported as "other," which included cases in which data were missing or in which the type of maltreatment was unspecified.[47]

Further differentiation of the 296,321 cases reported by this group was made according to the type of maltreatment: "major physical injury,"[48] "minor physical injury,"[49] "physical injury (unspecified),"[50] "sexual maltreatment,"[51] "deprivation of necessities,"[52] "emotional maltreatment,"[53] and "other maltreatment."[54] The breakdown is shown in the table below:

| Type | Percent |
|---|---|
| Major physical injury | 4.38 |
| Minor physical injury | 15.39 |
| Physical injury (unspecified) | 2.46 |
| Sexual maltreatment | 5.76 |
| Deprivation of necessities | 63.08 |
| Emotional maltreatment | 14.86 |
| Other maltreatment | 8.87[55] |

Some of the conclusions drawn in the report from the above data are self-evident. For example, neglect or—more specifically, deprivation of necessities—constitutes by far the major type of reported maltreatment, followed at some distance by minor physical injury, a recurrent pattern from prior reporting years.[56] Other conclusions are not as obvious on the face of the data. For example, the maltreatment category showing the most rapid growth in reporting in recent years is sexual abuse.[57]

A word of caution is in order. It would be misleading to think of the numbers used in this first report as anything more than approximations both of the total national incidence of abuse and neglect and of the incidence according to type of maltreatment. This is so because of the limitations on accurate measurement mentioned earlier[58] and noted in the report itself.[59] For example, the report observes that since collection of reporting data commenced in 1976, reported cases have increased by 71 percent. The report acknowledges that it is impossible to know whether the actual incidence of abuse and neglect has increased at the same rate during the same period, principally because of the lack of any universal definition of maltreatment and the variation among state reporting systems themselves.[60]

Despite the 71 percent increase in reported cases since 1976, the incremental increase each year has decreased,[61] which might lead one to conclude that we are moving toward a closer correlation between estimated incidence of abuse and neglect and actual incidence of abuse and neglect. The report advises caution here also, adding that the slowing rate of increase most likely signifies that as state reporting systems have become more sophisticated they are approaching their optimum capacity for handling reports.[62]

The second report mentioned above is a report of the findings of the National Study of the Incidence and Severity of Child Abuse and Neglect, also prepared for the National Center on Child Abuse and Neglect and also issued in 1981.[63] This study, unlike the first, is based on data collection resulting from sampling and a program definition of child maltreatment. By using such a methodology the study sought to avoid some of the inaccuracies inherent in use of actual reported cases.[64]

An underlying premise of the second study is that cases actually reported to child protective services (CPS) agencies as abuse and neglect represent only a portion of the actual incidence of abuse and neglect. This is so because there are other cases not known to CPS but known to other investigatory agencies (police, public health departments, and the courts) and to professionals in schools, hospitals, and social service and mental health agencies.[65]

The study developed a program design and methodology calculated to tap the unofficial sources of information and therefore to produce more realistic estimates of the incidence of child abuse and neglect. Its central features were: (1) use of a probability sample of twenty-six counties across the country, (2) assembly of data not only from official reporting agencies (CPS) but from the other sources mentioned as well, and (3) adoption of a program definition of maltreatment through which the data could be screened.[66]

*Maltreatment* for program purposes was defined as purposive behavior or marked inattention by a parent or other caretaker toward a child, resulting in foreseeable and avoidable injury or impairment to the child, or materially contributing to unreasonable prolongation or aggravation of an existing injury or impairment.[67]

Employing the program definition of abuse and neglect and the sampling methodology, the report arrived at a national incidence estimate of 651,900 cases of abuse and neglect (or maltreatment) for the one-year study period covering 1979–80.[68] This estimate was calculated as follows. The report estimated that 1,101,500 cases of maltreatment were reported to CPS agencies, but of this number only 470,500 cases were substantiated by the CPS agencies as cases actually involving maltreatment of children.[69] The latter figure was further reduced to 212,400 cases because only these cases fit the program definition of maltreatment.[70] To these 212,400 cases were added an additional 71,400 cases identified by other investigatory agencies (that is, police, public health authorities, and the courts) and another 368,100 cases identified by other study agencies (public schools, hospitals and mental health and social service agencies), for a total of 651,900 cases.[71]

The report itself concedes that this estimate is conservative for several reasons: (1) it is based on a narrow definition of maltreatment; (2) the non-CPS reporting sources were limited in range; (3) large and central city agencies were underrepresented in the non-CPS information gathering, and participation by some of the "participating" agencies was questionable; and (4) the study estimate excluded all unsubstantiated CPS cases.[72] Taking these factors into account the report conservatively estimates that the actual incidence of maltreatment is at least 1 million cases per year and quite possibly substantially more than that.[73]

The fact that two studies, using different methodologies, arrived at comparable estimates of the national incidence of abuse lends some credence to both studies, particularly when the study furnishing the lower estimate concedes that its total likely is conservative.[74] With occurrences of maltreatment in anywhere near these numbers, one might expect a fair number—indeed, an increasing number of cases—of maltreatment to reach the courts, which in fact has happened. Typically the focus in these cases is on various evidentiary issues including privilege, use of character evidence, and use of expert testimony. This is particularly true in sexual abuse cases, which are on the rise.[75] The remainder of this chapter is devoted to analysis of these evidentiary issues.

## Evidentiary Problems in Child Abuse Cases

The difficulties inherent in prosecution of child abuse cases have been chronicled elsewhere. For example:

> The evidence that is available from eyewitnesses is for the most part useless. Even if the child is alive and mature enough to testify, he may have changed his account of the incident to match the abuser's version. The victim of child abuse is far more susceptible to the influence of the alleged abuser than are most victims of other crimes. While other siblings often are present when the child is abused, they also are easily influenced and intimidated. Further, the husband-wife privilege may prevent the other parent from testifying. The defendant, who alone may know how the injury occurred, usually will maintain that the child was hurt accidentally. . . .
>
> Most of the available evidence in child abuse cases is circumstantial. The jury must weigh not only the credibility of the witnesses but also the probabilities of the inferences that the prosecution desires the jury to draw. Therefore, the sufficiency of the evidence frequently becomes an important question.[76]

For these and other reasons, child abuse cases are not among the easiest cases to prosecute. Four particularly troublesome evidentiary problems continue to plague courts: (1) the competency and credibility of a child victim as witness, (2) the admissibility of a child's out-of-court statements, (3) the applicability of the husband/wife and physician/patient privileges, and (4) the use of character evidence, either in the form of evidence of prior acts of abuse or expert testimony on the battering-parent profile.

### Competency and Credibility of Child Witnesses

The traditional test for determining a child's competency to testify is two-fold: whether the child understands the obligation to tell the truth and has sufficient capacity to observe, recollect, and relate.[77] Whether a child possesses such understanding and testimonial capacity is a decision within the trial court's discretion, and as with most discretionary decisions, will not be overturned except for abuse.[78]

Age is not a controlling factor.[79] Some relatively young children have been found competent to testify whereas older children have been found incompetent. For example, in *State v. Skipper*[80] the Louisiana Supreme Court upheld a defendant's conviction for cruelty to a juvenile over his claim that two witnesses—seven and five years old—were improperly allowed to testify. As to the seven-year-old, the court observed that

> he answered in the affirmative when asked if he understood the difference between telling the truth and not telling the truth, and also when asked if he understood why he was in court. . . . He was able to handle the defense attorney's questions concerning who had brought him to court, whether anyone had told him what to say, and whether what he told the judge was what he actually saw.[81]

Of the five-year-old, the victim, the court noted that he

> also answered in the affirmative when asked if he understood why he was in court and if he knew he had to be truthful (although he did not know what a "fib" was). He understood the judge wanted him to tell his story about what happened to him.[82]

Similarly, in *State v. Martin*[83] the Connecticut Supreme Court held that the six-year-old victim properly was allowed to testify because his testimony demonstrated that he possessed the capacity for intelligent recollection and the ability to relate what he had experienced.[84]

In *State v. Pettis*[85] the Rhode Island Supreme Court held that a thirteen-year-old sexual assault victim properly was allowed to testify even though she was mentally retarded and experienced difficulty explaining the difference between a falsehood and the truth. The trial judge concluded that on balance "I'm satisfied that in her own humble way she appreciates the necessity for telling the truth."[86]

On the other hand, the Georgia Court of Appeals in *Pace v. State*[87] reversed the defendant's conviction for child molestation on the ground that the eight-year-old victim improperly was allowed to testify.[88] The court's use of the actual transcript best illustrates the perceived deficiencies in the child's competency to testify while raising some question about the propriety of its decision:

By Mr. Sammons [the Assistant District Attorney]:
  Q. How old are you, Michelle?
  A. Eight.

Q. Do you know when your birthday is?

A. Huh-uh.

Q. Do you go to school?

A. Yeah.

Q. Where?

A. I don't know.

Q. Is it here in Dallas?

A. Yes.

Q. What grade are you in?

A. First.

Q. Who lives with you, Michelle?

A. Mama.

Q. Do you know that when you held up your hand just now with this fellow over here?

A. Yeah.

Q. Do you know what telling a story is?

A. Yeah.

Q. What is that?

A. Not supposed to tell lies.

Q. Is it right or wrong to tell a lie?

A. Wrong.

Q. Do you know where we are today?

A. Yeah.

Q. Where are we?

A. At court.

Q. Do you know that fellow up there?

A. Huh-uh.

Q. Do you know what he is called? You can't remember? Do you know where you are now?

A. At court.

The court:

Q. What does court do?

A. Help people.

Q. Do you know what my job is?

A. Huh-uh.

Q. Do you know what Mr. Sammons who is questioning you?

A. Yeah.

Q. Do you know what his job is? Let me ask you this: You said you knew what it meant to tell the truth. What happens when you tell an untruth?

By Mr. Sammons:

    Q. Is it bad to tell a story, Michelle?

    A. Yes.

By Mr. Farless [Defense Counsel]: . . .

    Q. Do you know what would happen to you if you don't tell the truth when someone asks you a question? Do you?

    A. No.

    Q. Do you go to church, Michelle?

    A. Yeah. But I used to.

    Q. How long has it been since you have been to church?

    A. I don't know.

    Q. Have you heard the expression, I swear to God?

    A. Yeah.

    Q. What does that mean to you? Michelle, where do you go to church when you go?

    A. I don't know.

    Q. Do you know how long it has been since you have been to church?

    A. I don't know how long. I don't know.

    Q. Does your mother ever read from the Bible to you?

    A. Huh-uh.

    Q. Does your grandmother ever read to you from the Bible?

    A. Huh-uh.

    Q. Does anyone ever talk to you about the Bible?

    A. Yeah.

    Q. Who?

    A. The preacher.

    Q. Do you know this preacher's name?

    A. Huh-uh.

    Q. Have you seen him in quite a while? How long has it been since you have seen him?

    A. I don't know.

    Q. Do you know what the Bible is supposed to be?

    A. I don't know.

    Q. Have you ever told fibs, made up stories?

    A. Huh-uh.

    Q. You never have had imaginary playmates, make up games to play?

    A. Huh-uh. . . .

    Q. . . . Michelle, when you play, you never make up games to play?

    A. Huh-uh.

    Q. Do you ever talk to your dolls?

    A. Yeah.

Q. Sometimes you pretend they talk back to you? They don't really, do they?

A. Huh-uh. . . .

Q. Have you ever been given a spanking for telling a story?

A. Huh-uh.

Q. When I say, tell a story, do you know what I mean?

A. Huh-uh.

Q. If I told you I could fly without an airplane, would you believe me?

A. Yeah.[89]

The examples illustrate that some deficiencies in a child's capacity are perceived as serious enough to disqualify the child from testifying whereas others are perceived as affecting only the credibility of the child. Thus, the fact that the five-year-old victim in *State v. Skipper* "did not know what a 'fib' was"[90] did not operate to disqualify him as a witness nor in *State v. Martin* did the fact that the six-year-old victim's memory was vague and limited as to some details[91] disqualify him as a witness. In the latter case the court noted: "Such shortcomings . . . are not unusual in the testimony of victims of a traumatic experience and are properly considered as going to the weight of the testimony rather than its admissibility."[92]

Two observations can be made regarding the preceding statement. First, the court perceives that testimony of victims following trauma—such as abuse, particularly sexual abuse—presents a unique problem in that the trauma itself can affect the victim's memory and ability to relate what happened. A case in point is *State v. Middleton*,[93] in which the Oregon Supreme Court in affirming a rape conviction held that expert testimony on familial child sexual abuse was properly admitted to explain inconsistencies in the fourteen-year-old victim's statements of what had happened to her.[94] This court, as did the court in *State v. Martin,* viewed the problem as one affecting weight rather than admissibility of the evidence.

This leads to the second observation. Some have argued that a child's testimony should be allowed into evidence for whatever credence the jury, in light of all the circumstances, may be inclined to give it.[95] Although the courts in *Skipper, Martin,* and *Pettis* purport to follow the traditional test they also can be perceived as supporting the more liberal view favoring admissibility, at least where the deficiencies in the child's understanding or memory are not too radical.

The problem is one of significant proportions. Prosecutors frequently are compelled to forgo putting the child-victim on the stand because the child—for reasons of age, embarrassment, reaction to trauma, awe, or shyness—will not pass the scrutiny required for testimonial competence.[96] In cases already noted for their paucity of evidence,[97] loss of the child's testimony can be devastating. The problem admits of only two solutions.

First, the prosecutor can seek to use the child's extrajudicial statements under existing exceptions or a specially formulated exception to the hearsay rule, which is discussed subsequently. Second, steps can be taken to reduce the trauma faced by the child-victim, permitting the child's testimony to be received in evidence. Both kinds of reforms have been suggested recently. Various commentators have suggested reforms such as use of youth examiners who would examine the child and present the child's statements in court, *in camera* examination of the child, use of a "child's courtroom" with the defendant "present" behind a one-way mirror, use of videotaped depositions, and closure of the courtroom to all persons whose presence is not necessary during the taking of the child's testimony.[98] Opinions have varied over whether such measures will pass constitutional muster in terms of the defendant's rights to confrontation, compulsory process, due process and public trial, and the right of the public and press to attend the proceedings.[99]

Some states already have added statutory provisions designed to facilitate the taking of children's testimony in sexual offense cases. These include, for example, provisions limiting access to child victims of sexual abuse, allowing use of videotaped depositions and use of closed circuit equipment to present testimony of a child victim, allowing use of anatomically correct dolls, and other measures designed generally to relieve the stress of child witnesses.[100] Such statutes are too new to permit a guess as to the courts' response to them, but early indications are that some of the provisions, at least, are not violative of a defendant's constitutional rights.[101]

On the other hand, in *Globe Newspaper v. Superior Court*[102] the United States Supreme Court held unconstitutional a Massachusetts statute requiring mandatory closure of the courtroom during testimony of a child victim in a sexual offense trial as violative of the first amendment right of the public and press to free access to criminal trials. Of course, *Globe Newspaper* does not address the issue of closure of noncriminal trials—for example, child abuse proceedings in juvenile court. Moreover, even in criminal trials it does not prohibit all closure only mandatory closure in a certain class of cases. The court recognized that closure might be appropriate in some cases, to be decided on a case-by-case basis.[103]

### Evidence of Child's Extrajudicial Statements

If the child's testimony is unavailable because of the child's incompetency or because the child will not make a credible witness, what can be done? A number of courts have allowed use of the child's out-of-court statements under various exceptions to the hearsay rule.[104]

An example is *Goldade v. State*[105] in which the prosecutor was forced to seek admission of the four-and-a-half-year-old victim's extrajudicial statements under an exception to the hearsay rule because of the trial court's ruling that she was incompetent to testify as a witness.[106] The trial court then allowed a pediatrician and a nurse to testify that the child had told them her mother had injured her, over the defendant's objection that their testimony constituted hearsay.[107]

The defendant's conviction for child abuse was affirmed by the Wyoming Supreme Court, which held that the testimony was properly admitted under the hearsay exception covering statements made to a physician for purposes of diagnosis and treatment.[108] The court recognized that ordinarily statements of fault are not admissible under this exception because they do not relate to diagnosis or treatment. Here, however, the physician's testimony clearly revealed that he was not simply treating bruises on the child's face but was attempting to diagnose the injuries as a case of child abuse, a diagnosis to which identity of the person causing the injuries was a pertinent fact.[109]

The Wyoming court has been sensitive to the special evidentiary needs in child abuse cases and has adopted a liberal view of admissibility in such cases.[110] In fact, in *Goldade* the court acknowledged that it "has pursued a policy in child homicide cases of developing rules which ultimately will assist in protecting the innocent victims of child abuse. . . . [N]o apology is necessary for this policy. Because of the manifest need to protect the most helpless members of our society from violence on the part of others, the policy is both necessary and proper."[111]

Such a liberal view is not always shared, however. For example, in *W.C.L. v. People*[112] the Colorado Supreme Court held that statements of a four-year-old victim of sexual assault were improperly admitted because they did not fall within any of the enumerated exceptions to the hearsay rule nor could their admission be justified under a general "residual exception" not recognized in Colorado.[113] As in *Goldade* the four-year-old child here was declared incompetent as a witness when called to testify because she did not know what "to tell the truth" meant.[114] A statement to the child's aunt identifying the child's uncle as the perpetrator lacked sufficient spontaneity, in the court's judgment, to fit within the excited utterance exception, and a similar statement made to a physician lacked the required relationship to diagnosis or treatment to fit within the medical diagnosis exception.[115]

The contrast in result between these two cases is symptomatic of a problem that has caused some to criticize the judicial practice of analyzing admissibility of children's extrajudicial statements in accordance with traditional hearsay dogma.[116] Routine, rigid adherence to traditional requirements is said to force a harsh result in most instances because it fails to take into account significant perceptual differences between children and adults that in many cases, especially those in which sexual abuse is alleged, renders statements of children more reliable than those of adults. The result is loss of a substantial amount of probative evidence that should be admitted.[117]

Perhaps in repsonse to such concerns some states recently have enacted statutes creating a new exception to the hearsay rule applicable in criminal prosecutions for sexual abuse of children.[118] Washington's statute, for example, provides as follows:

> A statement made by a child when under the age of ten describing any act of sexual contact performed with or on the child by another, not otherwise admissible by statute or court rule, is admissible in evidence in criminal proceedings . . . if:
>
> (1) The court finds, in a hearing conducted outside the presence of the jury, that the time, content, and circumstances of the statement provide sufficient indicia of reliability; and
>
> (2) The child either:
>
> (a) Testifies at the proceedings; or
>
> (b) Is unavailable as a witness: *Provided*
>
> That when the child is unavailable as a witness, such statement may be admitted only if there is corroborative evidence of the act.
>
> A statement may not be admitted under this section unless the proponent of the statement makes known to the adverse party his intention to offer the statement and the particulars of the statement sufficiently in advance of the proceedings to provide the adverse party with a fair opportunity to prepare to meet the statement.

The new Washington statute has been hailed as a positive innovation that allows courts greater discretion to consider alternative indicia of trustworthiness as opposed to consideration of only one factor—spontaneity—and that allows courts to consider the special characteristics of children that require differential treatment from adults as well as the special need for this type of evidence in sexual abuse cases.[119] Moreover, the new statute relieves courts from the often farcical task of distorting traditional hearsay analyses to bring children's statements within the confines of existing hearsay exceptions.[120] The claim is also made that the statute accomplishes these worthy objectives without infringing on the defendant's constitutional rights.[121]

In fact, both the Washington and Kansas statutes have been upheld against the claim they violate the defendant's constitutional right to confrontation.[122] Both courts held the statutes constitutional under the test announced in the United States Supreme Court's decision in *Ohio v. Roberts*[123]—that is, the confrontation clause is not violated if the declarant either is present or is shown to be unavailable and the out-of-court statement is shown to be reliable.[124]

Although the Kansas statute is not as limited, Washington's new hearsay exception is applicable only to sexual abuse cases, which means that in other kinds of abuse cases admissibility of a child's out-of-court statements still must depend on application of traditional hearsay analysis under recognized exceptions or a general exception. Nevertheless, because sexual abuse cases constitute the bulk of those in which problems are likely to arise with a child's in-court testimony,[125] the new statute is a welcome legislative response to a problem confronted by the courts alone, sometimes with unsatisfactory results, for a number of years.

## Waiver of Privilege

**Spousal Privilege.** Difficulty in obtaining the testimony of one parent against the other has been a recurring problem in child abuse cases.[126] Two types of husband/wife privilege—one a true privilege and the other a competency rule—occasionally have been invoked to exclude an otherwise valuable source of probative evidence.

*Testimonial Privilege.* The first type of privilege is not a privilege at all but rather is a remnant of the common law rule that declared both spouses incompetent to testify for or against the other. Eventually spouses were permitted to testify for the other as the disqualification gave way to a rule that allowed interest (that is, bias, interest in the outcome of the case) to be considered on the issue of credibility.

The rule that disqualified spouses from testifying against each other remained, however, at least in criminal cases, in the form of a testimonial privilege of the spouse against whom the testimony was offered to prevent the other from testifying. Many of these testimonial privilege rules have been altered today to declare the witness spouse the holder of the privilege, thus allowing a willing spouse to testify against the other.[127]

Even at common law certain exceptions were recognized—such as where one spouse was charged with a crime committed against the other or against the child of either or both.[128] Today, the practical effect of this exception is that in either a civil or criminal case alleging parental abuse of a child the other spouse is free to give adverse testimony.[129]

This is not to say, however, that application of the testimonial privilege always has been even. In states in which the privilege is applicable to civil and criminal cases alike, the exception is sometimes allowed in both kinds of cases,[130] but at other times allowed only in criminal cases alleging child abuse.[131]

Moreover, at times the exception has been construed so narrowly—for example, to be applicable only where one spouse is charged with abuse *of the other spouse*—that spousal testimony effectively is precluded in cases alleging parental abuse of a child.[132] In any event, regardless of how the statute creating the privilege might be worded, any question over its scope may be alleviated if the child abuse reporting statute provides for waiver of any privilege that otherwise might be applicable.[133]

*Marital Privilege.* The second type of spousal privilege is the marital communications privilege. Unlike the first type, it does not seek to disqualify a spouse from testifying but rather to preserve the confidentiality of communications between spouses. Thus, while a spouse is competent to testify against the other, he or she is not free to testify as to any confidential communcations made by the other spouse. The holder of the privilege is the communicating spouse.[134]

With this true privilege, also, an exception is sometimes provided to permit testimony even as to confidential communications in child abuse cases.[135] Additionally, as with the testimonial privilege, if the child abuse reporting statute contains a waiver provision, it operates as a waiver of the marital communications privilege.[136]

A couple of recent cases indicate how these privileges are being applied in child abuse cases today. In the first[137] the Alaska Court of Appeals upheld the trial court's order holding the appellant wife in contempt for failure to testify against her husband. The wife's refusal to testify was based on her claim of spousal privilege. Alaska recognizes both types of privilege discussed above—the testimonial privilege, which in Alaska belongs to the spouse against whom the testimony is offered,[138] and the marital communications privilege.[139] With respect to both, however, the rule creating the privileges provides that neither is applicable to a case in which one spouse is charged with "[a] crime against the person or the property of the other spouse or of a child of either."[140] In addition the child abuse statutes also provide for waiver of the husband/wife privilege in a child abuse proceeding.[141]

The only issue in the case centered on construction of the word *child*, specifically, whether the exception extends to a case, such as this one, in which the child is a foster child. Significantly, perhaps, the court held the exception broad enough to cover a foster child, for two reasons: (1) current research supports the view that spousal privilege should be construed narrowly because its effect is to prevent disclosure of probative evidence,[142] and (2) the privilege must yield in any event to the policy of prevention of child abuse.[143]

In the other case,[144] the Colorado Supreme Court reversed the trial court's dismissal of charges against the defendant husband following exclusion of his wife's testimony on the basis of husband/wife privilege. At his preliminary hearing the defendant was able to prevent his wife from testifying against him on a charge of sexual assault on a child by claiming the husand/wife privilege. Colorado's testimonial privilege, like Alaska's, is held by the spouse against whom the testimony is offered.[145] An exception is allowed under the privilege statute itself, but only "in a criminal action or proceeding for a crime committed by one [spouse] against the other."[146] The court observed that it was a moot point whether any crime committed by one spouse should be broadly construed as a crime "against the other" because the child abuse statutes provide that the husband/wife privilege cannot be claimed in a child abuse proceeding, which this clearly was.[147]

These cases are significant in that they indicate the tendency of courts to look both to the child abuse statutes as well as the statutes or rules creating the privileges when questions arise concerning the possible application of spousal privilege to child abuse cases. They also illustrate the further tendency of courts to give a somewhat narrower scope to spousal privilege than has traditionally been the case. The same is not necessarily true with respect to waiver of the physician/patient privilege in such cases.

**Physician/Patient Privilege.** In addition to spousal privilege, a number of states have eliminated the physician/patient privilege as well in child abuse proceedings.[148] In two recent cases, however, such statutes were given very narrow readings, casting some doubt on the scope to be accorded the physician/patient privilege in future cases as well as the breadth of application of any waiver of the privilege.

In the first case,[149] a clinical psychologist was subpoenaed to appear and bring certain of his records before a grand jury investigating charges of sexual abuse brought against one of his patients. He sought and obtained an order quashing the subpoena on the ground that disclosure would violate the psychotherapist/patient privilege recognized under the rules of evidence.[150] In the state's appeal from this order the Alaska Court of Appeals affirmed the trial court's decision.

The pertinent provision of the child abuse reporting statutes provides that the physician/patient privilege is not applicable to a child abuse proceeding "related to a report made under this chapter."[151] The language is very similar to that found in statutes of other states.[152] The court held that the provision eliminating the physician/patient privilege applies only in civil child protective proceedings brought under the child abuse reporting statutes and is not applicable to criminal proceedings alleging child abuse. The court based its decision on policy considerations and its reading of legislative intent.

The court's decision in this case is puzzling in view of its earlier decision in *Daniels v. State*[153] involving a similar refusal to testify but based on spousal rather than physician/patient privilege. There the same statute that eliminates both privileges in proceedings "related to a report made under this chapter"[154] was held applicable to a criminal prosecution for child abuse. Thus, the trial court's decision holding the wife in contempt for failure to give testimony against her husband was affirmed, in part because the spousal privilege must yield to the policy of prevention of child abuse.[155]

Other courts, when confronted with the same issue, likewise have concluded that elimination of the spousal privilege is applicable to criminal prosecutions for child abuse.[156] One legitimately might ask whether any different interpretation is warranted where the privilege concerned is the physician/patient privilege rather than the spousal privilege.

In the second case[157] narrowly construing statutory elimination of the physician/patient privilege in child abuse proceedings, the defendant was charged with criminal sexual abuse. The state sought discovery of his medical records and statements made by him to personnel in a psychotherapy program in which he voluntarily participated. The trial court denied the state's motion to discover statements made by the defendant in one-on-one sessions with psychotherapists but granted discovery of statements he had made in group sessions. The issue of the scope of the physician/patient privilege was certified to the appellate court for review.

The child abuse reporting statute provides that, notwithstanding the physician/patient privilege,[158] "[n]o evidence regarding the child's injuries shall be excluded in any proceeding arising out of the alleged neglect or physical or sexual abuse."[159] The purpose of this provision, said the Minnesota Supreme Court, is to encourage full, unfettered reporting of child abuse, which is consistent with the purpose of the reporting statutes themselves—that is, to protect children, not punish the wrongdoer. Thus, prior to reporting of abuse, the policy underlying the medical privilege must yield to the policy of protecting children.

Once abuse is discovered through required reporting, however, the purpose of child protection has been served. After that point it is no longer served by requiring full disclosure of confidential physician/patient communications. Therefore, the court construed the statute as a limitation on but not a complete abrogation of the privilege, allowing use only of evidence required to be reported under the child abuse reporting statute—that is, the "identity of the child, the parent, guardian, or other person responsible for his care, the nature and extent of the child's injuries and the name and address of the reporter."[160]

Such a construction by the court gives a very broad scope to the physician/patient privilege itself, which is contrary to the trend in recent years to narrow the scope of the privilege. Not all states recognize a general physician/patient privilege.[161] In those that do the privilege is noted for the kinds of cases to which it does not apply[162] and the ease with which it can be waived.[163] Moreover, the traditional underlying rationale of the privilege—that it is necessary to encourage communication by patients to their physicians—has been questioned.[164]

Perhaps the Alaska and Minnesota decisions are explained in large part by the fact that both involved confidential communications between psychotherapists and their patients. The psychotherapist/patient relationship, with its greater need for encouragement of communication, has become the last haven for a privilege that in recent years has struggled for survival.[165] Still, one might question whether the policy underlying the physician/patient privilege should be accorded greater weight than the policy underlying spousal privilege.[166]

## Use of Character Evidence

An axiom of evidence law is that evidence of a person's character is inadmissible to show his propensity to act in accordance with that character.[167] Several exceptions to the rule have been recognized; thus, under well-defined circumstances character evidence properly may be used to prove that a person acted in conformity with his character on a particular occasion. Thus, the accused in a criminal case may offer evidence of his good character to show that he is not a person with a propensity for crime, and once the defendant offers such evidence the prosecution may offer rebuttal evidence of the defendant's bad character to show a criminal disposition.[168]

The accused also may offer evidence of a pertinent character trait of the victim in a criminal case, and the prosecution then may offer rebuttal evidence; moreover, in a homicide case in which the victim is alleged to have been the aggressor, the prosecution may "open the door" by initially offering evidence of the victim's character for peacefulness.[169]

Character evidence also is admissible for the purpose of impeaching (that is, attacking) a witness's credibility.[170] It also is admissible in a case in which character is "in issue"—that is, in which a person's character or a trait of his character is an element of a claim or defense, as in a libel suit in which truth is alleged as a defense.[171]

Finally—and most germane to this discussion—character evidence may be admitted for purposes other than propensity to act in a certain way, for example, to prove identity, intent, motive, knowledge, absence of mistake or accident and the like.[172] A current model, Federal Rule of Evidence 404(b), for example, provides that

> Evidence of other crimes, wrongs, or acts is not admissible to prove the character of a person in order to show that he acted in conformity therewith. It may, however, be admissible for other purposes, such as proof of motive, opportunity, intent, preparation, plan, knowledge, identity, or absence of mistake or accident.

The language of Rule 404(b) states that evidence of character *may* be admissible for one of the stated purposes or a similar purpose. This is a reference to the admonition of Rule 403 that

> Although relevant, evidence may be excluded if its probative value is substantially outweighed by the danger of unfair prejudice, confusion of the

issues, or misleading the jury, or by considerations of undue delay, waste of time, or needless presentation of cumulative evidence.

Thus, evidence falling within one of the categories enumerated in Rule 404(b) is not automatically admissible but is subject to the balancing test set forth in Rule 403.[173] Decisions on admissibility of such evidence are left to the trial court's discretion, and courts are accorded considerable leeway in the exercise of this discretion.[174]

Recent cases involving evidentiary issues in child abuse proceedings indicate that use of character evidence in such proceedings is a recurrent issue. The cases generally are of two types: those in which character evidence is used for a permissible purpose (for example, as evidence of intent, identity, absence of mistake or accident, and similar purposes) and cases in which expert testimony on the "battering parent syndrome" is received, along with evidence that the defendant fits the profile, which courts have viewed as a use of character evidence. Each kind of case will be discussed in turn.

Both Alaska and Wyoming have adopted rules of evidence modeled after the Federal Rules of Evidence, in particular the rule that excludes evidence of character, if offered to show propensity[175] and the rule that allows evidence of character if offered for some other purpose, such as to provide identity, intent, or motive.[176] In recent decisions, however, courts in the two states reached different results in applying the rules to the question of admissibility of prior misconduct to show identity, intent, and like elements.

In *Grabill v. State*[177] in which the appellant's conviction for child abuse was affirmed, the Wyoming Supreme Court held that evidence of his prior misconduct—namely, abusive incidents involving other of his children—was properly admitted to prove (1) identity of appellant as the criminal agent and (2) intent or recklessness, either of which is an element of the crime of child abuse.[178] The evidence was in conflict regarding who— appellant or the child's mother—was the cause of the child's injuries. Therefore, identity was an issue in the case. Implicit in appellant's testimony was a denial that he was the agent of the child's harm.

Admissibility of character on such issues, the court conceded, must be balanced against the admonition in Wyoming Rule of Evidence 403 that prejudicial effect may outweigh probative value. In this kind of case, in which typically there exists a dearth of evidence, the need for evidence tending to establish the identity of the perpetrator outweighs any prejudicial effect likely occasioned by its admission. Therefore, the court held that admission of the evidence of prior misconduct was not an abuse of discretion.[179]

The Wyoming court's decision in *Grabill* has been criticized,[180] particularly the court's conclusions that appellant's denial that he had committed the crime made intent an issue in the case,[181] that evidence of appellant's prior misconduct tended to prove identity,[182] and that the need for evidence in child abuse cases justified admission of prejudicial evidence.[183] The only purpose of evidence of prior misconduct in the *Grabill* case, it is argued, was to show the appellant's propensity for violence, the kind of evidence intended to be excluded under Rule 404(b).[184] Because Rule 404(b) first states a prohibition[185] and then creates exceptions to the prohibition,[186] the writer maintains that judges should be especially vigilant in employing the balancing test of Rule 403[187] to ensure that the exceptions do not in fact become the rule.[188] The Alaska Supreme Court's decision in *Harvey v. State*[189] is offered as a case rightly decided by a court exercising the proper degree of caution.[190]

In *Harvey v. State* the appellant's conviction for negligent homicide of an eighteen-month-old child was reversed because evidence of prior misconduct was improperly admitted. The evidence in question was testimony that appellant had severely beaten another child on a previous occasion. The state argued on appeal that the evidence was properly admitted to establish general criminal intent. The court rejected this argument because a contrary decision would mean that in every case charging a felony, evidence of prior misconduct would be admissible to show general criminal intent. The exception thus would swallow up the rule.

More important, the court said, the issue in this case was causation, not intent. Appellant did not deny that he severely spanked the child; rather, he sought to show that the child was in the custody of his mother during the time immediately preceding his injuries and that she could have been the agent of his death.

The state also argued the evidence was admissible to show the harm was not the result of accident or inadvertence. The court conceded that evidence of prior misconduct is properly admissible to refute such a claim, but pointed out that appellant did not raise such a claim in this case; therefore, the evidence was inadmissible for this purpose as well.

These cases illustrate a difference in philosophy between courts as to what "triggers" use of character evidence. The Alaska court in *Harvey* views Rule 404(b) as first and foremost a rule of exclusion, with a few narrowly drawn exceptions that should be rarely considered and cautiously applied because of the high risk of prejudice. The court looks for some positive action on the defendant's part to place identity, intent, or the like in issue—such as raising accident as a defense, denying that the injury was inflicted intentionally, or claiming lack of knowledge.

To the contrary, most courts seem to follow the view of the Wyoming court in *Grabill* that Rule 404(b) is an inclusionary rule that allows evidence of character for certain purposes.[191] This view does not require the defendant to claim accident or lack of intent as a defense. The nature of the case and the other evidence introduced in it can determine whether one of these matters is an issue in the case.[192] For example, the defendant's plea of not guilty itself may place intent and absence of mistake in issue.[193]

Moreover, these courts generally view need for the evidence as a permissible consideration in child abuse cases, even at a risk of prejudice to the defendant.[194]

Although character evidence of the above kind, when offered for a permissible purpose, usually has been admitted, another kind of character evidence has routinely been rejected. Evidence of the latter kind consists of expert testimony on the battering parent profile, accompanied by testimony of other witnesses to the effect that the defendant fits the profile of the battering parent.[195]

Such evidence is to be contrasted with expert testimony on the battered child syndrome, which has been held admissible for years of the issue of cause of death of or injuries to the child victim.[196] Battering parent evidence, to the contrary, is evidence of the defendant's character because its only relevance lies in demonstrating the positive matchup between the defendant and the battering parent profile. Moreover, it is propensity evidence of the kind prohibited under Rule 404(a) and similar rules. In a leading case, [197] the Minnesota Supreme Court held such evidence inadmissible for the same reasons that character evidence to show propensity is usually held inadmissible:

> First, there is the possibility that the jury will convict a defendant in order to penalize him for his past misdeeds or simply because he is an undesirable person. Second, there is the danger that a jury will over-value the character evidence in assessing the guilt for the crime charged. Finally, it is unfair to require an accused to be prepared not only to defend against immediate charges, but also to disprove or explain his personality or prior actions.[198]

For these reasons the court held that battering parent evidence is inadmissible unless the defendant first puts his character in issue, a conclusion with which other courts uniformly have agreed.[199]

An interesting variant is found in a Washington case[200] in which the court held it error to allow an employee of a sexual assault center to testify that most of the perpetrators of sexual assaults on children in their program were parent figures, usually biological parents, where the defendant was the father of the eight-year-old victim. A further interesting point is that in all but one[201] of the latter cases the courts held that use of the inadmissible character evidence was harmless error in light of the overwhelming evidence of the defendant's guilt.[202] The conclusion one draws, then, is that as a general rule the use of character evidence, whether admissible for a permissible purpose or inadmissible because of the propensity rule yet harmless error, has not affected the outcome of cases to any appreciable degree.

# Conclusion

This chapter has reviewed three separate developments related to child maltreatment today: the changing concept of child maltreatment as evidenced by current statutes that give it an everexpanding definition; the most current efforts to measure the incidence of maltreatment and some of the difficulties limiting accurate measurement; and some of the most controversial and problematical evidentiary issues confronting the courts today in reviewing child abuse determinations by lower courts. Except in a very limited way no attempt has been made here to propose solutions to some of the problems reviewed.[203] Rather, the purpose has been to give the reader a fuller understanding of the nature and scope of child abuse and how they relate indirectly to the actual handling of child abuse cases by the courts.

Serious neglect of a child and certainly abuse of a child represent the most serious failure of the parent/child relationship. When a failure of such magnitude occurs, the state must intervene on the child's behalf pursuant to the state's interest in the welfare of children.[204] As outlined in the introductory section of this chapter, however, one of the chief difficulties in this troublesome area is in defining the point at which the failure is of sufficient gravity to warrant state interference with the parent/child relationship.

How much human behavior is defined as child abuse determines how many cases of abuse are measured as such, which determines in large part how many cases actually reach the courts. As more cases reach the courts, the more courts—and legislatures—will have an opportunity to resolve some of the unsettling issues presented here, based on a firmer understanding of the child abuse phenomenon itself.[205]

# Notes

1. *See, e.g.,* J. GOLDSTEIN, A. FREUD & A. SOLNIT, BEFORE THE BEST INTERESTS OF THE CHILD (1979); J. GOLDSTEIN, A. FREUD & A. SOLNIT, BEYOND THE BEST INTERESTS OF THE CHILD (1973); J. BOWLBY, CHILD CARE AND THE GROWTH OF LOVE (1965); Besharov, *"Doing Something" about Child Abuse: The Need to Narrow the Grounds for State Intervention,* 8 HARV. J.L. & PUB. POL'Y 539 (1985) [hereinafter cited as Besharov]; Wald, *State Intervention on Behalf of "Neglected" Children: A Search for Realistic Standards,* 27 STAN. L. REV. 985 (1975); Wald, *State Intervention on Behalf of "Neglected" Children: Standards for Removal of Children from Their Homes, Monitoring the Status of Children in Foster Care, and Termination of Parental Rights,* 28 STAN. L. REV. 623 (1976).

2. Wald, *Thinking about Public Policy toward Abuse and Neglect of Children: A Review of* Before the Best Interests of the Child, 78 MICH. L. REV. 645 (1980).

3. JUVENILE JUSTICE STANDARDS RELATING TO ABUSE AND NEGLECT, commentary to Standard 1.2 at 39 and cases cited therein (Tentative Draft 1977).

4. *Id.*, Standard 1.1.

5. *Id.*, Standard 2.1.

6. *See, e.g.*, ALA. CODE § 12-15-1(10).

7. *See, e.g.*, GA. CODE § 15-11-2(8); N.D. CENT. CODE § 27-20-02(5).

8. *See, e.g.*, D.C. CODE § 16-2301(9); WYO. STAT. § 14-6-201 (a)(xvi).

9. N.C. GEN. STAT. § 7A-517(21); *see* ILL. ANN. STAT. ch. 37, § 702-4; MINN. STAT. ANN. § 260.015(10).

10. N.C. GEN. STAT. § 7A-517(13); *see* ILL. ANN. STAT. ch. 37, § 702-5; MINN. STAT. ANN. § 260.015(6).

11. Other examples and the problem of vagueness in such statutes are discussed in H. RUBIN, JUVENILE JUSTICE: POLICY, PRACTICE, AND LAW 315–17 (2d ed. 1985).

12. *In re* D.T., 89 S.D. 590, 237 N.W.2d 166 (1975).

13. Roe v. Conn, 417 F. Supp. 769 (M.D. Ala. 1976).

14. *See, e.g.*, State v. Mattielo, 4 Conn. Cir. Ct. 55, 225 A.2d 507 (1966); District of Columbia v. B.J.R., 332 A.2d 58 (D.C. 1975); S.S. v. State, 299 A.2d 560 (Me. 1973); *In re* L.N., 109 N.J. Super. 278, 263 A.2d 150, *aff'd*, 57 N.J. 165, 270 A.2d 409 (1970); Patricia A. v. City of New York, 31 N.Y.2d 83, 286 N.E.2d 432, 335 N.Y.S.2d 33 (1972); *In re* Napier, 532 P.2d 423 (Okla. 1975); E.S.G. v. State, 447 S.W.2d 225 (Tex. Civ. App. 1969); Blondheim v. State, 84 Wash. 2d 874, 529 P.2d 1096 (1975). *Contra*, Gonzalez v. Mailliard, no. 50424 (N.D. Cal., Feb. 9, 1971), *excerpted in* 5 Clearinghouse Rev. 45 (1971), *rev'd on other grounds*, 416 U.S. 918 (1974).

15. The remaining material in this chapter is an adaptation of an article appearing in the North Dakota Law Review and is adapted here with permission of the North Dakota Law Review. The article is Davis, *Child Abuse: Pervasive Problem of the 80s*, 61 N.D.L. REV. 193 (1985).

16. Kempe, Silverman, Steele, Droegemuller & Silver, *The Battered Child Syndrome*, 181 J.A.M.A. 17 (1962) [hereinafter cited as Kempe].

17. *Id.*

18. Fontana, Donovan & Wong, *The "Maltreatment Syndrome" in Children*, 269 N. ENG. J. MED. 1389 (1963).

19. For an historical chronicle of earlier efforts to diagnose and publicize the phenomenon among professionals, *see* McCoid, *The Battered Child and Other Assaults upon the Family: Part One*, 50 MINN. L. REV. 1 (1965).

20. Some of the most important works include: THE BATTERED CHILD (R. Helfer & C. Kempe eds., 3d ed. 1980); V. FONTANA, SOMEWHERE A CHILD IS CRYING (1973); V. FONTANA & D. BESHAROV, THE MALTREATED CHILD (1979); THE ABUSED CHILD (H. Martin ed. 1976); HELPING THE BATTERED CHILD AND HIS FAMILY (C. Kempe & R. Helfer eds. 1972); M. LYNCH & J. ROBERTS, CONSEQUENCES OF CHILD ABUSE (1982); E. NEWBERGER, CHILD ABUSE (1982); Fontana, *The Maltreated Child of Our Times*, 23 VILL. L. REV. 448 (1978); Kempe, *Sexual Abuse, Another Hidden Pediatric Problem*, 62 PEDIATRICS 382 (1978); Kerns, *Child Abuse and Neglect: The Pediatrician's Role*, 21(7) J. CONTIN. EDUC. PEDIAT. 14 (1979); Schmitt & Kempe, *The Pediatrician's Role in Child Abuse and Neglect*, 5(5) CURRENT PROBS. PEDIAT. 3 (Mar. 1975). In addition, an international journal, CHILD ABUSE & NEGLECT, is published quarterly.

21. For accounts of these legislative developments, *see* V. DEFRANCIS & C.

LUCHT, CHILD ABUSE LEGISLATION IN THE 1970s (rev. ed. 1974); Paulsen, *The Legal Framework for Child Protection*, 66 COLUM. L. REV. 679 (1966); Paulsen, Parker & Adelmen, *Child Abuse Reporting Laws: Some Legislative History*, 34 GEO. WASH. L. REV. 482 (1966).

22. *See* Kempe, note 16 supra. *Cf.* WYO. STAT. § 14-3-202(a)(ii)(B) ("'Physical injury' means death or any harm to a child including but not limited to disfigurement, impairment of any bodily organ, skin bruising, bleeding, burns, fracture of any bone, subdural hematoma or subdural malnutrition").

23. *See, e.g.*, CAL. PENAL CODE § 11165(e), (g); FLA. STAT. ANN. § 415.503(7)(a); ILL. ANN. STAT. ch. 23, § 2053; N.Y. FAM. CT. ACT § 1012(f)(i)(B); WYO. STAT. § 14-3-202(a)(ii).

24. Indeed, a number of statutes simply include excessive corporal punishment as a part of the definition of physical abuse generally. *See, e.g.*, FLA. STAT. ANN. § 415.503(7)(a); WYO. STAT. § 14-3-202(a)(ii).

25. *See, e.g.*, People v. Jennings, 641 P.2d 276, 278–79 (Colo. 1982); Bowers v. State, 283 Md. 115, 126–27, 389 A.2d 341, 348 (1978).

26. *See generally* Ingraham v. Wright, 430 U.S. 651, 660–63 (1977), discussed in chapter 4.

27. *See, e.g.*, People v. Jennings, 641 P.2d 276 (Colo. 1982) ("cruelly punished"); Bowers v. State, 283 Md. 115, 389 A.2d 341 (1978) ("cruel or inhumane treatment"); State v. Sinica, 220 Neb. 792, 372 N.W.2d 445 (1985) ("cruelly punished"). *Contra*, State v. Meinert, 225 Kan. 816, 594 P.2d 232 (1979) ("unjustifiable physical pain" unconstitutionally vague).

28. *See. e.g.*, CAL. PENAL CODE § 11165(b), (g); FLA. STAT. ANN. § 415.503(7)(b); WYO. STAT. § 14-3-202(a)(ii).

29. Maryland's general definition of abuse, for example, provides:
"Abuse" means:

(i) The sustaining of physical injury by a child as a result of cruel or inhumane treatment or as a result of a malicious act by any parent [or custodian] under circumstances that indicate that the child's health or welfare is harmed or threatened thereby; or

(ii) Sexual abuse of a child, *whether physical injuries are sustained or not.*

MD. ANN. CODE art. 27, § 35A(a)(2) (emphasis added).

30. MD. ANN. CODE art. 27, § 35A(a)(4).

31. FLA. STAT. ANN. § 415.503(7)(b), (14)(g). Florida, like many other states (*see* note 32 *infra*), also makes sexual exploitation of children a criminal offense. *Id.* § 827.071.

32. In delivering the opinion of the Court in New York v. Ferber, 458 U.S. 747 (1982), Justice White indicated that the federal government and forty-seven states make sexual exploitation of children a criminal offense. 458 U.S. at 749 & n.2.

33. N.Y. PENAL LAW § 263.15.

34. 458 U.S. 747 (1982). The Court's opinion summarizes the concern legislatures and the public have expressed over the growing problem of sexual exploitation of children. *Id.* at 749–50 & nn.1–2, 757–58. Missouri's child pornography statute, MO. STAT. ANN. § 568.060, was upheld in State v. Helgoth, 691 S.W.2d 281 (Mo. 1985).

35. *See, e.g.*, FLA. STAT. ANN. § 415.503(7)(a), (10); WYO. STAT. § 14-3-202(a)(ii).

36. Wyo. Stat. § 14-3-202(a)(ii).

37. *See* S. Katz, When Parents Fail 68 (1971); Areen, *Intervention between Parents and Child: A Reappraisal of the State's Role in Child Neglect and Abuse Cases,* 63 Geo. L.J. 887, 933 (1975).

38. *See* note 5 *supra* and accompanying text. Standard 2.1 authorizes intervention in several different sets of endangering circumstances, including those in which children have suffered or are likely to suffer serious physical harm, are suffering emotional harm, or have suffered sexual abuse. Yet as a policy matter the Standards favor family autonomy and discourage state intervention except in egregious cases. *See* Standard 1.1 and commentary.

39. A Preliminary National Assessment of Child Abuse and Neglect and the Juvenile Justice System: The Shadows of Distress 9, Table 1 (U.S. Department of Justice, April 1980).

40. *Id.* at 13 & Table 1. Perhaps the variance between these most "recent" studies (one was based on 1973 data and the other on 1975 data) is itself evidence of the seriousness of the measurement difficulty.

41. *Id.* at 12.

42. National Analysis of Official Child Neglect and Abuse Reporting, 1979 (U.S. Department of Health and Human Services 1981) [hereinafter cited as National Analysis].

43. *Id.* at 77. The general reporting category *abuse* for analytical purposes is further broken down into types of maltreatment—such as *major physical injury, see* note 48 *infra; minor physical injury, see* note 49 *infra; physical injury (unspecified), see* note 50 *infra; sexual maltreatment, see* note 51 *infra; emotional maltreatment, see* note 53 *infra;* and *other maltreatment, see* note 54 *infra.*

44. *Id. Neglect* is more narrowly described as one of the program types of maltreatment, *deprivation of necessities,* see note 52 *infra.*

45. *Id.* at 5.

46. *Id.* at 22, 49.

47. *Id.* at 22. The report further explains that the *other* category "primarily represents 'at risk' cases." *Id.* at 5. *At risk,* in turn, is explained as a category "used when maltreatment itself is not reported, but the report indicates that the child is at risk of being maltreated and therefore needs attention because of the potential of abuse or neglect." *Id.* at p. 79.

The careful reader will note that when the separate figures for abuse, neglect, abuse and neglect, and other shown in the text are combined, they total 296,319, not 296,321. This discrepancy is inexplicable.

48. *Major physical injury* includes "brain damage/skull fracture, subdural hemorrhage or hematoma, bone fracture, dislocation/sprains, internal injuries, poisoning, burns/scalds, severe cuts/lacerations/bruises/welts, or any combination thereof, which constitute a substantial risk to the life and well-being of the child." *Id.* at 95.

49. *Minor physical injury* includes "twisting/shaking, minor cuts/bruises/welts or any combination thereof which do not constitute a substantial risk to the life and well-being of the child." *Id.* at 96.

50. *Unspecified physical injury* is a category used "when the maltreatment is clearly physical but the specific response cannot be placed accurately into the 'Major Physical' or 'Minor Physical' injury categories." *Id.* at 97.

51. *Sexual maltreatment* includes "the involvement of a child in any sexual act or situation, the purpose of which is to provide sexual gratification or financial benefit to the perpetrator; all sexual activity between an adult and a child is considered as sexual maltreatment." *Id.*

52. *Deprivation of necessities* includes "neglecting to provide the following when able to do so: nourishment, clothing, shelter, health care, education, [and] supervision or causing failure to thrive. *Id.* at 98.

53. *Emotional maltreatment* includes "behavior on the part of the caretaker which causes low self-esteem in the child, undue fear or anxiety, or other damage to the child's emotional well-being." *Id.* at 99.

54. *Other maltreatment* includes "types of maltreatment other than those mentioned above [notes 48–53 *supra*], including abandonment and tying/close confinement." *Id.* at 100.

55. *Id.* at 29. The careful reader will note here that the sum of the individual percentages is 114.8 percent. The report explains that more than one type of maltreatment may have been reported for a single child; therefore, the total for the figures shown is greater than 100 percent. *Id.* at 28.

56. *Id.* at 50.

57. *Id.* at 50–51.

58. *See* note 41 *supra* and accompanying text.

59. National Analysis, *supra* note 42, at 19, 23.

60. *Id.* at 19. A further word of caution is in order. One commentator has observed that while as recently as 1981 some 1.3 million cases of abuse were *reported,* about 65 percent of these cases turned out to be unfounded, leading him to conclude that overreporting results from increased public and professional sensitivity to the problem of child abuse. Besharov, *supra* note 1, at 545, 554–62.

61. *Id.* at 19, 49.

62. *Id.*

63. National Study of the Incidence and Severity of Child Abuse and Neglect (U.S. Department of Health and Human Services 1981) [hereinafter cited as National Study].

64. *Id. at 3.*

65. *Id.* at 2–3. This report also identified two other levels of abuse and neglect unknown to CPS: cases known to individuals such as the child, the abuser, friends or neighbors, and cases that are not known or recognized by anyone as abuse (that is, the abusing parent may not recognize his or her behavior as abusive, nor may the child or anyone else). The report described as "very difficult" the task of documenting the incidence of abuse at the latter level with an "only slightly less difficult" task at the former level. Because of concern for accuracy and reliability of information gathering at these levels, the decision was made not to attempt verification of data at these levels for inclusion in the report. *Id.* at 3.

66. *Id.* at 3.

67. *Id.* at 4.

68. *Id.* at 12, 16, 39, 41–42.

69. *Id.* at 16, 41. *Substantiated* means that a CPS caseworker followed through on the report by conducting a preliminary investigation, after which the incident was classified as *founded* or *indicated. Id.* at 11 n.2, 12.

70. *Id.* at 16, 41.

71. *Id.* at 16, 41–42.

72. *Id.* at 17.

73. *Id.* at 42. One should keep in mind that of the number of suspected incidents of abuse *reported* only a portion are substantiated as cases of abuse. One commentator has noted that although reported cases may number as high as 1.3 million, as many as 65 percent of these may prove to be unfounded. He attributes this overreporting to increased sensitivity among professionals and the public in response to expanded media focus on the problem of child abuse. Besharov, *supra* note 1, at 545, 554–62.

74. The second report refers to the "correspondence" between the totals arrived at in the two studies. National Study, *supra* note 254, at 11.

75. *See* note 57 *supra* and accompanying text. If this conclusion was accurate in 1981, it is even more accurate today with increased national media exposure of sexual abuse, particularly in schools and day care programs. *See, e.g.,* NEWSWEEK, May 14, 1984, at 30; *id.,* Aug. 20, 1984, at 44; *id.,* Sept. 10, 1984, at 14, 19.

76. Comment, *Evidentiary Problems in Criminal Child Abuse Prosecutions,* 63 GEO. L.J. 257, 259–61 (1974) [hereinafter cited as Comment, *Evidentiary Problems*]. As an example of the inconsistency between accounts as told by the victim and the abuser and the influence that parents have over their children, *see* State v. Hunt, 2 Ariz. App. 6, 10–11, 406 P.2d 208, 212–13 (1965).

77. E. CLEARY, MCCORMICK ON EVIDENCE 156 (3d ed. 1984) [hereinafter cited as MCCORMICK].

78. *See, e.g.,* State v. Martin, 189 Conn. 1, 454 A.2d 256 (1983); State v. Skipper, 387 So. 2d 592 (La. 1980).

79. MCCORMICK, *supra* note 77, at 156. A recent survey of child competency statutes and rules, plus suggestions for improving the process by which children are allowed to testify, is found in Melton, Bulkley & Wulkan, *Competency of Children as Witnesses,* in CHILD SEXUAL ABUSE AND THE LAW 125 (J. Bulkley ed. 1981) [hereinafter cited as Melton, Bulkley & Wulkan].

80. 387 So. 2d 592 (La. 1980).

81. *Id.* at 595.

82. *Id.*

83. 189 Conn. 1, 454 A.2d 256 (1983).

84. *Id.* at 9–10, 454 A.2d at 260 (reversed on other grounds).

85. 488 A.2d 704 (R.I. 1985).

86. *Id.* at 706.

87. 157 Ga. App. 442, 278 S.E.2d 90 (1981).

88. *Id.* at 443, 278 S.E.2d at 92.

89. *Id.* at 442–43, 278 S.E.2d at 91–92. Use of questions about church and Sunday school attendance has been questioned as having "little probative value today in view of changing norms regarding religion" and as having little likelihood "to shed light on the child's ability to apply moral principles." Melton, Bulkley & Wulkan, *supra* note 79, at 128.

90. 387 So. 2d at 595. *See* note 71 *supra* and accompanying text.

91. 189 Conn. at 10, 454 A.2d at 260.

92. *Id.*

93. 294 Or. 427, 657 P.2d 1215 (1983).

94. *Id.* at 438, 657 P.2d at 1221. *Cf.* State v. Myers, 359 N.W.2d 604 (Minn. 1984) (expert properly allowed to testify as to traits typically exhibited by child sexual abuse victim and also properly allowed to assist jury in evaluating credibility of child victim by testifying that in her opinion child was telling the truth, *where defense raised the credibility issue in cross-examination of child*); *see also* Hall v. State, 15 Ark. App. 309, 692 S.W.2d 769 (1985); People v. Roscoe, 168 Cal. App. 3d 1093, 215 Cal. Rptr. 45 (1985) (expert improperly allowed to testify about post-trauma syndrome for purpose of showing that witness was victim of molestation; but expert could so testify if witness's credibility is attacked, to disabuse jury of misconceptions about victims of rape or molestation and to assist jury in determining witness's credibility); People v. Bledsoe, 36 Cal. 3d 236, 681 P.2d 291, 203 Cal. Rptr. 450 (1984). Use of such expert testimony generally is discussed in Berliner, Canfield-Blick & Bulkley, *Expert Testimony on the Dynamics of Intra-Family Child Sexual Abuse and Principles of Child Development*, in CHILD SEXUAL ABUSE AND THE LAW 166 (J. Bulkley ed. 1981).

95. *See, e.g.,* McCORMICK, *supra* note 77, at 156. The Federal Rules of Evidence adopt this approach by doing away with all disqualifications. FED. R. EVID. 601. A recent report states that some thirteen states have adopted the Federal Rules approach by statute or rule. Melton, Bulkley & Wulkan, *supra* note 79, at 127 & n.20.

96. *See, e.g.,* Goldade v. State, 674 P.2d 721 (Wyo. 1984), in which the prosecutor was forced to seek admission of the child's extrajudicial statements when the child, a four-and-one-half-year-old, was declared incompetent to testify as a witness. The psychological problems experienced by child victims of sexual offenses and the evidentiary problems associated with use of their statements are chronicled in Parker, *The Rights of Child Witnesses: Is the Court a Protector or Perpetrator?*, 17 NEW ENG. L. REV. 643, 648-53 (1982) [hereinafter cited as Parker].

The victim might even experience a change of heart about testifying. As an example of perhaps a court's overraction to this dilemma, *see* State v. DeLong, 456 A.2d 877 (Me. 1983), in which the court affirmed the contempt conviction of a fifteen-year-old victim of sexual abuse for refusing to testify against her father.

97. *See, e.g.,* Comment, *Evidentiary Problems, supra* note 76, at 259-61; Note, *A Comprehensive Approach to Child Hearsay Statements in Sex Abuse Cases*, 83 COLUM. L. REV. 1745, 1745-46 (1983) [hereinafter cited as Note, *Child Hearsay*].

98. Melton, *Procedural Reforms to Protect Child Victim/Witnesses in Sex Offense Proceedings*, in CHILD SEXUAL ABUSE AND THE LAW 184, 185-93 (J. Bulkley ed. 1981) [hereinafter cited as Melton]; Parker, *supra* note 96, at 664-73.

99. Melton, *supra* note 98, at 185-93; Parker, *supra* note 96, at 686-715.

100. *See, e.g.,* ALA. CODE §§ 15-1-2, 15-25-1 to -6.

101. *See In re* Appeal in Pinal County Juvenile Action, 147 Ariz. 302, 709 P.2d 1361 (Ariz Ct. App. 1985) (confrontation clause rights of two juveniles were not violated by closed circuit presentation of testimony of six-year-old brother of murder victim).

102. 457 U.S. 596 (1982).

103. *Id.* at 607-09. *See, e.g.,* Florida Publishing Co. v. Morgan, 253 Ga. 467, 322 S.E.2d 233 (1984) (statute providing for closed juvenile court hearings valid if public or press has opportunity to present evidence and argument that in given case state's or juvenile's right to privacy is overridden by public interest).

104. Without getting into the technicalities of the hearsay rule itself, some of the exceptions under which children's out-of-court statements have been admitted include the spontaneous exclamation exception, the statement of physical condition exception, a specially formulated "tender years" exception and the "catch-all" or residual exception often allowed under hearsay evidence rules. For a discussion of the cases as well as a criticism of such specialized use of recognized hearsay exceptions, *see* Note, *Child Hearsay, supra* note 97, at 1753–63.

105. 674 P.2d 721 (Wyo. 1984).

106. *Id.* at 723. Because of shyness, awe, or both the child was unable to answer questions when called as a witness by the state.

107. *Id.* at 723–24.

108. *Id.* at 725.

109. *Id.* at 725–26. The court also gave considerable weight to its function in this case, which it perceived as pursuing "the transcendant goal of addressing the most pernicious social ailment which afflicts our society, family abuse, and more specifically, child abuse." *Id.* at 725.

110. *See, e.g.,* Grabill v. State, 621 P.2d 802 (Wyo. 1980) (evidence of prior acts of abuse admissible to prove identity and intent or reckless disregard of consequences).

111. 674 P.2d at 727.

112. 685 P.2d 176 (Colo. 1984).

113. *Id.* at 181–83. *See also* State v. Campbell, 299 Or. 633, 705 P.2d 694 (1985) (child's statement to mother inadmissible under residual exception).

114. 685 P.2d at 178 & n.1.

115. *Id.* at 179–81.

116. *See, e.g.,* Note, *Child Hearsay, supra* note 97, at 1755–58, 1761, 1763.

117. *Id.*

118. *See, e.g.,* Kan. Stat. Ann. § 60-460 (dd); Wash. Rev. Code Ann. § 9A.44.120.

119. Note, *Child Hearsay, supra* note 97, at 1764–65; Comment, *Sexual Abuse of Children—Washington's New Hearsay Exception*, 58 Wash. L. Rev. 813, 819–20 (1983) [hereinafter cited as Comment, *Washington's New Hearsay Exception*].

120. Comment, *Washington's New Hearsay Exception, supra* note 119, at 817–19.

121. Note, *Child Hearsay, supra* note 97, at 1765–66; Comment, *Washington's New Hearsay Exception, supra* note 119, at 825–29. The latter commentary concludes, however, that under some circumstances the new statute could be applied in such a way that the defendant's rights would be compromised, and therefore courts are urged to examine specific applications of the exception on a case-by-case basis to determine whether the right to confrontation has been violated. Comment, *Washington's New Hearsay Exception, supra* note 119, at 826–27.

122. State v. Ryan, 103 Wash. 2d 165, 691 P.2d 197 (1984) (reversed on other grounds); State v. Myatt, 237 Kan. 17, 697 P.2d 836 (1985); *see also* State v. Slider, 38 Wash. App. 689, 688 P.2d 538 (1984) (statement of two-and-a-half-year-old child victim properly admitted under statutory exception); State v. Pendelton, 10 Kan. App. 2d 26, 690 P.2d 959 (1984) (statements of seven-year-old child victim properly admitted under statutory exception).

123. 448 U.S. 56 (1980).

124. *Id.* at 66.

125. *See* note 96 *supra* and accompanying text.

126. *See generally* Comment, *Evidentiary Problems, supra* note 76, at 260.

127. McCORMICK, *supra* note 77, at 161–62; *see generally* Trammel v. United States, 445 U.S. 40 (1980).

128. McCORMICK, *supra* note 77, at 162 & n.11.

129. *See, e.g.,* TEX. CODE CRIM. PROC. art. 38.11.

130. *See, e.g.,* CAL. EVID. CODE § 972(d), (e)(1).

131. *See, e.g.,* MINN. STAT. ANN. § 595.02(1).

132. *See, e.g.,* State v. McGonigal, 89 Idaho 177, 403 P.2d 745 (1965); State v. Riley, 83 Idaho 346, 362 P.2d 1075 (1961). The Idaho statutes later were amended to extend the exception to child abuse cases. *See* IDAHO CODE §§ 9-203(1), 19-3002(2).

133. *See* notes 141 and 147 *infra* and accompanying text.

134. For the distinction between the two privileges and their origins, see McCORMICK, *supra* note 77, at 188–91.

135. *See, e.g.,* FLA. STAT. ANN. § 90.504(3)(b).

136. *See* notes 141 and 147 *infra* and accompanying text.

137. Daniels v. State, 681 P.2d 341 (Alaska Ct. App. 1984).

138. ALASKA R. EVID. 505(a)(1).

139. *Id.* 505(b)(1).

140. *Id.* 505(a)(2)(D)(i), (b)(2).

141. ALASKA STAT. § 47.17.060.

142. 681 P.2d at 343–45, citing among other authorities, Trammel v. United States, 445 U.S. 40 (1980). *Cf.* State v. R.H., 683 P.2d 269 (Alaska Ct. App. 1984), in which the court reached a contrary result with respect to the physician/patient privilege. *See* notes 149–156 *infra* and accompanying text.

143. 681 P.2d at 345. *Cf.* Goldade v. State, 674 P.2d 721, 725, 727 (Wyo. 1984).

144. People v. Corbett, 656 P.2d 687 (Colo. 1983).

145. COLO. REV. STAT. § 13-90-107(1)(a).

146. *Id.*

147. 656 P.2d at 688–89. The pertinent provision of the child abuse statutes is COLO. REV. STAT. § 19-10-112 (1978). *Cf.* State v. R.H., 683 P.2d 269 (Alaska Ct. App. 1984), in which the Alaska court held a similar provision eliminating the physician/ patient privilege inapplicable to criminal prosecutions for child abuse. *See* notes 149–156 *infra* and accompanying text.

148. *See, e.g.,* ALASKA STAT. § 47-17-060; COLO. REV. STAT. § 19-10-112; OR. REV. STAT. § 418.775(1); VA. CODE § 63.1-248.11.

149. State v. R.H., 683 P.2d 269 (Alaska Ct. App. 1984).

150. The physician/patient privilege is recognized under ALASKA R. EVID. 504(b).

151. ALASKA STAT. § 47.17.060.

152. *See* statutes cited note 148 *supra.* Virginia's statute, for example, provides:

> *In any legal proceeding resulting from the filing of any report or complaint pursuant to this chapter,* the physician-patient and husband-wife privileges shall not apply.

VA. CODE § 63.1-248.11 (emphasis added). Similarly, the Oregon statute provides:

> In the case of abuse of a child . . . the physician-patient privilege . . . shall not be a ground for excluding evidence regarding a child's abuse, or the cause thereof, *in any judicial proceeding resulting from a report made pursuant to [the reporting statute].*

OR. REV. STAT. § 418.775(1) (emphasis added).

153. *See* notes 137–143 *supra* and accompanying text.

154. ALASKA STAT. § 47.17.060.

155. *See* note 143 *supra* and accompanying text.

156. *See, e.g.,* People v. Corbett, 656 P.2d 687 (Colo. 1983); State v. Suttles, 287 Or. 15, 597 P.2d 786 (1979). In these states, also, the statutes eliminating the spousal and physician/patient privileges contain language similar to that in the Alaska statute—that is, indicating that the abrogation applies to "any judicial proceeding resulting from a report made pursuant to [the child abuse reporting statute]." OR. REV. STAT. § 418.775(1); *see also* COLO. REV. STAT. § 19-10-112.

157. 342 N.W.2d 128 (Minn. 1984).

158. The physician/patient privilege is MINN. STAT. ANN. § 595.02(4).

159. *Id.* § 626.556(8).

160. The child abuse reporting statute, from which the quotation is taken, is MINN. STAT. ANN. § 626.556(7). The current language is slightly different from the statute in effect at the time of the court's decision.

161. McCORMICK, *supra* note 77, at 184, 244 & n.5.

162. *Id.* at 257-58.

163. *Id.* at 254-57.

164. *Id.* at 244. The latter concern led to rejection of a general physician/patient privilege when the Federal Rules of Evidence were proposed. *See* PROPOSED FED. R. EVID. 504, Advisory Committee's Note, 56 F.R.D. 241-42.

165. McCORMICK, *supra* note 77, at 244-45. Indeed, some jurisdictions do not recognize a general physician/patient privilege but do recognize a psychotherapist/patient privilege. *Id.* at 245 & nn. 9 & 10.

166. All states recognize some form of spousal privilege, whereas most, but not all, states recognize a physician/patient privilege. *Id.* at 183-84. *See* notes 161-64 *supra* and accompanying text.

167. *Id.* at 554. FED. R. EVID. 404(a) states the general rule:

Evidence of a person's character or a trait of his character is not admissible for the purpose of providing that he acted in conformity therewith on a particular occasion.

168. McCORMICK, *supra* note 77, at 566-70; FED. R. EVID. 404(a)(1).

169. McCORMICK, *supra* note 77, at 571-74; FED. R. EVID. 404(a)(2).

170. McCORMICK, *supra* note 77, at 574; FED. R. EVID. 404(a)(3).

171. McCORMICK, *supra* note 77, at 551-53; FED. R. EVID. 405(b).

172. McCORMICK, *supra* note 77, at 557-65.

173. *See* FED. R. EVID. 404(b), Advisory Committee's Note, 56 F.R.D. 183, 219.

174. McCORMICK, *supra* note 77, at 544-48. For an example of a decision finding no abuse of discretion by the trial court in admitting evidence of character for a permissible purpose, *see* the discussion of Grabill v. State, 621 P.2d 802 (Wyo. 1980), *infra* notes 177-79 and accompanying text.

175. ALASKA R. EVID. 404(a); WYO. R. EVID. 404(a). The Federal Rule is set forth in the text *supra*.

176. ALASKA R. EVID. 404(b); WYO. R. EVID. 404(b). The Federal Rule is set forth in the text *supra*.

177. 621 P.2d 802 (Wyo. 1980).

178. *Id.* at 808-11. WYO. STAT. § 6-2-503 provides:

a person is guilty of child abuse . . . if:

(i) The actor is an adult or is at least six years older than the victim; and

(ii) The actor intentionally or recklessly inflicts upon a child under the age of sixteen (16) years:

(A) Physical injury [as elsewhere defined]; or

(B) Mental injury [as elsewhere defined].

179. 621 P.2d at 810–11. In State v. Tanner, 675 P.2d 539 (Utah 1983), the court also emphasized the need of evidence, especially in child abuse cases, as a factor to be considered in the balancing process. 675 P.2d at 547.

180. Note, 16 LAND & WATER L. REV. 769 (1981).

181. *Id.* at 777–80.

182. *Id.* at 781–82.

183. *Id.* at 783–85.

184. *Id.* at 779–80, 782.

185. Rule 404(b) is set forth in the text *supra*. The first sentence is a particularized statement of the general rule prohibiting use of character evidence if offered to show propensity.

186. Reference here is to the second sentence of Rule 404(b), set forth in the text *supra*.

187. Rule 403 is set forth in the text *supra*.

188. 16 LAND & WATER L. REV. at 774–75.

189. 604 P.2d 586 (Alaska 1979).

190. 16 LAND & WATER L. REV. at 778–79.

191. *See, e.g.,* Huddleston v. State, 695 P.2d 8 (Okla. Crim. App. 1985); State v. Tanner, 675 P.2d 539 (Utah 1983), and decisions cited therein at 545–49.

192. State v. Tanner, 675 P.2d at 545–46.

193. McMichael v. State, 94 Nev. 184, 577 P.2d 398 (1978).

194. State v. Tanner, 675 P. 2d at 547. For a general description of the balancing analysis between prejudice and probative value, *see* McCORMICK, *supra* note 77, at 544–48.

195. *See, e.g.,* State v. Loebach, 310 N.W.2d 58 (Minn. 1981).

196. *See, e.g.,* State v. Tanner, 675 P.2d 539 (Utah 1983); State v. Loebach, 310 N.W.2d 58 (Minn. 1981); State v. Wilkerson, 295 N.C. 559, 247 S.E.2d 905 (1978).

197. State v. Loebach, 310 N.W.2d 58 (Minn. 1981).

198. *Id.* at 63.

199. Sanders v. State, 251 Ga. 70, 303 S.E.2d 13 (1983); Duley v. State, 56 Md. App. 275, 467 A.2d 776 (1983). In *Sanders* the court also said that battering parent evidence would be admissible if the defendant raises a defense to which such evidence would be relevant in rebuttal. The latter use would appear to be a Rule 404(b) kind of use. *See* notes 172–74 *supra* and accompanying text.

200. 35 Wash. App. 287, 667 P.2d 96 (1983).

201. The exception in State v. Maule, 35 Wash. App. 287, 667 P.2d 96 (1983), in which the court held admission of the prejudicial evidence (*see* note 200 *supra* and accompanying text) to constitute reversible error.

202. Sanders v. State, 251 Ga. at 76–77, 303 S.E.2d at 18; Duley v. State, 56 Md. App. at 283, 467 A.2d at 783; State v. Loebach, 310 N.W.2d at 64.

203. To the extent solutions were mentioned they were solutions proposed by others. *See* notes 98–101, 118–125 *supra* and accompanying text.

204. *See* chapter 4 for a discussion of the permissible scope of the state's interest in the welfare of children.

205. Legislatures, for example, can enact legislation controlling admissibility of children's out-of-court statements based on a better understanding of children's credibility versus that of adults. *See, e.g.,* notes 118–25 *supra* and accompanying text. Courts similarly can reach more informed decisions on competency of children to testify based on a better understanding of the psychology of victims of traumatic

crime, particularly child victims of sexual offenses. *See* notes 90–94 *supra* and accompanying text. And courts can make more informed decisions on the admissibility of character evidence based on increased awareness of policy considerations and whether there is a genuine "need" for such evidence. *See* notes 177–79 *supra* and accompanying text.

# 10
# Conclusion:
# Balancing the Interests

### Paternalism versus Autonomy

Earlier in this book the observation was made that in some areas the law takes a paternalistic stance toward children, whereas in others it accords them (or their parents) varying degrees of autonomy. The law is protective of children, for example, in the areas of contracts, employment, and to a great extent, medical decision making in life-threatening cases. The law grants a measure of autonomy to children or their parents in other areas—for example, abortion decision making (but only to a limited extent), torts (but more as a result of a policy favoring compensation of victims than of a desire to grant children greater responsibility), non–life-threatening medical decision making, and emancipation decision making. These disparate results stem from an inherent conflict in the law—a kind of schizophrenia—between the desire to accord children a greater degree of control over their lives and freedom of choice, and the need, on the other hand, to protect them from others, their surroundings, and, sometimes, from their own folly.

Some have argued that children should not be treated the same for all purposes but rather should be treated differently—in some cases as adults—depending on the purpose. They categorize children's entitlements or claims of rights and maintain that in some areas—for example, child abuse, child pornography, employment—children must be protected, whereas in others—for example, the area of constitutional rights—they must be given equal status with adults.[1] Some, of course, have argued for total autonomy for children in all respects.[2] What is most likely to happen is that writers urging radical or more moderate change in the law's attitudes toward children will provoke dialogue leading to legislative and judicial reassessment of some of the traditional limitations on children's personal freedom, capacity to act, and authority to make certain decisions for themselves.

### Private Law

In the area of private law, for example, some old assumptions need to be rethought and new developments taken into account in according children greater authority—for example, to enter into contracts, dispose of their property, and in short, earn their own way in the world. More and more states allow for increased emancipation of children, which has the effect of removing the disabilities of minority and granting adult status to children for most purposes.[3] In addition, model proposals such as the *Juvenile Justice Standards* have urged that in each area of law statutes should specifically deal with children and their legal capacity. For example, the statutes dealing with contracts generally should include provisions addressing when and under what circumstances children can enter into binding contracts.[4] In the absence of a specific provision, the standards would treat as emancipated any child who is self-supporting and living separately from his parents.[5]

Children—for some purposes but not necessarily for all purposes—should be regarded as adults. Attainment of adult status, however, should not necessarily occur for all purposes at the same age. On those occasions on which children are to be treated differently from adults, some rational reason for the differential treatment should be set forth.[6]

## Public Law

### General

In the public (that is, constitutional) law area as well one sees a conflict between paternalism and autonomy. In some areas—such as child pornography—children are in need of protection from harmful influences, even over their objection or the objection of their parents.[7] In addition, parents are often accorded considerable authority to make decisions for children on the dual theories that children sometimes lack capacity to make decisions for themselves and that parental control and authority are necessary to preserve the stability of the family unit, so vital to our societal structure.[8]

On the other hand, children are sometimes accorded autonomy—that is, adult status—to make decisions for themselves, even in some rather sensitive areas. Thus, a mature minor may decide to obtain an abortion over the objection of her parents or even without their knowledge.[9] And yet a state may constitutionally impose a parental notification statute (as opposed to a parental permission requirement), if it so chooses.[10]

Just as in the area of private law, old assumptions of children's incapacity need to be rethought and new information on child development and changes in our social structure need to be taken into account in reassessing the respective roles of children, parents, and the state in decision making for children. This is particularly true in relation to constitutional rights, whether in regard to a child's decision on whether she will obtain an abortion, what he will read or view, or whether he will wear an armband in school or pass out leaflets on the streets. Reassessment, however, does not mean abandonment. Many age restrictions or other limitations on children's rights might be retained, but only if based on current knowledge about child development and parental and other roles.

### Right to Life

As a part of the package of constitutional rights to life, liberty, and property, the right to life viewed in its broadest sense is the right to be let alone. In the family context, the right to life embraces the right to make decisions—such as medical decisions—without governmental interference. In some instances—for example, in the abortion context but not necessarily limited to it—older children should be able to consent to medical treatment or procedures on their own, without the necessity of parental consent.[11] In others—as in non–life-threatening cases and even life-threatening cases involving defective newborns—parents, in consultation with medical personnel, ought to be allowed to make medical decisions for children without governmental interference. The state should be permitted to intervene and make a medical decision on a child's behalf only in cases in which the child has a chance to lead a meaningful life and is being deprived of that chance by the parent's refusal to give consent to treatment.

Unfortunately, such decisions arouse the most basic emotions, those related to self-preservation and protection of the helpless. In a period of general judicial activism, the trend is toward more, not less, state involvement in the medical decision-making process. Thus, whereas courts traditionally authorized state intervention in family decision making only in life-threatening cases, they now someitmes authorize such intervention in non–life-threatening cases as well. This area of law has been characterized by legislative indifference until recently, but now Congress and some state legislatures are beginning to enact legislation in this area in which courts have been acting without guidance for several years.

### Right to Liberty

The liberty right encompassed in the triology of rights to life, liberty, and property includes a wide spectrum of personal freedoms, including the right to marry and raise a family, to engage in the common occupations of life, to acquire knowledge, and to enter into contracts. In its most basic rather than its broadest form, it means freedom from bodily restraint. Curfew laws constitute one of the most direct limitations on personal freedom to move about. Their impact is even more forceful when directed against only one segment of American society—children.

At one time courts distinguished between laws that banned the mere presence of children on the streets at certain hours—holding such laws unconstitutional—and laws that banned children from remaining on streets at certain hours after being asked to move indoors—holding such laws constitutional as a reasonable, limited restriction on personal freedom. In recent years, however, courts have abandoned this distinction and have struck down laws banning children outright from being on the streets absent an emergency or riot situation, while upholding other laws constituting, in their view, reasonable limitations on use of the streets. In the latter cases, even presence laws were upheld where sufficient exceptions to the ban were allowed—such as in the cases of children accompanied by a parent, children on the way to or from work, and the like.

What has emerged in this area, then, is a desirable tension between state authority and individual freedom. Neither is absolute, and each must accommodate a reasonable tolerance of the other within certain well-defined limits. In any setting in which individual freedom is curtailed, however, the burden is on the state, not the individual, to show that the restriction on freedom is rationally related to some legitimate state objective—such as protecting children from actual, demonstrated harm or protecting society from a clearly established threat of juvenile crime. Absent any well-defined state interest and a statute carefully drawn and reasonably calculated to achieve it, any such statute is likely to fall.

### Right to Property

The constitutional property interest of children was viewed in a very broad sense, encompassing claims of a constitutional right to attend a certain school, to belong to an organization, to play a particular sport, or to participate in another extracurricular activity. In this area, also, the state's authority to regulate a particular activity, especially a public institution such as the public schools, is often in conflict with the perceived right of the individual to participate in that activity.

The courts, especially the United States Supreme Court, have been reluctant to interfere in the state's day-to-day decision making in maintaining and operating such institutions. This reluctance is evidenced by an unwillingness to characterize every claimed expectation that people might have as a property interest entitled to constitutional protection. This reluctance is seen clearly in the Supreme Court's very limited definition of a property interest in *Board of Regents v. Roth*.[12] The reluctance perhaps stems from a deep-seated belief that there are some kinds of disputes that should not be resolved by the courts.

The examples given at the end of chapter 7 illustrate this point. In one case, the court did not view a disputed result in a high school football game as a judicial controversy, whereas in the other case a trial court did view a dispute between parents and their eighteen-year-old daughter as a justiciable matter and actually resolved the controversy between them.

The Supreme Court itself, however, has not given much support to the notion of governmental intervention into such decision making. In recent years, the Court has indicated an unwillingness to interfere in institutional academic decision making (as opposed to disciplinary decision making) on the ground that eductional decision making is largely subjective in nature and is best left to educators themselves rather than courts.[13] The Court's hesitance to enter into this arena of controversy perhaps flows from a conviction that some institutions—such as the schools, but arguably the family as well—should be left alone by the courts because unnecessary interference might have a negative effect on relationships between persons who must continue to function within the institution—for example, the continuing relationships between teachers and students and between parents and children.[14] Under this *laissez-faire* theory, such disputes must be worked out within the institution through administrative procedures or through nonjudicial external procedures such as arbitration or mediation.

## Right to an Education

Children's rights in education have largely stemmed from the concept of equality of opportunity to receive an education. To the extent that a state provides a free public education to its children—and all states do—it must make such an education available to all. This has been true particularly where differential treatment was based on race or sex.

The educational sphere has been characterized generally by full-scale intervention by the courts, particularly the federal courts, to ensure the equal availability of educational opportunity and to ensure the fair administration of educational policies and practices. The process of massive intervention commenced with the desegregation cases, but once the process began it soon spread to other facets of education as well.

Right to educational opportunity has not been an exclusive province of the courts. Congress, for example, has sought to ensure equality of educational opportunity for handicapped children.[15] Although the courts have been supportive in enforcing the requirements of such legislation,[16] there are limits beyond which they have not ventured, leaving certain freedom to local school authorities to devise an appropriate plan of education for handicapped children.[17]

Aside from assuring fair access to educational opportunity, courts and legislatures have been actively involved—although in different respects—in resolving recurring conflicts between religion and the state. Legislatures more often than not have been engaged in efforts to restore prayer in schools or to offer financial and other assistance to parochial schools. The courts, on the other hand, have been engaged in a countereffort to maintain the strict separation ween church and state. Although these cases have not generated as much emotion as, for example, the abortion controversy, they do touch on competing notions of what our fundamental values as a society should be. As such, they are not likely to disappear soon, particularly because such fundamental debates tend to await philosophical shifts in the membership of the Supreme Court to produce a swing of the pendulum in the opposite direction.

## Protection from Inadequate Parenting

Perhaps as much as any other area covered in this book, the issue of state intervention to protect children from neglect or abuse illustrates the stark contrast between the competing interests of protectionism versus autonomy. The fundamental issue is one of deciding when the state should step in and assume the parental function when parents have failed a child in a significant way, and when it should not do so, either because the family has a fundamental right to be left alone or because intervention will do more harm than good.

As in the area of medical decision making for children, the area of child abuse and neglect is characterized by deep philosophical differences over the appropriate level of state intervention. One's view of the appropriate level of intervention is often a response to the perceived magnitude of the problem—that is, one's perception of how much abuse occurs. The magnitude of the problem is in turn dependent on how the problem—abuse—is defined.

After enactment of child abuse reporting statutes in the mid-1960s the definition of abuse steadily expanded, as did state intervention. Recent literature, however, has tended to question whether broad intervention by the state in the lives of families is desirable.[18]

On the other hand, courts and, increasingly, legislatures have tended in recent years to foster state intervention in the family by fashioning rules facilitating increased use of certain kinds of evidence in child abuse cases, particularly those alleging sexual abuse. Child abuse is increasingly perceived as a "pernicious social ailment,"[19] and when a problem is perceived as reaching national proportions, it is often met with massive marshalling of resources, including increased governmental intervention.[20]

As the definition of abuse continues to expand and the level of state intervention increases accordingly, more and more cases are likely to reach the courts, bringing about increased pressure for relaxed evidentiary rules to facilitate prosecution of abuse cases. These developments make it clear that the child abuse area is another area, like child pornography or employment, in which the state will continue to assume a highly protective attitude toward children. Few can argue against the protective posture itself. Given the validity of a protective policy, the real issue is how far it should go. Children should be protected from harm, but not at the cost of greater harm resulting from the intervention itself, with its consequent disruption of the family unit and important relationships. At the moment, an interventionist philosophy prevails, but this area also is one of those awaiting a shift in philosophy, in which movement back and forth will continue until a proper balance between protection and autonomy is reached.

## A Final Word

The law has never assumed a monolithic attitude toward children. As illustrated here, for most purposes the law has been protective of children because of their perceived vulnerability and incapacity to make decisions or act for themselves. For some purposes, however, the law has granted autonomy to children to make decisions for themselves or to be responsible for themselves.

As mentioned earlier in this book, the basic issue is one of authority of who will decide for a child—the child, the parents, or the state. In any given area of law, this issue should be decided in reference to the various interests at stake. The interests of the child, the parents, and the state in any given case must be identified and balanced against each other to determine the appropriate rule of law to govern such cases.

Some interests of children include

adequate parental care,

educational opportunity,

certain constitutional rights,

freedom to contract, dispose of property, and engage in employment,

medical care.

Interests of parents might include

preservation of family unity,

maintenance of parental authority,

protection of children,

education of children.

Interests of the state might include

preservation of life, health, safety, and general well-being of all citizens,

maintenance of order (such as in schools).

Occasionally, the interests of children, parents, and the state touch on the same area but are diametrically opposed. The case of *Wisconsin v. Yoder*[21] is an example. All parties were concerned about education, but the state insisted on universal compulsory attendance until age sixteen, whereas Amish parents and their children insisted on education in the public schools through eighth grade only (age fourteen or fifteen) followed by vocational education in the Amish community. Of course, another interest was at stake in that case as well—the right to religious freedom under the first amendment.

More often than not, the applicable interests are in conflict. In another religious freedom case, *Prince v. Massachusetts*,[22] the parental interests in religious freedom and parental authority had to yield to the state's interest in preserving the health and well-being of children. What explains the difference between the two decisions? A balancing of the interests in each case revealed that in *Yoder* the state's interest in having an educated citizenry was furthered by the Amish practice of self-education after the eighth grade, whereas in *Prince* the state's interest in protecting children from unwholesome street influences was frustrated by the aunt's insistence on having the children hand out religious pamphlets.

This analysis permits some conclusions, admittedly very broad, to be drawn. The state should act against parental wishes and children's wishes only to protect children from significant harm or to further some significant, overriding state interest. This approach would apply to laws against child pornography and sexual exploitation of children, laws addressed to the problem of child neglect and abuse, and laws requiring compulsory school attendance (except as they might conflict with religious belief, which is probably limited to the Amish). Children should be entitled to the same constitutional rights as adults, except where some paramount state interest applicable only to children is at stake (such as the juvenile curfew laws).

The hands-off approach is equally applicable to private law. Perhaps children under a minimum age (for example, seven, to use the age of criminal responsibility) should not, by reason of age alone, be allowed to enter into contracts, dispose of their property, or work or be held responsible for their torts. Children over this age, however, perhaps should be allowed to do these things if they can demonstrate the sort of maturity required for such activities. Whether this level of maturity has been reached should be decided on a case-by-case basis, as in the abortion decision-making cases.

Where parental interests and children's interests are in conflict, parents should be able to make most decisions for children in the interest of preserving family unity and parental authority. Every difference of opinion over diet, curfew, and clothing should not become a matter for the courts to decide. Parents must be given an area in which to operate, and parents and children alike should have a clear idea of where the boundary line is.

Parents should also be given a zone free from unwarranted state interference in decision making for a child. Only if the parents have failed in some significant way (as in neglect or abuse cases and cases of refusal to consent to life-saving medical treatment) should the state be able to intervene and make a decision on the parents' behalf. Absent such a failure, the parents should be able to make decisions respecting the child's education, discipline, and medical care.

This book, for the most part, has sought to relate not what ought to be or what is fair but what is. What has emerged in recent years is a body of law that might be described as children's law, although until now it has not been perceived as an area of law in itself but rather as a fragmented collection of tort law relating to children, contract law relating to children, constitutional law relating to children, and so on. This book has sought to bring all of these areas—many of them inconsistent with one another—together in one place as related parts of a whole. To the extent that it has talked of what ought to be—of the balancing of interests at stake in decision making for children—it has done so with the goal of promoting dialogue about the proper interaction between children, parents, and the state. In that respect, this conclusion is prologue to the future of children's law.

## Notes

1. *See* the references to Wald, *Children's Rights: A Framework for Analysis*, 12 U.C.D. L. Rev. 255 (1979) [hereinafter cited as Wald], in chapter 4, notes 105–14 and accompanying text, as well as the references to F. Zimring, The Changing Legal World of Adolescence (1982) [hereinafter cited as F. Zimring], in chapter 1, notes 19–20 and accompanying text.

2. *See, e.g.,* R. FARSON, BIRTHRIGHTS (1974); J. HOLT, ESCAPE FROM CHILD-HOOD (1974).

3. *See e.g.,* ALASKA STAT. § 09.55.590; CAL. CIV. CODE §§ 60 *et seq.;* CONN. GEN. STAT. ANN. §§ 46b-150 *et seq.;* TEX. FAM. CODE ANN. §§ 31.01 *et seq.* Others are listed in Comment, *The Uncertain Status of the Emancipated Minor: Why We Need a Uniform Statutory Emancipation of Minors Act (USEMA),* 15 U.S.F. L. REV. 473, 477-79 (1981). The California statutory scheme is discussed in Note, *California's Emancipation of Minors Act: The Costs and Benefits of Freedom from Parental Control,* 18 CAL. W.L. REV. 482 (1982).

4. JUVENILE JUSTICE STANDARDS RELATING TO RIGHTS OF MINORS, Standard 2.1(A) and commentary at 30-31 (1980). The STANDARDS specifically provide that a child is entitled to his own wages and that child and parent can sue one another for tortious behavior, *id.,* Standard 2.1(B) and commentary at 31-32, and also contain provisions on child support, *id.,* Standards 3.1-3.4, consent for medical care, *id.,* Standards 4.1-4.9, youth employment, *id.,* Standards 5.1-5.8, and contracts, *id.,* Standard 6.1.

5. *Id.,* Standard 2.1(C) and commentary at 32-33.

6. *See* F. ZIMRING, *supra* note 1, at 111-15.

7. *See, e.g.,* New York v. Ferber, 458 U.S. 747 (1982); *see also* Prince v. Massachusetts, 321 U.S. 158 (1944) (child employment).

8. Wald, *supra* note 1, at 259; Hafen, *Children's Liberation and the New Egalitarianism: Some Reservations about Abondoning Youth to Their "Rights,"* 1976 B.Y.U. L. REV. 605. The Supreme Court's decisions in H.L. v. Matheson, 450 U.S. 398 (1981), Parham v. J.R., 442 U.S. 584 (1979), and Wisconsin v. Yoder, 406 U.S. 205 (1972), are examples of cases advocating parental authority. *See also* Ingraham v. Wright, 430 U.S. 651 (1977) (supportive of authority of school personnel to discipline students).

9. Bellotti v. Baird, 443 U.S. 622 (1979).

10. H.L. v. Matheson, 450 U.S. 398 (1981).

11. For examples in which, in the abortion context and otherwise, courts and legislatures have given children authority to consent to medical treatment or procedures, *see* chapter 5, notes 69-81 and accompanying text, *supra.*

12. 408 U.S. 564, 576-77 (1972). *See* the quote from Justice Stewart's opinion in *Roth* at the beginning of chapter 7.

13. Regents of the Univ. of Mich. v. Ewing, 106 S. Ct. 507 (1985); Board of Curators v. Horowitz, 435 U.S. 78 (1978).

14. Rehnquist, *The Adversary Society: Keynote Address of the Third Annual Baron de Hirsch Meyer Lecture Series,* 33 U. MIAMI L. REV. 1, 2, 8-9, 14-15 (1978).

15. *See, e.g.,* Education for All Handicapped Children Act of 1975, Pub. L. 94-142, 20 U.S.C.A. §§ 1401-1461.

16. *See, e.g.,* Irving Indep. School Dist. v. Tatro, 468 U.S. 883 (1984); Espino v. Besteiro, 520 F. Supp. 905 (S.D. Tex. 1981).

17. *See, e.g.,* Board of Educ. v. Rowley, 458 U.S. 176 (1982).

18. *See* the authorities in chapter 1, note 1, *supra.*

19. Goldade v. State, 674 P.2d 721, 725 (Wyo. 1983). *See* NEWSWEEK, May 14, 1984, at 30; *id.,* Aug. 20, 1984, at 44; *id.,* Sept. 10, 1984, at 14, 19.

20. The same is true, for example, of the drug problem in this country. Recently the House of Representatives voted to use extraordinary means to combat the growing menace of drug abuse, including use of the armed forces and reinstitution of the federal death penalty for some drug dealers. N.Y. Times, Sept. 12, 1986, at A1, col. 2.

21. 406 U.S. 205 (1972).

22. 321 U.S. 158 (1944).

# Index

# About the Authors

**Samuel M. Davis** is J. Alton Hosch Professor of Law and Associate Dean at the University of Georgia School of Law. Admitted to the Bar in Mississippi and admitted to practice before the United States Supreme Court and other lower federal and state courts, he is the author of *Rights of Juveniles: The Juvenile Justice System* (1980) and co-author of *Children in the Legal System* (1983). He lectures nationwide on juvenile justice and child welfare issues.

**Mortimer D. Schwartz** is Professor of Law and Associate Dean for Law Library at the University of California, Davis. Admitted to the Bar in California, Oklahoma, and Maine, he has served as a member and an officer in state and local child welfare associations. He has authored research on children's rights and has presented findings at meetings of international organizations concerned with the rights of the child and the law.

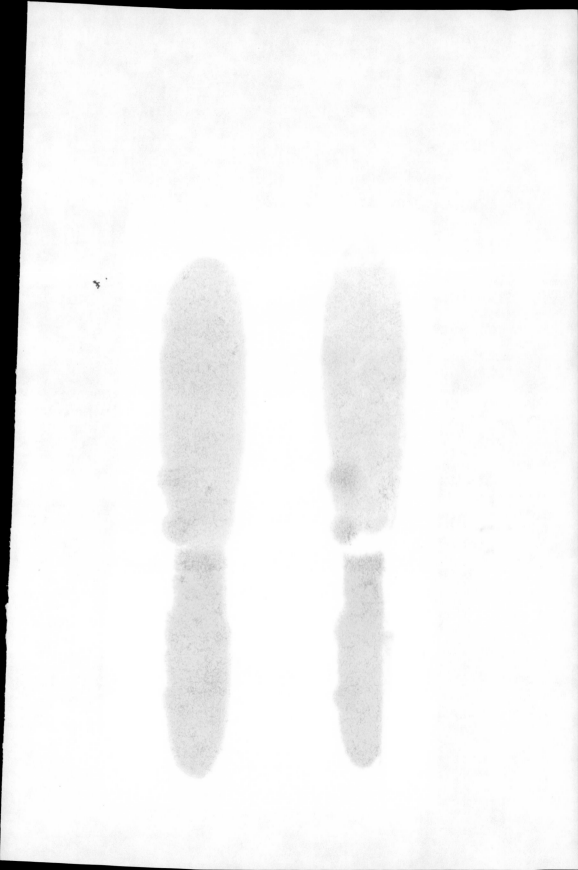

## DATE DUE

| | |
|---|---|
| MAR 14 1994 | |
| OCT 08 1995 | |
| | |
| | |
| | |
| | |
| | |
| | |
| | |
| | |
| | |
| | |
| | |
| | |
| | |
| | |

GAYLORD                    PRINTED IN U.S.A.